EXPLORING WILD CENTRAL FLORIDA

*purchased at
Loxahatchee NWR Visitor Center
May 1996*

Central Florida Natural Areas

1. Archie Carr National Wildlife Refuge
2. Avon Park Air Force Range
3. Canaveral National Seashore
4. Chassahowitzka National Wildlife Refuge
5. Crystal River National Wildlife Refuge
6. Hobe Sound National Wildlife Refuge
7. Merritt Island National Wildlife Refuge
8. Pelican Island National Wildlife Refuge
9. Kissimmee River Trail
10. Hoover Dike Trail
11. Arbuckle State Forest & Lake Arbuckle State Park
12. Blue Cypress Lake
13. Blue Spring State Park
14. Bull Creek Wildlife Management Area
15. Caladesi Island State Park
16. Dupuis Reserve State Forest
17. Fort Cooper State Park
18. Fort Pierce Inlet State Recreation Area
19. Green Swamp
20. Hickory Hammock Trail
21. Highlands Hammock State Park
22. Hillsborough River State Park
23. Homosassa Springs State Wildlife Park
24. Honeymoon Island State Recreation Area
25. Hontoon Island State Park
26. Jonathan Dickinson State Park
27. Lake Kissimmee State Park
28. Lake Manatee State Recreation Area
29. Little Manatee River State Recreation Area
30. Lower Wekiva River State Preserve
31. Myakka River State Park
32. Oscar Scherer State Recreation Area
33. Rock Springs Run State Reserve
34. Savannas State Reserve
35. Sebastian Inlet State Recreation Area
36. Three Lakes Wildlife Management Area
37. Tosohatchee State Reserve
38. Van Fleet State Trail
39. Wekiwa Springs State Park
40. Withlacoochee State Forest
41. Withlacoochee State Trail
42. Alderman's Ford Park
43. Archbold Biological Station
44. Babson Park Audubon Center
45. Barley Barber Swamp
46. Big Bend Manatee Viewing Center
47. Blowing Rocks Preserve
48. Boyd Hill Nature Park
49. Charlotte Harbor Environmental Center
50. Disney Wilderness Preserve
51. Edward Medard Park & Reservoir
52. E.G. Simmons Park
53. Eureka Springs Park
54. Fort DeSoto Park
55. Fred H. Howard Park
56. John Chestnut, Sr. County Park
57. Lake Okeechobee Sanctuaries
58. Lake Park
59. Lettuce Lake Regional Park
60. Lithia Springs Park
61. Pinellas Trail
62. Saddle Creek County Park
63. Savannas Outdoor Recreation Area
64. Sawgrass Lake Park
65. Starkey Wilderness Park
66. The Hammock
67. Tiger Creek Preserve
68. Upper Tampa Bay Park
69. Weedon Island Preserve
70. Wilderness Park
71. Withlacoochee River Park

EXPLORING
WILD
CENTRAL
FLORIDA

A Guide to Finding the Natural Areas
and Wildlife of the Central Peninsula

SUSAN D. JEWELL

Susan D. Jewell

PINEAPPLE PRESS, INC.
Sarasota, Florida

If you really want to feel alive,
surround yourself with living things

For Howard and Marian Jewell

Library of Congress Cataloging-in-Publication Data

Jewell, Susan D. (Susan Diane)
  Exploring Wild central Florida: a guide to finding the natural
areas and wildlife of the central peninsula / by Susan D. Jewell.
    p.   cm.
  Includes bibliographical references (p.   ) and index.
  ISBN 1-56164-082-4   (pbk. : alk. paper)
  1. Natural history—Florida—Guidebooks.   2. Natural areas—
Florida—Guidebooks.   3. Parks—Florida—Guidebooks.   4. Florida—
Guidebooks.   I. Title
QH105.F6J485   1995   95-32924
508.759—dc20   CIP

Inquiries should be addressed to:
Pineapple Press, Inc.
PO Drawer 16008
Southside Station
Sarasota, Florida 34239

Composition by Octavo
Printed and bound by Quebecor/Fairfield, Fairfield, Pennsylvania

10 9 8 7 6 5 4 3 2 1

CONTENTS

VII. NATURAL AREAS—COUNTY, CITY, PRIVATE, AND LOCAL PARKS   197

ACKNOWLEDGMENTS

Many people contributed their time patiently to answer my questions about their particular areas of expertise. All spoke with pride of the natural resources they were protecting. I would like to extend sincere appreciation to Rob Bennetts, Barabara Bolt, Scott Coulter, Elizabeth Gehron, Jim Gibson, Joyce Kleen, Barry (Chop) Lege, Fred Lohrer, Burkett Neely, Eileen Nunez, Kevin Pedicord, Bill Pranty, Bob Przekop, Don Progulske, Joe Schwagerl, Vicki Thomae, Keith Thompson, Paul Tritaik, Pat Walsh, and Blair Wrackley. Wayne Hoffman contributed numerous hours to improve my bird checklist. Tony Gola and Hank Smith made numerous improvements to the text. Any errors are the responsibility of the author.

My task was made more enjoyable by the companionship of Tony Gola, who accompanied me on many exploring trips and otherwise assisted me with the production of this book. Last, but most important to me, is the faithful moral support of my family, who hardly saw me while I was writing.

Dedicated to the memory of
Herbert W. Kale, II, Ph.D.
1933–1995
Outstanding Ornithologist
Dedicated Conservationist
Friend

Dr. Kale was ornithologist for the Florida Audubon
Society, author of *Florida's Birds,* and worked tirelessly
in the unsuccessful effort in the 1980s to save the dusky
seaside sparrow (shown here) from extinction.

INTRODUCTION

Florida is a paradise—warm climate, ample sunshine, flowers, fruits, bounty from the sea, miles of beaches and warm waters, flatwater canoeing, and so on. But it was not always so inviting. Before the land was "tamed," the early settlers had to contend with swarms of mosquitoes, no-see-ums, chiggers, and deer flies. They had alligators, rattlesnakes, and cottonmouths. They had panthers, red wolves, and black bears. They had either swamps and marshes or desertlike scrub, but not much in between. They had malaria, yellow fever, and typhoid. They had thorny shrubs. Blistering summers. Dripping humidity. Hurricanes.

Actually, not much has changed. True, we don't have red wolves in Florida anymore, and the panthers, what few there are, are not very prime physical specimens. Most of the human diseases are under control. But we have drained the wetlands to farm the underlying rich soil. We have air-conditioned our endless summers, chemically bombed our mosquitoes, cleared or paved our yards to repel snakes and alligators, and amply warned our residents of impending hurricanes.

Now you want to see the *real* Florida. That does *not* mean a high-tech theme park. The real Florida is tucked quietly away in nature parks, preserves, and refuges across the state. No obnoxious advertising to lure people. No gimmicks. Just wildlife and habitats similar to what was here before Europeans arrived 500 years ago.

Central Florida is full of diversity. Sandhills and cypress swamps, mangroves and marshes, pinelands and prairies, springs and scrubs shelter a wide variety of plants and animals. Wading birds, shorebirds, songbirds, waterfowl, raptors, and alligators are easy to spot. Bears, river otters, panthers, manatees, and snail kites remain for the patient wanderer to find. Central

Florida has at least 35 currently existent species of native amphibians, 84 of reptiles, 46 of mammals, and 341 of birds.

There is nothing like camping in a remote woods to calm the daily stresses. It's easy on the wallet, too. The network of federal, state, county, city, and private preserves provide ample choices for short or long excursions. In fact, the Florida government has one of the best land-buying plans for preservation of any state. Its Conservation and Recreation Lands fund and Preservation 2000 fund together provide for the purchase of the highest priority lands—those with the most endangered habitats or species that are being threatened by development.

This intense protection is not by coincidence. Florida has one of the greatest needs to protect land. About a thousand people move into the state *every day*! The pressures to develop are immense. Perhaps the crux of the issue is that immigrants rarely have the strong ties to the land as do families who have homesteaded in one place for several generations. Newcomers can't see how things formerly were—they have only the present to gauge the future by. Thus, it takes an increased effort to preserve the land for the future.

I
AN OVERVIEW

HOW TO USE THIS BOOK

Geographically, this book concentrates on central Florida. The northern range of this book is New Smyrna Beach on the Atlantic coast and Yankeetown on the Gulf coast. The southern range of this book is Martin County on the Atlantic coast and Charlotte County on the Gulf coast. Not all parks and natural areas within this range could be included.

If you are traveling from the northern states or another country, hopefully you'll have access to "Exploring Wild Central Florida" several weeks or months before departing on your trip. Then you can use it to plan your itinerary, saving you time (and possibly money) when you arrive. Use the time before your trip to write or call for more information on hours of operation, entrance fees, and tour schedules.

Newcomers to central Florida may want to stick to the better known natural areas. From Orlando, you can easily drive to Blue Spring State Park, Lake Kissimmee State Park, Wekiwa Springs State Park, and Withlacoochee State Forest. From Tampa–St. Pete, the drive is easy to Fort DeSoto Park, Myakka River State Park, and Weedon Island Preserve. From the Cape Canaveral Area, Merritt Island National Wildlife Refuge, Bull Creek Wildlife Management Area, and Canaveral National Seashore are easily accessible.

No conscientious naturalist would divulge specific locations of rare plants and animals. While most people respect the regulations protecting our natural resources, an unscrupulous collector may not. Therefore, only general locations will be given.

This book is not intended to be a field guide to plants and animals, and no attempt is made to be all-inclusive. Some species of special interest are discussed in greater detail.

1

Distances and measurements are given in miles, feet, and acres. Temperatures are given in degrees Fahrenheit (°F). Some conversions that travelers may find helpful:

1 mile = 1.6 kilometers	1 kilometer = 0.62 miles
1 foot = 0.3 meters	1 meter = 3.3 feet
1 acre = 0.4 hectares	1 hectare = 2.47 acres
1 pound = 0.45 kilograms	1 kilogram = 2.2 pounds
(°F–32)5/9 = °C	(9/5 °C)+32 = °F

Each area has a suggested best time of year to visit it, in case the reader is able to choose the season. Written directions are given, but it is suggested that the reader use them in conjunction with a road map (such as *DeLorme's Atlas and Gazetteer* or American Automobile Association maps). The written directions include the following abbreviations for roads: 'US' for a federal highway, 'SR' for a state road, 'CR' for a county road, and 'Alt' for an alternate road.

Information on pet regulations in the parks is included for a very important reason. Florida can become very hot even in the winter. A Florida statute prohibits leaving pets in unattended vehicles because they can suffer greatly or die from the heat. Since many parks don't allow pets (except guide dogs), and pets usually cannot be left unattended at a park or motel, your visit may be greatly restricted if you bring Fido with you. If possible, leave your pets at home with a friend or relative.

Information on private concessions is offered solely for the reader's convenience and does not constitute endorsement by the author.

"Primitive backpack camping" refers to designated sites along a hiking trail where camping is permitted but where there is usually nothing more than an open patch of ground.

PLANNING YOUR TRIP
Getting to central Florida
Because of the tourist business, central Florida is very accessible. Major airports serve Orlando and Tampa–St. Petersburg.

Fort Pierce, Punta Gorda, Vero Beach, and Sarasota all have fairly large airports. Buses and trains also serve the area. Major highways connect the coastal cities and Orlando directly and the inland cities indirectly. It takes about two hours to drive between Fort Pierce and Merritt Island and about one and one-half hours between Orlando and Tampa.

Central Florida weather

Central Florida's climate is subtropical in some places and temperate in others. Summer temperatures are high and winter temperatures are mild, even when the occasional cold front pushes into the peninsula from the north. This may drop the temperature to 30°–40°F for two or three days. Many cold fronts from the interior of the continent never reach central Florida. Table 1 shows representative air temperatures for several towns in this area.

The table shows the mild winter air temperatures. Three-digit temperatures occur mostly in the interior, away from the moderating influences of the Atlantic Ocean and the Gulf of Mexico. Lake Okeechobee is so large that it causes a "lake effect" similar to the climatic effects caused by the ocean. In this case, temperatures are moderated around the lake shore.

The infrequency of temperatures in the 100s doesn't seem to matter—the relative humidity makes it feel just as hot! Hence, there is the southern equivalent of the wind-chill factor, called the "heat index." The National Weather Service defines the heat index as "the temperature that a human body would feel when

Table 1.   Average air temperatures (°F) of selected locations in central Florida (NOAA 1992)

Month	Orlando	Tampa	Avon Park
Jan	60.5	59.8	61.8
Apr	72.0	73.6	72.9
Jul	82.4	82.2	82.3
Oct	74.9	74.5	75.2

humidity and air temperature are factored in"—and it's frequently above 100 in the summer, meaning the air *feels* like it's over 100°F. A formula would be used for the following example: If the air temperature is 90°F and the relative humidity is 60 percent, the heat index is 100. Relative humidities on a typical summer morning are often 80–90 percent. In the winter, they are often around 50 percent.

Almost every visitor learns that Florida is known as the Sunshine State. Why the nickname? Because, aside from Arizona, Florida receives more sunshine in proportion to the amount of daylight possible than all the other states.

Central Florida's seasons are not very distinct. While the air temperature extremes range from the 20s to the low 100s, a normal year would register from the upper 30s to the upper 90s. It is precipitation more than temperature that gives central Florida two seasons—wet and dry. The wet season extends from mid-May to mid-October, and the dry season is November to April.

All of central Florida is south of the 30°N latitude, the general demarcation between the westerly and the easterly prevailing winds. South of 30°N, the prevailing winds blow from the east and are known as the trade winds. Thus, most often, the winds blow in from the Atlantic, causing the greatest influence along the east coast. By the time the wind reaches the Gulf coast, the land mass has moderated the temperature and softened the wind speed.

Most of the 50–60 inches of rain that occurs annually falls between late May or early June and November, with peaks in June and September. The precipitation from May to August frequently falls in short, intense daily rainstorms. A visitor to Florida during those months can expect rain (usually in the form of a thunderstorm) for 10 to 30 minutes almost every day. The clouds form from the sun's rays evaporating water in the lakes, marshes, and ocean. The precipitation in September and October tends to fall less frequently but in larger amounts per event. This is because tropical storms are more frequent then and often drop many inches of rain at once. Table 2 shows the average rainfalls for the region.

Table 2.   Average rainfall (inches) of selected
locations in central Florida (NOAA 1992)

Month	Orlando	Tampa	Avon Park
Jan	2.10	2.17	2.25
Apr	2.19	1.82	2.59
Jul	7.78	7.35	7.81
Oct	2.82	2.34	3.53

The most reliably good weather (less chance of thunderstorms, tropical storms, cold fronts, intense heat, or mosquitoes) is in March and April. The weather is truly delightful. In
fact, it's often so dry that some species of tropical trees lose their
leaves regularly every April, and great piles of crunchy leaves can
be raked from beneath barren trees. A New England "fall" is in
the autumn, while central Florida's "fall" is in the spring. Some
species of deciduous trees shed their leaves a few at a time all
year, while temperate species lose them in the autumn.

The months of November and December are also good times
to visit for several reasons. The rainy season has ended, but the
vegetation is still lush. The weather is cooler and less humid.
There is only a small chance of a cold front strong enough to discourage you from exploring. As a bonus, the lodging rates are
usually lowest until mid-December.

WHEN YOU ARRIVE

What to wear

The weather information above should give you an idea of the
type of clothing you'll need. Most of the year, shorts or lightweight pants are comfortable. Any time you plan to go on a trail,
it's better to wear lightweight long-sleeved shirts and long pants
to prevent mosquito, chigger, poison ivy, and sunburn problems. Clothing should be loose so that it doesn't stick to you from
the humidity.

It's amazing how cold it can get in Florida during a winter cold
front, when the temperature is in the 40s or 50s (°F), the wind is

5

blowing, and it's damp. At these times (usually from December to March), it's good to have several lightweight layers of sweaters and jackets.

Sunglasses and a sun hat are useful most of the year. Comfortable walking shoes or jogging shoes will be suitable for the trails, especially if you don't mind getting them wet.

Most restaurants are casual in central Florida. Even in restaurants that serve gourmet food, most people wear casual clothing. Shorts are not uncommon in restaurants.

Fishing Licenses

State saltwater fishing licenses are required, with the following exceptions: 1) an individual under 16 years of age, 2) an individual fishing from a charter boat that has a vessel saltwater fishing license, 3) a Florida resident 65 years of age or older, and 4) a Florida resident fishing in saltwater from land or from a structure fixed to the land. Residents may obtain a 10-day, 1-year, 5-year, or lifetime license, and nonresidents may obtain a 3-day, 7-day, or 1-year license. Licenses are also required for freshwater fishing. The "cane pole law" allows a person to fish without a license in the county of his or her residence, with a pole not equipped with a reel, and using live or natural bait (catch and size limits still apply). Licenses may be obtained from county tax collectors' offices or from bait and tackle shops.

The State Park System

The many state parks (including recreation areas, preserves, and reserves) are maintained to keep the lands in or restore them to their conditions when the first Europeans arrived. The historic sites preserve the cultural heritage. Fees are charged at most sites. People who plan to explore a number of parks, or who live near a park that they visit frequently, should consider buying an annual individual or family pass.

The parks are open from 8 AM to sunset every day of the year including holidays (a few open earlier and are noted below in the park entry). The gate may close at an odd time, such as 7:22 PM.

Parks with campgrounds generally allow check-ins after sunset. Primitive campsites have no facilities, and campers must pack out their trash. Pets are permitted only in designated areas and must be kept on a 6-foot (maximum) hand-held leash. Pets are not allowed in swimming, camping, beach, or concession areas. Guide dogs for the disabled are welcomed in all areas. Horses (where permitted) must have proof of a recent negative Coggins test.

The National Wildlife Refuge and National Park System

The National Wildlife Refuge system is composed of over 500 refuges across the country. Many were established to protect habitat for migratory birds, such as waterfowl. The first refuge, Pelican Island in central Florida, was created to protect a colony of nesting water birds. Recently, many refuges have been established to protect habitat for a single endangered species, such as Crystal River National Wildlife Refuge for manatees, Florida Panther National Wildlife Refuge for panthers, and so on. St. John's National Wildlife Refuge was established to protect habitat for the dusky seaside sparrow. The refuge has been closed to the public to protect the sparrows. However, since the dusky became extinct in 1990, the refuge may open to the public in the near future. The first refuge established to protect endangered habitat is in central Florida—the Lake Wales Ridge National Wildlife Refuge.

Unlike national parks, the refuges were created solely for protecting natural resources. Only compatible activities are permitted. This is why few public amenities are offered. Many have educational facilities, such as a visitor center. Some have concessions that rent canoes or offer guided tours. None of the central Florida refuges permit camping. When you visit a refuge, come prepared with drinking water and anything else you may need. Pets may or may not be permitted (see separate entry or call the refuge to confirm).

The national park system was established to protect our natural resources while providing a way for people to enjoy them.

Thus, they usually have more tourist facilities than the refuges. The only national park site in central Florida is Canaveral National Seashore.

Purchasers of a federal Duck Stamp (available at post offices and refuges; currently $15) are allowed free admission to all national wildlife refuges. Duck stamps are good for one year from July 1 to June 30, and nonhunters may purchase one. The funds from the stamps are used to buy habitat for more refuges. Purchasers of a Golden Eagle pass (currently $25), good for one year from the date of purchase, are allowed free admission to any federal fee area. This includes all national parks, monuments, seashores, historic sites, and national wildlife refuges anywhere in the United States. Handicapped individuals may obtain a free Golden Access pass (good for free admission to any federal fee area). Senior citizens may obtain a Golden Age pass for a modest one-time fee, good for free admission to any federal fee area. All passes may be obtained at any federal fee area.

Conservation tips

Good conservationists bring their creed with them wherever they go. Because of the tremendous volume of tourists coming to Florida every year, the natural resources are being severely stressed. You can help insure that your visit here has a minimal environmental impact by observing a few suggestions:

1. *Conserve water.* Except during periods of heavy rainfall, central Florida often has a critical water shortage. This shortage usually occurs during the winter dry season, which coincides with the tourist season. During droughts, a county may impose water restrictions. Historically (and ridiculously) these have come when there was already a water shortage—not earlier, when it could have prevented one. Restrictions can include a requirement by restaurants that waiters serve water only on request. You should refuse water at restaurants unless you plan to drink it. Don't criticize the restaurant for poor service if water is not automatically provided.

Other restrictions include watering lawns and washing cars. Keep your showers short, and use your ingenuity to think of other ways you can save water. The lack of water is bad enough, but a compounding problem is that it drives engineers and city planners to find new ways to retrieve water (like drilling a new well), usually at a cost to the environment.

2. *Drive carefully to avoid hitting wildlife.* Watch for snakes warming themselves on roads in the winter as the air cools in late afternoon or escaping high water after heavy rains. Drive slower than the maximum speed limit, especially at night. Headlights, particularly high beams, temporarily blind animals and cause them to freeze in their tracks; keep this in mind when driving in rural areas at night.

If you are motorboating, watch the water ahead of you for ripples that might indicate a manatee is surfacing. If you are near a manatee, cut your motor to neutral gear until the manatee has moved away. Observe posted signs that warn of manatee areas.

3. *Be a responsible angler.* Remove monofilament line from the water and shore—many animals have been slowly strangled or dismembered by discarded fishing lines. Resist fishing just for sport, because this harasses the fish and accomplishes nothing for the angler. The fish do not play games for fun with anglers—they fight for their lives. Those games frequently cause the exhausted and stressed fish to succumb to predation or disease. Catching and releasing fish for sport does not qualify an angler as a conservationist; leaving them alone does. Fish that are to be released should be handled carefully with wet hands and placed promptly and gently underwater.

4. *Don't collect souvenirs from the wild.* All national and state parks prohibit the collection of plants, animals, rocks, etc. This is a good policy to follow everywhere. Take photographs instead.

5. *Don't feed wild animals.* Alligators, raccoons, and other wildlife learn to associate food with humans. This has caused some attacks on humans by alligators looking for

handouts. The alligator usually gets shot as punishment. Most human food causes health problems to wild animals. All state parks, national parks, and national wildlife refuges strictly prohibit feeding wild animals.

6. *Recycle your containers.* Shamefully, there has never been a "Bottle Bill" in Florida. Most state and national parks have bins for recyclable beverage containers.

7. *If you witness a violation against wildlife, call the Wildlife Alert Hotline:* for the Lakeland region at (800)282-8002, for the West Palm Beach region at (800)432-2046. You may receive a reward if your tip results in a conviction.

Local precautions

There are probably no more hazards in central Florida than anywhere else in the country . . . just some different ones. You have chosen an adventurous and occasionally risky hobby. Everyone should have a safe and enjoyable trip. However, every person is different and has varying reactions to adverse conditions. While park rangers and other staff are well-trained, they cannot predict the weather, wildlife-people interactions, and the experience level of each person they advise. You must rely on your own common sense and recognition of your experience level to have a safe trip. *Please note that the rules and regulations listed below for the natural areas are not all-inclusive. Additional regulations may apply and may be obtained by contacting the areas.*

Your trip to Florida should be perfectly delightful, without any of the misfortunes mentioned below. The chance of a safe trip is increased if you are aware of the following situations.

Weather
Thunderstorms and Lightning

The thunderstorm season begins around May and lasts till November, the duration of the wet season. The heaviest rainfall months are June to September. Within these months, it is possible to have a thunderstorm almost daily. The Tampa area leads the country in the number of days with thunderstorms per year, averaging 80 to 90 days. Most of the rest of central Florida averages 80 to 85, while the east coast averages 70 to 80 days. Thunderstorms may occur at any time of the year. They are often caused by heat rising from the warming land, creating unstable air above. A cumulonimbus cloud (or "thunderhead") indicates a potential thunderstorm.

The major hazard of these storms is the lightning they produce. In Florida, a single day of intense thunderstorms can cause 10,000 lightning strikes. Next to being at the center of a thunderstorm, the most dangerous place to be is under the leading edge. Don't assume you are safe if the storm hasn't quite hit. Don't underestimate lightning. It causes about 10 deaths and 25 injuries a year in Florida, or about 10 percent of lightning-caused deaths in the United States.

If you are out on the water, try to get to land, where you are not as exposed. Do not get into the water, because water conducts electricity. Never stand under the tallest object around. Drop anything metal you are carrying (sorry, that means binoculars and cameras, too). If you find yourself in the midst of lightning strikes with no shelter, as on an open boat, kneel down on your hands and knees, away from the motor, antennas, and console. The hands and knees posture makes a "path of least resistance" for the electricity to follow and gives you a better chance of survival than by sitting or lying down. Try to find a ditch or depression to crouch in.

Other hazards from thunderstorms include high winds and hail. High winds are almost always associated with thunderstorms, while hail is infrequent. High winds can be a problem for canoeists, who should always be vigilant for thunderstorm development.

Hurricanes

Florida has the highest probability of any region in the country of getting struck by a hurricane. The National Weather Service designates June 1 to November 30 as the official hurricane season. There have been hurricanes or tropical storms in the Atlantic Ocean during every month of the year except April. The height of the tropical activity (tropical waves, depressions, storms, and hurricanes) is late August to mid-October. There-fore, you can minimize the possibility of encountering a tropical storm or hurricane by avoiding these months for your trip.

Hurricanes play an important ecological role. During the summer and fall, when the temperature of tropical waters can become dangerously high for marine organisms, hurricanes function by cooling the water. The heat rises from the water and is carried northward to cooler waters by the clouds and the wind. That is why higher ocean temperatures increase the chance of a hurricane forming and why global warming can set off an increase of hurricanes. Hurricanes are vital to maintaining the balance of life in the oceans.

Don't count on the local municipal emergency shelters being able to accommodate tourists during a storm. Shelters cannot even support all the residents. If you travel to coastal central Florida during the hurricane season, it is possible you will be mandated to evacuate inland to higher ground. A storm surge (a wall of water pushed by the wind) can raise tides 20 feet or more above normal, causing more deaths than the wind itself. Before heading to Florida during hurricane season, check the National Weather Service for tropical weather activity.

Tornadoes and Waterspouts

Tornadoes are common in Florida, particularly March through May. They may occur in any month and often accompany trop-ical storms and hurricanes. Tornadoes are not as common in the southern tip of the peninsula as in the central and northern parts. Florida also has the aquatic version of a tornado—the waterspout. A waterspout forms over a large body of water, such as the ocean. Most often, a waterspout is short-lived, relatively weak, and never reaches land. The funnel may never even touch the surface of the water. Such a waterspout is not hazardous, but if you see a funnel cloud of either type, seek shelter in a sturdy building.

Poisonous plants

The initial panic an amateur botanist feels when seeing central Florida plants for the first time is that so many of them look alike. The generic morphology (form) of leaves exposed to heavy seasonal rains is a leathery surface with smooth edges and pointed tips. This facilitates shedding rainwater. The myriad of look-alike plants presents a problem to the careful naturalist who won't touch any plant that he or she can't identify. Some plants in this region have parts that are toxic if ingested or if touched by a sensitive person. Poison ivy is the only one commonly found in the area. It has a compound leaf with three leaflets, hence the expression "leaves of three, don't touch me." It grows as a creeping ground cover, as a shrub, or as a fuzzy vine climbing the trunk of a tree. You should expect to find it just about anywhere around Florida, especially where there has been disturbance (such as the side of a trail).

To be safe from an irritating rash or worse, always identify a plant before touching it. If you find you have bumped against a poisonous species, wash your skin with plenty of sudsy cold water as soon as possible. See also Brazilian pepper under "Exotic Plants."

Vertebrate Animals
Snakes

There are four kinds of venomous snakes in central Florida: the eastern diamondback rattlesnake, the dusky pygmy rattlesnake, the Florida cottonmouth (also known as the water moccasin), and the eastern coral snake. Encounters with these snakes are rare. The nonvenomous Florida water snake is often mistaken for the less common cottonmouth, and the nonvenomous scarlet snake and scarlet kingsnake can be confused with the coral snake. Coral snakes are nocturnal and burrow under loose litter, so it is unlikely you will encounter one by accident. If you see a brightly colored (red, yellow, and black) banded snake with a black nose whose identity you are unsure of, recall the adage "Red touch yellow kills a fellow" to remind you that if the red and yellow bands are touching each other, you are looking at a venomous snake.

Sharks

Sharks are common in the warm Florida waters. The vast majority are small, nonaggressive, and nonthreatening to humans. In the very few attacks that have occurred, the sharks were not intentionally seeking humans. Swimmers in shallow murky water are at risk because the sharks can smell something nearby, but they can't see what it is. Spear-fishermen have had fish they just caught snatched from their hands. One diver lost her hand this way. Some sharks eat lobsters, so sport lobsterers should be cautious when catching them. But keep this in mind— for every shark bite we endure, we kill about a million sharks.

To decrease your chances of getting bitten by a shark, avoid standing or swimming in shallow, murky water and don't hold fish or lobsters in your hand underwater. This is a good reason for divers and snorkelers to refrain from attracting reef fish by feeding them.

Alligators

Although they appear lethargic and slow-moving, these giant reptiles can react with blinding speed when provoked. Normally, alligators that have never seen a human are no threat to people. The problem arises when an alligator that lives near houses or a park becomes accustomed to people feeding it. Thereafter, that alligator recognizes humans as a source of food. Since an alligator has little intelligence, it can't distinguish that the food ends at the tip of the extended hand. A state law prohibits people from feeding alligators. It is extremely important to observe this regulation for your safety and the safety of people who visit after you.

In the wild, female alligators are extremely protective of their young. Since they may guard them for over a year, no time of year is without defensive females. Therefore, if you are walking in an area where there are alligators, look and listen carefully, and be ready to back off if you hear the babies' squeaky, whimpering "yurt, yurt" calls for help.

Alligators look at dogs and cats as the perfect dinner items. Therefore, keep your pets under your control at all times, and keep them well away from canals, ponds, and other wetlands.

Insects

Most people deal with insects by applying repellents. While this works, repellents are not without hazards sometimes worse than the original problem. The active ingredient in most repellents, called DEET (N,N-diethyl-m-toluamide), has been linked to seizures and several deaths in the United States (MMWR 1989). It is absorbed through the skin and into the circulatory system. About 10–15 percent of the amount applied to the skin passes into the urine. Insect repellents with DEET can eat through vinyl and plastic. Watchbands and car seats can be damaged if your DEET-covered skin contacts them. Some of the hazards of frequent applications of insect repellent were discovered when Everglades National Park officials conducted investigations to determine why their rangers were experiencing frequent headaches and nervous disorders.Here is a summary of some precautions to take when using repellents (MMWR 1989):

- wear long sleeves and pants and apply repellent only to exposed skin or to clothing
- use low concentrations of DEET
- never apply repellent to wounds
- apply once every 4–8 hours; over-application will not improve effect
- wash skin after returning indoors

Certain people, such as children, are more sensitive to repellent than others. Be courteous by not spraying repellent near other people or indoors.

Mosquitoes

From June to November, coinciding with the wet months, the mosquitoes can be plentiful. Many months of the year can be devoid of mosquitoes. December to May is usually dry enough to prevent mosquitoes from hatching, and cold fronts often kill the adults.

Mosquito eggs need water coverage to hatch. The eggs hatch after flooding by rains or high tides, and the larvae mature in 5 to 10 days. Standing water, such as accumulates in old tires, flower pots, and gutters, is perfect for the proliferation of mosquitoes. Therefore, many people contribute to their own mosquito problems by allowing mosquito breeding places in their yards.

You are more likely to encounter mosquitoes in the coastal mangrove areas and hammocks than in the freshwater marshes. The common saltmarsh mosquito shuns strong sunlight, so you are better off in the open than in the shade and better off in the daytime than at night.

The female mosquito needs the protein from blood to form her eggs; thus it is only the females that bite. The males feed on nectar; they do for marsh flowers what bees do for meadow flowers—they pollinate them. We need mosquitoes.

Fire ants

Some people can ignore swarms of mosquitoes, listlessly swat at horseflies, and calmly step around rattlesnakes. But have you ever seen a human do anything other than frantically explode at the attack of fire ants? The ants in question are the red imported fire ants (*Solenopsis invicta*), which were accidentally introduced into Alabama from Brazil in the 1920s. Since then, they have spread all over the southeastern United States, eventually reaching central Florida in the 1960s.

These fire ants are red and less than an eighth of an inch long. They are not often seen unless their mound is stepped on. Fire ants have one of the quickest reaction times to nest agitation of any ant, and it's usually too quick for the agitator. They leave itchy raised pustules that persist for weeks. The nest mounds are piles of dirt about 6 to 12 inches high and can most often be found in disturbed areas, such as the side of a road.

Lovebugs

The dread of automobile drivers in central Florida at certain times of the year is a perfectly harmless insect. The problem is that this insect, the lovebug (*Plecia neartica*, Order Diptera), swarms over roads in dense courtship flights twice a year in April–May and late August–September. The bugs are very sticky and create a nasty mess to clean from windshields. In fact, they may even damage the paint if not promptly washed off. Lovebugs can also clog your radiator. If you plan to drive during those months, avoid the daytime after 10 AM, when the lovebugs are most active.

Lovebugs are about a third of an inch long and are black with a red thorax. They feed on nectar and pollen and do not bite. Their common name derives from their mating flights in the spring and fall, when males and females fly clasped together in amplexus (mating position). Love bugs are native to Mexico and the Gulf Coast of Texas, but they invaded central Florida in the 1960s.

Other insects and arthropods

"No-see-ums" (or "sand-gnats") (*Culicoides furens*, Order Diptera) are minuscule insects that take painful bites and leave itchy welts. No-see-ums are so small and quick that most people don't see what bit them, hence the colloquial name. They appear at dawn and dusk, usually near mangroves and salt water, and stay for a brief but nasty hour. Because of these tiny insects, camping tents must have the fine-meshed no-see-um-proof netting, not just mosquito netting.

The scorpions (*Centruroides gracilis*, Class Arachnida) in Florida are not the same as the ones in the southwestern United States. Ours are not fatally venomous, but their stings can make a person ill. Scorpions are found throughout Florida, but you will not be likely to see one unless you are searching for it. Scorpions prefer to hide under wood (such as fallen branches or lumber) rather than rocks. Instead of using your bare hands, use a walking staff or tripod leg to flip a piece of wood over. Always put the wood back exactly as you found it, so unseen creatures are not left homeless.

Deerflies (*Tabanus* spp., Order Diptera), which resemble giant house flies, are large and slow enough so that it's hard to miss them even before they bite. This is lucky, because their bites take a disproportionately large share of your skin. They are active during broad daylight, usually in the summer.

Chiggers (Family Trombiculidae, Class Arachnida) are almost microscopic orange larval mites that burrow into the skin and feed on lymph. Their saliva causes itchy welts that can last for weeks. The best prevention for chiggers is wearing long pants tucked into your socks, not sitting on rocks or logs, and showering immediately after hiking (a chigger may crawl over your skin for hours before settling on a suitable place).

Miscellaneous

Humidity

Photographers beware! The central Florida humidity and salt spray can insidiously destroy your delicate equipment. Binoculars and spotting scopes are often victims, too. Wipe moisture and salt spray off the exterior surfaces frequently. Carry a heavy plastic bag with you in case of a sudden downpour. Additionally, there is the intense heat to contend with. Keep your equipment and film in the shade or in a cooler.

Sunburn

Locals can usually tell who the tourists are—they have the peeling sunburns or the dark tans. People who have lived a long time in Florida have learned how harmful the sun's rays can be. They protect their skin and consequently look pale compared to visitors. Skin cancer is prevalent in the South and getting more common every year as the protective ozone layer in the atmosphere is depleted. No time of the year is safe. In winter, although the Earth's axis is tilted away from the sun, the Earth is closer to the sun, so the rays are very strong. In summer, the Earth is farther but the rays are more direct. If you are swimming, boating, or just wading through water, you'll get a double whammy, because the rays will reflect off the water, too. Use sunblock, or wear a hat and long sleeves to keep the sun off your skin. Prolonged exposure to strong ultra-violet (UV) rays can damage the retinas of your eyes and cause cataracts, so wear sunglasses that block UV rays.

Crime

Regrettably, the metropolitan areas of Florida have attained high crime rates, some of which is aimed at tourists. Thieves watch people for signs of vulnerability, such as being lost or in unfamiliar surroundings. Crime is not common in most of the places mentioned in this book, but disguising yourself as a local and using common sense will go a long way toward deterring it.

A BRIEF HUMAN HISTORY
OF CENTRAL FLORIDA

The first Europeans to gaze upon the shores of Florida were the Spanish explorers, lead by Juan Ponce de León in 1513. Ponce de León, who was seeking riches and natives to capture as slaves, claimed the area for Spain. He bestowed the name "La Florida" because he landed on the shore on Easter, the holiday of "Pascua Florida." More than likely, few conspicuous flowers greeted his eyes. The assortment of showy flowers presently gracing the state is primarily from other continents!

The Seminoles and Miccosukees, the two Native American tribes currently in southern and central Florida, were not the original inhabitants. These two tribes descended from Creeks who settled here after being chased from their ancestral lands in present-day north Florida, Georgia, and Alabama by intolerant Europeans. Both tribes preferred to live quietly without interference from Europeans. They retreated farther and farther south until they ended up in the Everglades, a vast wetland scorned by the Europeans. Still, the federal government, supported by wealthy white landowners eager to acquire more land, wanted all the native people expelled. The Indian Removal Act of 1830 forced the southeastern Indians, including the Seminoles, to march on foot over 800 miles to a reservation in what is now Oklahoma. The forced exodus is known today as the "Trail of Tears," because so many died of hunger, exhaustion, cold, heat, and disease. Some Seminoles resisted the removal, including the Seminole leader Osceola. Osceola led his people in this struggle against the federal government, which became known as the Second Seminole War (1835–42). The Seminoles never surrendered, but the war wound down after the federal government lost 1,500 men and $30 million.

The Seminoles and the Miccosukees are recognized as separate tribes by the federal government. The Seminoles' Brighton Reservation (one of five reservations in Florida) is in Glades County, near the northwest part of Lake Okeechobee. Most Miccosukees live on several reservations in south Florida. Both tribes try to keep their cultures flourishing by hunting and selling crafts.

Before the Seminoles and Miccosukees arrived, the Tequesta inhabited southeast Florida from the present Palm Beach area to Homestead. The Jeaga lived in a small area around Jupiter and Hobe Sound. The Ais lived north of the Jaega around Melbourne. Much of the northern half of the Florida peninsula was occupied by the Timucuans. Along the west coast, the Tocobaga dwelt from Tarpon Springs to Boca Grande. The Calusa inhabited southwest Florida, from the present Punta Gorda to Marco. All the native Florida tribes disappeared soon after the arrival of the Europeans. They were either killed by Europeans or chased to West Indian islands, where their blood eventually mingled with the West Indians'.

The Spaniards and Americans alternated ownership of the peninsula until 1845, when Florida attained statehood (only to secede from the Union in 1861). As recently as the 1800s, few people of European origin lived in central Florida. Much of the area was marsh, swamp, and scrub. The narrow strip of coastal ridge along the Atlantic was dry enough for development, with nearby fertile lands for farming. There were few roads; travel was mostly by boat along the coast, rivers, and lakes. Steamboats plied the St. Johns and the Oklawaha Rivers, while sailing vessels skimmed the coastal waters.

Rich beds of phosphate, known locally as "white gold," were discovered in central Florida in 1889. The find set off a stampede of prospectors, a small-scale version of the Californian quest for yellow gold. To this day, the largest deposits of phosphorus in United States are in Florida, which produces one-third of the world's supply. Phosphate rock underlies most of the state.

Of all the gifts Florida has bestowed, the citrus industry has been the king. The story began in the 1500s, when the Spanish explorers imported orange trees. Some seeds were scattered (probably by natives) on high ground in many places, and to this day it is possible to find descendants of these trees growing in otherwise wild places. Central Florida was a prime location for citrus groves because of the climate and soil. Grapefruits did not arrive, however, until 1809. The great freezes of 1835 and the winter of 1884–85 destroyed many trees, causing localized economic depressions. The latter loss encouraged the industry to reestablish its groves farther south. The southward migration continues today, causing losses of some remaining natural areas. The scrub areas are particularly favored.

A traveler in central Florida can hardly miss the traces of an era when cattle ranching was a bigger business than producing citrus. Many cattle ranches still thrive, but the ranching methods have become modernized. In the 1800s, a typical rancher allowed his cattle to roam the scrub. Thus, the cattle were called scrub cows. The ranch hands who drove the cattle to market were known as "cow hunters," because they did not want to be called "boys" and because they truly did have to hunt down the cows in the scrub. They rode horseback and carried long whips that they used to control the animals. Historians say that the cow hunters never used a whip on an animal, but rather cracked the whip in the air so fast that it sounded like a gunshot and served as the only control needed. This is where the term "Florida Cracker" originated, although the term is frequently used to refer to a native Floridian.

Coastal communities became popular as winter vacation spots in the 1800s with wealthy people from northern states. The interior was attractive to farmers for the nearly year-round growing season and ample water.

In the early 1900s, minds were merged to solve the pesky mosquito problem. In 1927, St. Lucie County began to dig ditches to drain the marshes where mosquitoes bred. Instead, the ditches retained water and increased the problem. Now, sea water is pumped into the marshes and the problem has abated.

A QUICK LOOK
AROUND CENTRAL FLORIDA

Geologically speaking, Florida is the youngest of the contiguous states, having emerged from the sea about 20 million years ago. This occurred when the Earth's climate was cooling, causing sea levels to subside when so much water became frozen in the polar ice caps. Several physiographic features define central Florida. For the most part, the terrain is extremely flat. However, a north-south ridge forming a spine down the middle provides modest but ecologically significant elevations. The elevation of central Florida ranges from sea level to 298 feet above sea level (at the Bok Tower hill). The lake region lies east of the ridge. Hundreds of miles of coastline along the Gulf of Mexico and the Atlantic Ocean contain sandy beaches, salt marshes, and mangroves. Perhaps the most prominent single feature is Lake Okeechobee, the largest freshwater lake entirely within U.S. boundaries. At 730 square miles, it is so immense that it is recognizable from space.

The ridges that rise out of the central prairies are ancient reminders of pre-Pleistocene islands that were once all that existed of Florida. As waves and wind piled sand higher onto the islands, giant sand dunes were born. The ridge was formed as a prehistoric coastline, causing the shape of the Florida peninsula then to mimic the current shape, but on a much narrower scale. When the islands became isolated from the mainland, several species of plants and animals evolved separately from their nearest relatives. One species, the Florida mouse, originally was part of a population of mice that inhabited the land all around the Gulf of Mexico before the sea level rose. As the water rose, these mice were separated from their relatives. Once the water receded and the islands rejoined the mainland, the mice were still spatially separated from their nearest relatives, which were in Guatemala. Similar stories can be told about many other animals and plants on the ridges.

The ridges are composed of layers of sand up to several hundred feet deep. Water percolates so quickly and thoroughly through the sand that the plants must survive on very little moisture. Most of the nutrients are also quickly leached from sand, so the plants must be adapted to finding nutrients in other ways. Differences of inches in elevation can dramatically alter the vegetation types. Due to the dryness, even in the wet season, this scrub habitat has evolved to be not only fire-tolerant, but fire-dependent.

The arid scrub habitat resembles the American Southwest desert. Indeed, even some of the species that thrive here are found in the desert, such as the scrub jay and an agave-like plant (*Nolina brittoniana*). The Florida ziziphus, once thought to be extinct, is found here on only three sites. Although a specimen sat in an herbarium since 1948, the plant was not described until 1984! Possibly the only reason it avoided extinction was that it has thorny branches, which cattle will not eat. The ziziphus' closest relative is a Southwest species. Other scrub plants include scrub plum, Carter's mustard, and wireweed. The first lichen ever federally listed, Florida perforate lichen, is found here. Endemic animals include the Florida mole skink (which feeds on cockroaches, spiders, and crickets), sand skink, Florida pine snake, and Florida scrub lizard. Other scrub species have become isolated by intervening recent wetlands.

The most prominent ridge is the Lake Wales Ridge, about 100 miles long, from 4 to 13 miles wide, and rising to an elevation of almost 300 feet. Most of the ridge has been converted to citrus groves or residential development. The U.S. Fish and Wildlife Service recognized the value of the remaining ridge and created the 499th national wildlife refuge on scattered parts of it. Located only 60 miles from the first refuge in the national system (Pelican Island), the Lake Wales Ridge National Wildlife Refuge was established in 1994 to conserve a variety of endangered plants and animals endemic to the central ridge scrub. The area has 13 endangered and threatened species of plants, 13 rare plants, and four federally listed wildlife species—the greatest concentration of listed species in eastern North America. The refuge will get a slow start due to the immense funding requirements for purchasing the goal of 19,630 acres on 12 separate parcels in Highlands and Polk counties. Realistically, approximately 13,000 acres will be purchased. Habitat management, such as prescribed burns, will be practiced to maintain healthy scrub. As of press time, the parcels are scattered and not accessible to the public. For more information, contact Merritt Island National Wildlife Refuge (see separate entry). Parts of the refuge may become accessible in the near future, especially if public support aids in obtaining funds to operate and manage the refuge. Another smaller ridge runs through Withlacoochee State Forest and several other small ones are nearby.

The lake region of central Florida, located primarily in Lake, Polk, Osceola, and Highlands counties, is underlain by limestone. Some lakes are caused by dissolving of the rock and some are caused by sinkholes. Only a few were formed by rivers. Most obtain their water from rainfall and groundwater seepage. Most of the lakes are shallow, with depths less than 16.5 feet (including Lake Okeechobee). The riverine lakes, such as Lake Kissimmee and Lake Hachineha, flow into the Kissimmee River and ultimately into Lake Okeechobee. These smaller lakes are the source of much of Okeechobee's water.

All of the Atlantic coast and most of the Gulf coast of Florida are protected by barrier islands. These long, narrow islands block the full force of the waves and wind, which is particularly important during storms. Barrier islands are more necessary on the Atlantic coast than the Gulf because the continental shelf has a steeper slope on the Atlantic and thus the waves are bigger. The shallow slope and small waves on the Gulf are what allow shells to roll gently ashore, making the barrier islands along the Gulf coast one of the best places in the world for shelling. The islands are formed as sand is washed along the shore by the currents. The barrier islands are dynamic—their shape is constantly changing because of shifting sand. When a major storm blows in from the sea, barrier islands are the most vulnerable and dangerous places for people to be.

Behind the sheltering islands, where the wind and waves are calmed, mangrove stands and estuaries can form. These habitats are the primary nurseries for many of the fish and crustaceans we depend on for food. It is here that many larval fish, crabs, shrimp, scallops, oysters, and lobsters find the nourishment they need to grow.

Lake Okeechobee is full of history and human-made tragedy. Once teeming with fish, it was treated for many years as a reservoir that existed mostly to serve the water needs of south Florida. Historically, the lake had a shallow bank that held the water in. When heavy rains fell, as during the summer wet season, the water overflowed the southern bank into the low-lands that were once part of the Everglades. There the water started a gradual sheet flow south toward Florida Bay and the Gulf of Mexico. Thus the soil just south of the lake, which received an annual flush of the lake's nutrients, became extremely fertile. In fact, it was (and may still be) some of the most fertile farmland in the country. However, during the hurricanes of 1926 and 1928, massive amounts of wind-driven water breached the southern bank and an estimated 400 and 2,000 people, respectively, died from the floods. As a result, the Central and Southern Flood Control District was established. One of the first tasks undertaken was to build a dike around the southern end of the lake. Obviously, the quenching water and nourishing components could no longer bathe the northern Everglades. The intricate link between Lake Okeechobee and the Everglades had been broken. The Everglades, now divided by canals and levees, has lost much of its sheet flow and its surface area.

Lightning-caused fires are an integral part of central Florida's natural health. Most habitats, such as scrub and pinelands, are adapted to fire. Prior to development, the native peoples frequently set fires to aid the process. Most natural fires occur from May through August, when the end of the dry season overlaps with the start of the thunderstorm season. After the wet season has progressed a few months, the land normally becomes too wet to kindle large fires.

If ever a river had an identity complex, it's the Kissimmee (Seminole for "long water"). Once a graceful, meandering 102-mile waterway, carrying millions of gallons of clean water to feed Lake Okeechobee, the Kissimmee fell victim to well-intentioned but naïve state and federal engineers. The concept was to straighten the river into a diked channel half the original length to prevent flooding and increase farmland. The construction began in 1961. But the 300-foot-wide, 30-foot-deep channel caused a loss of over 35,000 acres of wetlands and a 90 percent reduction in migratory waterfowl. No sooner had the Army Corps of Engineers completed the project in 1971 when it became obvious that the results were disastrous. No longer could the floodplains filter the agricultural and residential nutrients and pollutants. Straight into Lake Okeechobee they went! So devastating was the situation that environmentalists immediately began to lobby to dechannelize the river (by then known by the denigrating name of C-38, where the "C" stands for canal). In 1994, after two decades of feasibility studies, the South Florida Water Management District began the first step to recreate some of the original meanders by backfilling 25 miles of a straight channel. That should restore 56 miles of the river. The environmental world holds its breath with hope while the project progresses. The financial cost of undoing this fiasco is too incredible to print.

II
HABITATS

It is always difficult to separate a large land mass into distinct habitats, since they may be intertwined. In central Florida, where elevation changes are so subtle, a small hill may constitute one habitat, while the surrounding depression may be another. An ecosystem is usually composed of several types of habitats that must all function together.

In Florida, the influence of weather is profound. The balmy Caribbean breezes would govern the type of vegetation were it not for the occasional cold front that barrels down from the north. Many of the fronts weaken before reaching the peninsula, but some of the stronger ones survive to reach the Florida Keys and even Cuba. Those few cold fronts, especially if they carry frosts, dictate the type of vegetation that will survive. Such tropical species as the mangroves can grow well only as far north as (approximately) Citrus County on the Gulf and Brevard County on the east. In general, the coastal regions, which are warmer in winter because of the moderating influence of the sea, support tropical species farther north than inland.

SWAMP

A swamp is a wooded wetland. Several types occur in central Florida. They surround lakes and ponds, line the shallow banks of rivers and streams, and fill depressions in the land. The primary tree cover types are cypress and red maple. In all types of swamps in central Florida, it is common to find epiphytes growing on the tree trunks. Bromeliads, orchids, and ferns grow best in damp, warm, shady habitats.

Cypress

Scattered throughout the freshwater wetlands of central Florida are vast stands of conifers known locally as cypresses, although they are not true cypresses but bald-cypresses. Unlike most conifers, cypresses shed their needles around November each year (hence look bald) and sprout new ones in February or March. Taxonomists argue whether the pond-cypress is a separate species or a variety of bald-cypress. Pond-cypresses grow in still water, while bald-cypresses frequently grow along rivers and slow-moving waters.

Cypresses grow best with their roots in water and are the most flood-tolerant freshwater trees in Florida. Two of their most recognizable characteristics, the swelling buttresses and spindly "knees," are adaptations to their watery environment. The knees are projections of the roots that emerge from the water, probably to assist with respiration when the oxygen levels surrounding the roots are low. Oddly, although the seeds need to soak in water, they won't germinate under water. Vast cypress swamps across the southeastern United States were logged for their rot-resistant lumber. Cypress lumbering is still big business in some areas.

Places to look for cypresses are Barley Barber Swamp (with some of the oldest cypresses in Florida), Green Swamp, Dupuis Reserve State Forest, Bull Creek Wildlife Management Area, John Chestnut, Sr. County Park, Tosohatchee State Reserve (with one of the last virgin stands), Highlands Hammock, Hontoon Island, Jonathan Dickinson, and Hillsborough River State Parks.

Some wildlife species that commonly use cypress habitats are swallow-tailed kites, red-shouldered hawks, prothonotary warblers, fox squirrels, river otters, and alligators.

Hardwood Swamp

Other types of trees besides cypresses grow along rivers, such as black gum and southern redcedar. Rivers with major flood-plains are the St. Johns, Withlacoochee, Fisheating Creek, Loxa-hatchee, Hillsborough, and Alafia.

Bromeliad-clad cypress trees stand with their roots in shallow water at the end of the dry season (Susan D. Jewell)

Swamps that lie in depressions typically support red maples, bays (sweet, swamp, loblolly, and redbay), and pond-apples. Maple swamps are quite common. The red maples lose their leaves for the winter even in central Florida.

Hardwood swamps can be found at Green Swamp, Sawgrass Lake Park, Lettuce Lake Regional Park, Wekiwa Springs State Park, Lower Wekiva River State Preserve, and along the Peace and Withlacoochee Rivers.

HAMMOCK

Hammocks are "islands" of trees generally growing on higher elevations than the surrounding landscape. They have evolved from lack of fire exposure and are the upland climax community. They grow on rich organic soils and are generally densely canopied and diverse in flora. Tropical hardwood hammocks are dense stands that contain primarily West Indian tree species. They are the only tropical hardwood forests in the continental United States and are probably the most endangered habitat in

Live oaks draped with Spanish moss. Note the open understory (Susan D. Jewell)

the country. The current land-grab and development boom along the coastal resort areas (where the tropical hammocks are primarily located) is destroying the remainder of this already geographically limited area. Conservation groups must work very hard to save the remaining tropical hardwood hammocks.

Other types of hammocks include subtropical, temperate, and oak hammocks. Oak hammocks typically consist of live oaks laden with epiphytes (such as Spanish moss and resurrection fern), and the understory is very open.

Blowing Rocks Preserve and Fort Pierce Inlet State Recreation Area have tropical hardwood hammock habitats. Live oak hammocks are found in numerous locations, including Hickory Hammock Trail, Avon Park Air Force Range, Merritt Island National Wildlife Refuge, Highlands Hammock State Park, Myakka River State Park, Tosohatchee State Reserve, Lake Kissimmee State Park, and Fort DeSoto Park.

PINELAND

There are several types of pinelands in central Florida, often difficult to separate. They share a few characteristics. They prefer infertile, well-drained soil and depend on fire to regenerate. Fires eliminate the competition for space by the invading hardwoods and cause the pine cones to open quickly and spread their seeds. Without the lightning-caused fires that swept through the pines over the centuries, the pinelands would have reverted to hardwoods. Much of the original pinelands have been lost that way, since we newcomers have suppressed fires. The suppression has been direct in many cases and indirect in many others. The roads, canals, and farms throughout the area have been effective firebreaks. Natural resource managers in parks containing pinelands (such as Myakka River, Oscar Scherer, Tosohatchee, Lake Kissimmee, and Jonathan Dickinson) practice prescribed burning, however, to keep the pines regenerating. The pine flatwoods, high pines, and pine scrub are the three primary types of pinelands.

Pine flatwoods at Tiger Creek Preserve (Susan D. Jewell)

Pine Flatwood

Pine flatwoods occur on level, often low-lying and poorly drained, terrain. This is the most extensive habitat type in central Florida. The three overstory species comprising the central Florida flatwoods are longleaf, slash, and pond pine. The canopy is rather open, with a well-developed low shrub layer and an often sparse herbaceous layer. The plants are fire-adapted and able to withstand months of drought in the dry season and months of inundation in the wet season. Typical shrubs found in the flatwoods are gallberry, wax myrtle, saw palmetto, and rusty lyonia. Wiregrass is characteristic of the herb layer. It has a beneficial relationship to longleaf pine. It forms persistent clumps of dead foliage which burn easily, and the resulting fires prevent the growth of shade-producing shrubs that outcompete longleaf seedlings.

Some herps that are common in pine flatwoods are the pine woods treefrog, pine woods snake, eastern diamondback rattlesnake, eastern glass lizard, and Florida box turtle. Typical mammals are fox squirrels, eastern moles, black bears, gray foxes, and bobcats. Brown-headed nuthatches, red-cockaded woodpeckers, Bachman's sparrows, and pine warblers typify the bird life.

Pine flatwoods can be found at Jonathan Dickinson, Highlands Hammocks, Hontoon Island, and Myakka River State Parks, as well as Avon Park Air Force Range, Dupuis Reserve State Forest, Weedon Island Preserve, and Upper Tampa Bay Park.

High Pine (Sandhill)

Slightly higher in elevation than the flatwoods is the high pine. In fact, the adjective refers to the elevation rather than the height of the trees. The terrain is rolling hills and the soil is sandy, giving rise to the synonym and more commonly used "sandhill." Historically, much of the sandhills were composed of longleaf pine, which was a fire-resistant and long-lived species. Longleaf pines can attain ages of 500 years or greater. This makes them valuable to red-cockaded woodpeckers, which may use the same tree cavities for nesting for many generations. Recently, much of the longleaf has been replanted by short-lived slash pines after the former were logged. An understory of deciduous oaks (primarily turkey oak) and sparkleberry, with wiregrass as a ground cover, is common to the sandhills. Only one federally listed plant, the clasping warea, is found in the high pine, contrasting to the many species found in the scrub pine.

A hike through the xeric sandhills may reveal such herps as gopher tortoises, Florida scrub lizards, Central Florida crowned snakes, eastern indigo snakes, and oak toads. Red-cockaded woodpeckers and Bachman's sparrows prefer the high pines. Florida mice, Sherman's fox squirrels, and southeastern pocket gophers are three mammals that are typical of the sandhills. The pocket gophers' burrows can easily be spotted by the light-colored mounds of soil next to the two-to-three-inch-wide round burrow entrances. Gophers play a vital role in soil exchange and distribution of nutrients in the soil layers.

Look for sandhills in Withlacoochee State Forest, Lower Wekiva River State Preserve, Rock Springs Run State Reserve, Fort Cooper State Park, Arbuckle State Forest and State Park, and Avon Park Air Force Range.

Pine Scrub

On the highest elevations of central Florida are the scrub habitats, and those supporting pines are the pine scrubs. They are characterized by the presence of sand pines, which often grow to a mere 20 feet in height. The soil is loose and sterile, making it difficult for large trees of any species to grow. Pine scrub is dependent on fire to regenerate itself. Sand pine scrubs thrive with fires every 10 to 100 years. If irrigated, pine scrub is good for growing citrus, and this has been the cause of the destruction of much of the habitat. Rosemary is an understory plant which is a common component of pine scrub.

Pine scrub is a harsh place for wildlife. It can get extremely dry in the winter and extremely hot in the summer, with little or no shade. Rainwater percolates quickly through the sandy soil, leaving no puddles for thirsty animals. A small number of species have adapted. Sand skinks, Florida worm lizards, gopher tortoises, scrub jays, and Florida mice are some of those hardy species. Aside from the jays, these species are all able to seek shelter underground, where it is cooler.

Most of the sand pine scrub is on the Lake Wales Ridge and along the coastal ridges. Look for it at Jonathan Dickinson, Highlands Hammock, Wekiwa Springs, and Blue Spring State Parks; Rock Springs Run State Reserve; Lower Wekiva River State Preserve; Little Manatee River and Lake Manatee State Recreation

Sand pines on the coastal ridge at Jonathan Dickinson State Park (Susan D. Jewell)

Areas; Archbold Biological Station; and Hobe Sound National Wildlife Refuge.

SCRUB

If you want to see a desert but can't afford to go to New Mexico, drive to central Florida. While it's not officially called a desert, it resembles one in many ways.

Scrub is a term applied to habitats that are generally xeric and nutrient-poor. The soils are sandy and do not hold moisture. The plant species that grow are adapted to long periods of little or no rainfall, low nutrients, and hot sunlight. Tree growth is stunted. Most of the plants have waxy-coated, hairy, or curled leaves to reduce moisture loss. About 40 percent of the plant species growing in the scrub are endemic, one of the highest rates in the continental United States. The scrub vegetation is adapted to fires between 30 to 80 years apart. If left unburned, the oaks grow densely but produce few acorns and the understory is shaded out. If burned too often, some species don't reach reproductive maturity.

Most of the terrestrial animal species are fossorial or semi-fossorial to escape the sun's rays. That is, they dig underground or use another animal's burrow. Examples are the Florida mouse, bluetail mole skink, sand skink, short-tailed snake, and the peninsula crowned snake. So specialized are the plants and animals that live in the Florida scrub that more than 30 species are not found anywhere else in the world. The scrub of central Florida more closely resembles the deserts of the American Southwest than anything else. In fact, some of the floral and faunal species are related to southwestern desert species.

Scrubs are situated on the highest elevations in central Florida. The scrubs along the Lake Wales Ridge are probably the oldest ecological community in the state. They were developing when the seas were lapping at the edge of the ridge and the rest of Florida was underwater. A difference in elevation of a few inches may determine which type of scrub will grow. The pine

An ancient sand dune near Sebring on the Lake Wales Ridge, about 60 miles from either coast (off-road vehicle tracks in foreground) (Susan D. Jewell

scrubs were discussed above. Two other types are the oak and coastal scrubs.

Oak Scrub

The oak scrubs are similar to the sand pine scrubs. In fact, they are often adjacent and intermingled. The oak scrubs are characterized by a short overstory with such species as myrtle oak, sand live oak, Chapman's oak, scrub oak, scrub hickory, and silk bay. The understory may include rusty lyonia, rosemary, and scrub palmetto. Lichens often cover the sandy ground, or the ground may be bare. One of the rarest shrubs in North America, the Florida ziziphus, was thought to be extinct until small groups were found on the Lake Wales Ridge. Other federally endangered plants are the scrub blazing star, scrub plum, and Carter's mustard. Rare or threatened animals include the sand skink, bluetail mole skink, Florida mouse, and Florida scrub jay. The sand skink is adapted to the loose sand by having tiny legs that fit into grooves when the legs are pressed against the body. This enables the skink to "swim" through the sand, staying hidden from predators and strong sunlight. It is found only in Florida and is the only member of its genus in the world. In central Florida, this federally threatened species is rarely found outside of the Lake Wales Ridge area.

Archbold Biological Station, Arbuckle State Forest and State Park, and Avon Park Air Force Range contain oak scrub.

Coastal Scrub

Along the barrier islands and the more recent former shorelines, sandy ridges rise from the mangroves and estuaries. Some of the coastal scrubs are sand pine scrub (see above) and some are dune scrub. The dunes are unstable and shift with the wind and tides. On these current or recent dunes, such plants as seagrape, scrub palmetto, cabbage palm, prickly-pear, rosemary, sand live oak, and staggerbush grow. Herps that thrive on coastal scrubs include gopher tortoise, peninsula crowned snake, Florida scrub

Coastal scrub at Savannas State Reserve, composed primarily of sand live oak and myrtle oak (Susan D. Jewell)

lizard, Florida pine snake, and Florida gopher frog. The scrub jay is typical of this habitat but is becoming rare.

Coastal scrubs may be seen at Hobe Sound and Merritt Island National Wildlife Refuges, Canaveral National Seashore, Blowing Rocks Preserve, Jonathan Dickinson State Park, Savannas State Reserve, and Caladesi Island State Park.

FRESH WATER BODIES

Most of Florida is low-lying and flat and receives a large annual rainfall. The Floridan Aquifer lies beneath most of the state, and the water table is relatively high. Aside from the sandy soil of the ridges, most of the soils are capable of retaining water for at least short periods. These factors result in the establishment of large pools of surface water. Lakes, rivers, and springs are abundant in central Florida. Much of the history of the settlement of Florida is tied to transportation along the waterways.

Lake Russell at Disney Wilderness Preserve, with a typical shoreline of cypresses (Susan D. Jewell)

Lake

Two lacustrine features are outstanding in the region. One is Lake Okeechobee in south-central Florida, so large it is identifiable from space. The other is the lake district, a series of variably sized lakes that runs north-south through the center of the state. Most of the lakes are relatively shallow and contain warm water. Often there is a rim of picturesque cypress trees along the shallow banks. Lake Okeechobee was formed in a depression in the bedrock. The lake is fed primarily by rainfall and inflowing rivers like the Kissimmee and Fisheating Creek. It has no natural outflowing rivers. Before the dike and canals were built, the water would slowly spill over the natural bank at the south end and flow imperceptibly through the Everglades. The lake is so shallow that the average maximum depth is less than 16 feet. Historically, it had a broad littoral zone in the northwest section—a zone with water only a few inches to 2 feet deep, where aquatic plants flourished and much of the animal life was concentrated. The artificial manipulation of water levels by humans, aided by pumping structures and a massive dike built around the entire lake, has destroyed much of this rich nursery, where many species of fish reproduce. The man-made connections from the lake to the Gulf Coast via the Caloosahatchee River and the St. Lucie Canal have greatly altered the lake's ecological components. Fishermen lament that the sport and commercial fisheries have suffered substantially from these alterations. The South Florida Water Management District, the U.S. Army Corps of Engineers, and numerous other agencies are working to restore the ecological functions of the lake, but it is a monumental project.

The lake district surpasses any other area in the United States by the number of lakes it contains. Many of the lakes were created from sinkholes. They have neither inflowing or outflowing streams. They acquire water from rainfall and seepage through the ground and lose it through evapotranspiration and groundwater. Other lakes and ponds are formed from springs and still others by the flow of rivers.

Some lakes, such as Blue Cypress and Tsala Apopka, are relatively pristine. Others have been drastically altered. Lake

Apopka, northwest of Orlando, is considered one of the most polluted lakes in the state. Water clarity is about 10 inches, whereas it was as much as 10 feet in 1947. The lake formerly covered 48,000 acres, but 18,000 acres were diked off for farming. The farms are below the level of the lake. The farms are flooded to kill nematodes, then the water is pumped back into the lake. The agricultural runoff is causing eutrophication (premature aging) and has nearly destroyed the sport fisheries. At least one of the major farm industries, however, has built a system that successfully recycles its irrigation water.

River

The rivers of central Florida are generally sluggish, due to the shallow grade. Whitewater exists only where a rock breaks the surface and causes a ripple. This feature made many rivers ideal for travel in the early days of Florida's history. The color of the water is usually brownish, caused by tannins from oak and other leaves. Rivers that arise from springs are usually quite clear.

The major rivers of central Florida are the Kissimmee, St. Johns, Withlacoochee, Caloosahatchee, and Peace. The Kissimmee is so

The cypress-lined Withlacoochee River in Withlacoochee State Forest (Susan D. Jewell)

41

steeped in history that it is explored elsewhere in this book. The St. Johns is unusual because it flows northward and because its source is an inland estuary created by a series of lakes. The 75-mile-long Caloosahatchee was named for the Calusa Indians that once cherished it as their larder and highway. It was channelized and connected to Lake Okeechobee by the famous swamp-drainer Hamilton Disston in the 1800s. The Peace and the Withlacoochee are two of the larger rivers left nearly undeveloped and natural.

During many months of the year, manatees feed in the rivers, sometimes swimming many miles inland. Some may spend the winter in a river, if they can find adjacent warm springs.

Spring

Juan Ponce de León was looking for the Fountain of Youth when he encountered Florida. Had he heard rumors of the myriad of springs that gushed mysteriously from the center of the earth here? We will never know, since he never found his special fountain.

Springs form when rain falls on the sandy ridges and percolates deep into the porous bedrock. The water reappears downhill miles away, where it is forced to the surface. Florida has more than 300 springs. Most of them are artesian, meaning the water is forced upward by immense underground pressure (as opposed to gravity springs, which flow down from a hole in a hillside). Like celestial stars, springs are ranked by magnitude, such that the lower numbers correspond to the greater flows. Five first-magnitude springs occur within the range of this book: three in Citrus County (Chassahowitzka, Crystal, and Homosassa Springs), one in Hernando County (Weeki Wachee Springs), and one in Volusia County (Blue Spring).

The water that flows from them ranges in temperature from an average low of 66.2°F to an average high of 77°F, or about 72°F overall. There is great variability in the components of the water: calcium, magnesium, sodium, bicarbonate, chloride, and sulfate. One characteristic that varies little is the water's superior clarity. Flow rates depend on the height of the water table. Since humans have lowered the water table in some areas, some springs have significantly decreased their flows, and some have ceased altogether.

Most springs either create rivers or contribute to existing ones. The stretch of water that flows from the spring to where it meets an adjoining river is called a "run." Where the spring exits the underlying rock is a hole that may appear bottomless. Many diving students have taken their open water check dives in these springs, because they can dive to 50 or more feet with little concern for the weather. The water is clear but appears in beautiful shades of blue. Numerous species of fish, invertebrates, and plants thrive in springs and runs.

Development of tourist attractions around some springs has contributed to the deterioration of water quality. Pollution from runoff, destruction of the littoral zone, and erosion of the banks (from people climbing on them) are all factors. The water from Florida's springs is among the cleanest in the world. It is vital that we exercise care when using the springs for our own recreation.

Springs may be found at Blue Spring State Park, Fort Cooper State Park, Wekiwa Springs State Park, Homosassa Springs State Wildlife Park, Alderman's Ford Park, Eureka Springs Park, Lithia Springs Park, and Chassahowitzka and Crystal River National Wildlife Refuges.

FRESHWATER MARSH

Because of its flat topography and high water table, much of Florida is covered by wetlands. Freshwater marshes are very common along the central longitudinal axis of the state. Marshes surround the lakes in the lake region and rivers (such as the Kissimmee and St. Johns), acting as floodplains during the wet season. Marshes are characterized by shallow standing water with primarily herbaceous vegetation (submergent, emergent, and floating). Trees may be scattered or clumped into small tree islands. In Florida, marshes generally have hard water (a result of the limestone substrate), seasonal water levels, and occasional fires. The fires occur mostly during the wet season

Freshwater marsh at Savannas State Reserve, sawgrass in foreground (Susan D. Jewell)

(from lightning), when moisture levels are high. Thus, the fires effectively prevent the encroachment of trees and shrubs but have little impact on the marsh plants.

Typical plant species of central Florida marshes include bladderwort, arrowhead, spike rush, pickerel-weed, Tracy's beakrush, sawgrass, and St. John's-wort. White waterlily is characteristic of deeper, more permanent water, such as that found in sloughs. Other types of marshes are sawgrass and prairies.

Sawgrass grows in freshwater marshes throughout Florida, some of which are characterized by deep organic soils (peat) and inundation for more than nine months a year. The name "sawgrass" is both accurate and misleading. The blades do indeed have sawlike edges, but the plant is a sedge rather than a grass. Mixed in with the sawgrass are spike rush, bladderwort, pickerel-weed, muhly grass, and many other wetland plants. Sawgrass marshes are adapted to periodic lightning-caused fires. The growing bud of the sawgrass plant lies protected just under the soil. After the passage of the fire, it responds with growth so rapid it can out-race the rising water levels of the rainy season. Saw-

The vast wet prairie on the edge of Lake Kissimmee (Susan D. Jewell)

grass marshes can be seen in Savannas State Reserve, Merritt Island National Wildlife Refuge, and Sawgrass Lake Park.

Prairies are flat, grassy, treeless areas. The two types in Florida, wet and dry, depend on the length of inundation. Wet prairies are seasonally flooded for about 50 to 150 days per year. They support a greater variety of plant species than any other marsh type. Typical plant species include Tracy's beakrush, St. John's-wort, white-topped sedge, cordgrass, muhly grass, and sawgrass. Wildlife species you may encounter include limpkins, grasshopper sparrows, sandhill cranes, and round-tailed muskrats. Several places to find wet prairies are Lake Kissimmee State Park, Three Lakes Wildlife Management Area, Starkey Wilderness Park, Dupuis Reserve State Forest, and Avon Park Air Force Range.

Dry prairies may be flooded only a few inches after a heavy rainstorm. Scattered pines or cabbage palms may dot the landscape, and saw palmettos may provide varying amounts of coverage, with wiregrass and other grasses as the dominant ground cover. Burrowing owls, crested caracaras, and sandhill cranes depend on dry prairies. Look for dry prairies at Myakka River State Park and Avon Park Air Force Range.

ESTUARY

Where the rivers meet the oceans is a nebulous area of half land, half water. This is where the estuaries lie—those rich nurseries where many species of fish, crustaceans, and mollusks start their lives. Wading birds, dolphins, sea turtles, and small sharks are attracted to the bonanza of prey that thrive in the brackish water. Oysters, conchs, blue crabs, shrimp, mullet, and snook are some of the prey that humans are attracted to. The high productivity of commercially valuable fish and shellfish cannot be disputed or ignored. The estuaries include salt marshes, lagoons, seagrasses, mangroves, and hardwood edges.

Salt marshes are one of the most highly productive habitats in the world. They are periodically flooded treeless coastal areas that depend on the tides to wash in nutrients and flush out detritus regularly. They act as filters by keeping pollution from upland development from entering estuaries. They stabilize the shore so that sediment isn't continually eroding. Cordgrass, salt-wort, and glasswort are three plant species common to Florida salt marshes. Raccoons feed on fiddler crabs and wading birds feed on fish in the marsh. Marsh rabbits and cotton rats are also common. Salt marshes may be found at Merritt Island, Chassa-howitzka, and Crystal River National Wildlife Refuges, Upper Tampa Bay Park, and E. G. Simmons Park. Salt marshes are not necessarily located near emptying rivers, but often they are.

Seagrasses are flowering plants that grow completely submerged and are rooted to the bottom. They provide the forage for such grazing animals as manatees, sea turtles, and some ducks. Turtle grass and widgeon grass are two examples. Many small fish, seahorses, crabs, and shrimp forage in the dense cover of seagrasses.

Some of the larger estuaries in central Florida are the Indian River Lagoon, Tampa Bay, and Matlacha Pass. They are exciting places to canoe because of the variety and abundance of

Mangroves on the Indian River estuary at Jack Island Preserve. The dead mangroves were killed by a freeze (Susan D. Jewell)

wildlife, although novice canoeists should not attempt such trips due to the winds, tides, and risk of getting lost. A lagoon is a confined body of water located near the ocean but with few openings to it. Water doesn't flush well from it and may remain for months or years, until an extremely high tide occurs. The Indian River Lagoon system stretches 156 miles from Volusia to Palm Beach Counties. It has an average depth of 3 to 4 feet (9 to 10 feet in the Intracoastal Waterway). It is composed of three interconnected lagoons: Mosquito, Indian River, and Banana River. It has the highest species diversity of any estuary in North America (1,350 plants and almost 3,000 animals). The Atlantic salt marsh snake and a snail are found here and nowhere else. The lagoon is designated an "Estuary of National Significance," as are Tampa Bay and Sarasota Bay.

MANGROVE

Four tree species are collectively considered mangroves: red mangrove, black mangrove, white mangrove, and buttonwood.

The stiltlike prop roots of the red mangrove surrounded by sprouting propagules (Susan D. Jewell)

Only red mangrove, however, is in the mangrove family (Rhizophoraceae). All four share the common traits of being very tolerant of salinity and water level changes. Hence, they thrive in tidal zones and represent the transition between the sawgrass marshes and the ocean. Black and white mangroves have mechanisms to excrete salt (you can see the salt glands at the base of each white mangrove leaf), while red mangroves don't allow salt to enter their tissues. Therefore, mangroves do not need salt water and can thrive in freshwater habitats, though they are rarely found there because they are outcompeted by freshwater-adapted trees.

Red, black, and white mangroves have seeds, called propagules, that begin germinating while still on the tree. Even the roots start growing! This gives them a quick start to anchor in the mud before a strong tide comes. Try this experiment the next time you find a red mangrove tree with mature propagules (the cigar-shaped pods about 6 inches long): float a propagule in the water and watch how it orients itself. It will float with the root end down—ready to grow as soon as it drifts onto a mudflat. This is because it is weighted like a bowling pin, with the bottom being heavier. Mangrove propagules and roots can anchor well only on low-energy shorelines—that is, shorelines with such shallow slopes that the waves and tides are barely noticeable. Much of Florida, especially the southwest coast, is like that. Another environmental requirement is a warm climate; branches exposed to frost usually die. Together, these reasons make central and southern Florida home to the most extensive mangrove swamps in the United States.

Mangrove systems are vital as rich nursery grounds for fish and invertebrates, such as snook, tarpon, mullet, mangrove snapper, spiny lobster, pink shrimp, oyster, and blue crab. Many birds, such as wood storks, roseate spoonbills, brown pelicans, and mangrove cuckoos, nest on mangrove trees.

Red mangrove trees are easily recognized by their stiltlike prop roots that resemble a spider's legs. Black mangroves (and occasionally white mangroves) have pencil-like root appendages, called pneumatophores, that grow under the tree like new shoots of asparagus and function like breathing organs at low tide. Buttonwoods have no distinguishing root structures.

Mangroves are protected from human destruction by Florida law because of their vital roles as nursery grounds and shoreline stabilizers. Part of the legal penalty is the requirement that the guilty party plant five mangrove seedlings for every one destroyed. Good examples of mangrove habitat are at Weedon Island Preserve, Caladesi Island State Park, Honeymoon Island State Recreation Area, E. G. Simmons Park, Jack Island State Preserve, Hobe Sound National Wildlife Refuge, and Pelican Island National Wildlife Refuge.

BEACH AND DUNE

Along the seaward sides of the barrier islands and the coasts without barrier islands, the beaches and dunes lie restlessly. They shift with the winds, the tides, and the currents. One storm alone can remove 6 to 8 feet of sand from a beach. When left unaltered by humans, however, beaches and dunes have a way

The beach and dune on the Atlantic coast (Susan D. Jewell)

of equilibrating—that is, where the sand is removed from one place, it is deposited somewhere else. The salt-tolerant dune plants (such as sea oats, sea purslane, and bay-cedar) are the sole stabilizers. This is why it is so important for them to be left undisturbed. Sea oats, which can have 5-foot-deep roots and rhizomes that ably bind the sand, are protected by state law. Southeastern beach mice and sea turtles depend on the sandy beaches and dunes.

Beaches and dunes can be seen at Blowing Rocks Preserve, Archie Carr National Wildlife Refuge, Hobe Sound National Wildlife Refuge, Canaveral National Seashore, Fort Pierce Inlet State Recreation Area, Sebastian Inlet State Recreation Area, Caladesi Island State Park, and Honeymoon Island State Recreation Area.

III

A PEEK AT THE
SPECIAL WILDLIFE

FLORIDA PANTHERS

While settlers from the 1600s to the 1900s were systematically destroying the wilderness haunts of the panthers and hunting them almost to extinction (they were hunted for bounty until 1950), a small population survived in the untamed haunts of central and southern Florida. The Florida panther is a sub-species of the mountain lion (or cougar), which roamed almost every habitat from the Atlantic to the Pacific Oceans. In 1958, the panther gained protection in Florida, and in 1967 the U.S. Fish and Wildlife Service listed it as endangered. Today, only 30 to 50 panthers roam Florida, mostly from Lake Okeechobee south. The number is not increasing in spite of intensive cooperative efforts by the U.S. Fish and Wildlife Service, Florida Game and Fresh Water Fish Commission (FGFWFC), the National Park Service at Everglades National Park and Big Cypress National Preserve, and other agencies. Radio-tagged panthers are being tracked by National Park Service staff in Big Cypress and Everglades National Park and by the FGFWFC. A captive breeding program has been established by the agencies listed above and will be conducted by zoos in Florida.

Known mortality is due primarily to malnutrition and collisions with automobiles. Of 21 panther deaths investigated from 1978 to 1988, 11 were the result of motor vehicle hits.

A decrease in the number of white-tailed deer (the preferred prey item) has caused the panthers to feed on smaller prey (such as raccoons and young alligators) in some areas. Panthers may survive on small prey items, but they are not likely to reproduce

on this inadequate diet. Studies have shown that a female panther needs large prey items like deer to procreate and raise cubs.
Another problem is arising with the switch from large to small
prey. The fresh waters of some lakes and marshes are contaminated with mercury, a toxic metallic element which becomes
concentrated in predators of aquatic animals, such as raccoons,
otters, and alligators.

Florida panthers resemble western mountain lions with a few
minor differences. Panthers are more red than the tawny mountain lions, have a "cowlick" in the middle of their backs, and have
a sharp bend in the distal end of their tails. They also are slightly
smaller, weighing about 50 to 100 pounds for females and 100 to
140 pounds for males. However, some of these morphological
features may be artifacts of inbreeding. Other subspecies introduced or escaped from captivity into Florida have intergraded
with the native cats, so some individuals do not carry the above
traits. As part of its recovery plan, the U.S. Fish and Wildlife Service is interbreeding western mountain lions with Florida panthers, since the Florida race is doomed by genetic weaknesses.

MANATEES

One of the most treasured experiences a naturalist can have in
Florida is to encounter a West Indian manatee in the wild. This
graceful relative of the elephant may be visible in central Florida
in any month of the year. The colder the winter, the more likely it
is to find a manatee in the larger springs, especially those near
the ocean. Manatees are sensitive to cold water, and the springs
have a relatively constant mild temperature of about 72°F.

Manatees are also known as "sea cows" because they are large
marine mammals that graze on underwater vegetation. They are
even more harmless than cattle, because they have no hooves,
horns, or front teeth to inflict injury. In fact, manatees are so
nonaggressive and defenseless because, as adults, they have no
natural predators (most of the large sharks remain in deeper
water than the manatees). This lack of defense makes them easy
prey to humans, who hunted them for meat in earlier decades.

Manatees are protected from hunting now, but they face more modern dangers. One is from motor boats. Since manatees are mammals, they must breath air. They dwell in shallow water where they can surface easily to breathe. This puts them squarely in the path of thousands of motor boats with deadly propellers and hulls that killed 223 in Florida from 1989 to 1993 and about 50 in 1994. Out of a population of about 1,800 manatees in the United States, that is a high percentage. Many manatees are identified individually by the propeller scars they bear. Manatees are a federally endangered species.

Adult manatees may weigh up to 3,000 pounds and attain 15 feet in length, although the average is closer to 8 to 10 feet and 1,200 pounds. This great size requires them to eat 60 to 100 pounds of aquatic plants every day, which they find in both fresh and salt water. Manatees may live for 50 to 80 years.

If you are searching for manatees, here are a few places to try: the Intracoastal Waterway (ICW) and associated rivers and canals (such as Hobe Sound National Wildlife Refuge, Loxahatchee River), coastal beaches, especially near ICW inlets (such as St. Lucie Inlet, Blowing Rocks Preserve), Crystal River, Homosassa Springs State Wildlife Park (guaranteed views), Blue Spring State Park, the St. Johns River, Merritt Island National Wildlife Refuge, and Big Bend Manatee Viewing Center. In the warmer months, manatees utilize Lake Okeechobee and the St. Lucie, Caloosahatchee, and St. Johns Rivers. In the winter, they prefer the Upper St. Johns (Blue Spring area), Merritt Island area, coastal St. Lucie and Martin counties, Tampa Bay, and the Chassahowitzka-Crystal River area. In Fort Pierce, try the H.D. King Power Plant on Indian River Drive (CR 707). It is opposite a yachting center and an art gallery, just south of the South Bridge Seaway that leads to Hutchinson Island. In the winter, manatees loaf along the canal (Moore's Creek) that flows under Indian River Drive. A pedestrian bridge allows viewers to watch safely off the road.

Manatees frequent canals near the ocean, where residents treat them to fresh water from garden hoses. Because humans have interfered with the flow of fresh water that should be naturally available, manatees can sometimes be stressed for fresh drinking water. Although it is very tempting to attract a manatee by feeding or watering it, *it is illegal* and can cause harm. Feeding and watering induces them to lose fear of humans and linger around canals and docks. This places them dangerously close to a concentration of potentially deadly motor boats.

If you are fortunate enough to encounter manatees while you are canoeing, don't panic. They are very docile and will swim sluggishly around you. If you make a sudden move that startles them, you'll be amazed at the energy they display when they turn tail and flee. It is legal to swim with these gentle giants *as long as you do not alter their behavior,* for example, you can't cause them to swim in a direction other than that in which they were headed. If you find an injured or dead manatee, call the Manatee Hot Line at (800) 342-1821 or the Florida Marine Patrol at (800) DIAL-FMP.

ALLIGATORS

Few creatures in North America evoke as much fear and curiosity as the two largest native reptiles, the American alligator and the American crocodile. So much myth and mystery surrounds them.

Alligators are found from North Carolina to Florida and west across the Gulf states to Texas. They number in the millions— perhaps a million in Florida alone. Once reduced to near extinction, alligator populations have recovered and the species has been removed from the endangered species list. Alligators prefer fresh water, although occasionally they'll be found swimming in salt water along the Gulf Coast. Crocodiles, which number 500 to 600 and are endangered, have a limited U.S. range, occurring only in southern Florida—on the east coast as far north as Broward County and on the west coast as far north as Lee County. They prefer salt water, but will occasionally wander into fresh water, never venturing far from the sea.

Differences in appearance between the two crocodilians are subtle. An alligator's skin color is black (although it often

Female alligator fixing nest material on nest (Susan D. Jewell)

appears and is depicted as green), while a crocodile's is gray. An alligator has a wide snout, while a crocodile has a narrow one with the large fourth tooth from the lower jaw protruding when the mouth is closed. Neither species is especially dangerous to humans; see "Alligators" under "Local Hazards."

Alligators disperse during the wet season and may be difficult to locate. During the dry season, they may be seen at Jonathan Dickinson State Park, Highlands Hammock State Park, and Myakka River State Park.

GOPHER TORTOISES

The gopher tortoise is the only species of land tortoise in the eastern United States. It is found throughout the drier parts of Florida and is known as a "keystone species" because so many other types of animals depend on tortoise burrows for survival. More than 100 species of vertebrates and invertebrates, including indigo snakes, gopher frogs, Florida mice, burrowing owls, lizards, and many insects, regularly retreat to the burrows

Gopher tortoise at Fort Pierce Inlet State Recreation Area (Susan D. Jewell)

or at least seek refuge during fires. As many as 250 more species have been found to use the burrows at least occasionally.

A tortoise digs its burrow with its shovel-like front feet. The burrow may be 10 feet deep and as much as 40 feet long. It provides cooling shade during the heat of the day and insulating warmth during cold fronts. The soil must be well-drained and loose, which is just the type of substrate that developers seek. This competition for scrub habitats has caused the tortoise to lose substantial habitat, such as the coastal ridges along the Atlantic seaboard. A distinguishing feature of the tortoise burrow is that the entrance is oblong, unlike the round armadillo and pocket gopher burrows. This accommodates the tortoise's shell, which is wider than it is high. A large sandy mound a foot or more in diameter next to the hole (called the "apron") makes it easy to spot gopher tortoise burrows.

An additional assault on gopher tortoises is a respiratory disease that can be passed from one tortoise to another. It may have been spread by the release of tortoises at Sanibel Island. The relocation of gopher tortoises from areas slated for development was a standard mitigation method until this disease was discovered. It is a clear example of what wildlife biologists have been trying to convince people of for years—that releasing an animal anywhere besides its own territory can have serious repercussions. Relocations of most species of animals by the U.S. Fish and Wildlife Service and state agencies are usually preceded by quarantines and veterinary examinations.

Gopher tortoises and their burrows may be seen at Jonathan Dickinson State Park, Myakka River State Park, Archbold Biological Station, Oscar Scherer State Park, Highlands Hammock State Park, Withlacoochee State Forest, and many other places. Anywhere you see prickly-pear cactus growing, you may see a gopher tortoise, since that's a favored food. Another favored food is gopher apple. Gopher tortoises are listed as a "Species of Special Concern" by the state.

SEA TURTLES

Florida is well-known to tourists for its thousand miles of white, sandy beaches with warm waters and gentle tides that make them perfect for sunbathing and swimming. For these same reasons, sea turtles also think Florida beaches are the greatest and flock by the tens of thousands to lay their eggs here every year. The densities of nests at Archie Carr National Wildlife Refuge are among the highest in the world. Sea turtles spend most of the year at sea or feeding along a coast. When the nesting urge overtakes the females, they head for their own birth place, even if it's thousands of miles away. No one knows for sure how they navigate, but it is probably a combination of methods which include using the sun, landmarks on the ocean floor, currents, and scents. If they do use olfactory cues to guide them to ancestral beaches, imagine how confused they are when we dump our sewage into the water.

Sea turtles have suffered directly from drowning in shrimp nets. The nets are dragged along the ocean floor, scooping up the scavenging shrimp. When a turtle gets caught, it drowns because it can't escape to the surface to breathe. Special devices that attach to shrimp nets and allow turtles to escape (called Turtle

Excluder Devices or "TEDs"), are now mandatory for most shrimp boats. Plastic bags are another nemesis of those sea turtles which prey on jellyfish. Floating plastic bags so resemble jellyfish to the nearsighted turtles that they eat them and die from blocked digestive systems.

Causes of reduced nesting include the presence of garbage on the beach, which interferes with the turtles crawling on the sand and digging their nests. A major culprit is fishing line, which entangles the turtles. The roots of the exotic tree Australian-pine prevent turtles from digging. Hatching turtles become disoriented from artificial lights on the beach at night. Since the hatchlings are drawn towards the lightest horizon, which is normally the ocean, the lights turn them inland where they die or are killed by raccoons, snakes, opossums, and so on.

Four species of sea turtles found in Florida are federally endangered. The most common nesting species is the threatened loggerhead, which may weigh up to 350 pounds (although historically they reached 1,000 pounds). The reddish-brown carapace color is the easiest way to distinguish the species. Loggerheads lay their eggs from May through August on both the Atlantic and Gulf coasts.

Green turtles nest from June to September and only on the Atlantic coast. They are common in the Caribbean, where they were hunted for food for centuries. They have a green carapace and can weigh up to 450 pounds. Leatherback turtles are the largest of all living turtles; they can grow to 1,200 pounds. Their carapaces don't have scutes (thus no hard shell) but are covered instead by dark, leathery-looking skin. Although they are not hunted for their meat, their eggs are sought for food. The Atlantic hawksbill rarely nests in Florida but may be seen in Florida waters. The Atlantic ridley does not nest in Florida but feeds offshore.

The following places have sea turtle nesting beaches: Atlantic coast—Canaveral National Seashore, Archie Carr and Hobe Sound National Wildlife refuges, Blowing Rocks Preserve; Gulf coast—Fort DeSoto Park, Honeymoon Island State Recreation Area, and Caladesi Island State Park.

RAPTORS

Many of the local raptors are familiar to birders from other parts of North America because the birds have migrated from those parts. Red-shouldered hawks, kestrels, and ospreys are three examples. Our resident red-shouldered hawks, however, differ slightly in appearance by having very pale gray heads.

Raptors pass through the region as they migrate farther south to Central and South America. Coastal islands with undeveloped salt marshes and uplands attract concentrations of many raptors, including bald eagles, peregrine falcons, ospreys, and northern harriers. The raptors often cluster at the southern ends of such coastal islands as at Fort DeSoto, Honeymoon Island, Fort Pierce Inlet, Hobe Sound, and Merritt Island. A few residential species of special interest and where to find them are highlighted here.

Snail kites are medium-sized hawks that require shallow fresh water where their staple food, the apple snail (*Pomacea paludosa*), dwells on sawgrass, spikerush, and other aquatic plant stems. The kites are present in central Florida throughout the year, although they may concentrate at Lake Okeechobee and the Kissimmee region during periods of extended drought in the Everglades. It may take several years of suitable water levels after a marsh dries out to restore the snail populations and attract the kites again.

A 1994 statewide survey revealed a total of 996 kites, higher than any previous year. This is partly because biologists using radio transmitters on some kites have followed the birds to roosts they may not have otherwise found. The snail kite has been listed as an endangered species since 1967. The primary problem facing snail kites is the loss of habitat, both by development of wetlands and artificial manipulation of the remaining wetlands. Another problem is the presence of exotic plants such as water lettuce and water hyacinth. These cover the water and prevent the kites from seeing their prey, the snails. Snail kites nest around Lake Jackson, Lake Okeechobee, Lake Kissimmee (particularly Bird and Rabbit Islands), Lake

Tohopekaliga, E. Lake Tohopekaliga, and the St. Johns marshes. Look for them also at Savannas Outdoor Recreation Area, the marshes around the Upper St. Johns River (that is, the St. Johns Marsh in Brevard County), the Kissimmee River drainage area, and around western Lake Okeechobee.

Swallow-tailed kites are fairly common between March and August over pinelands and cypress and mangrove swamps. They may be seen gliding gracefully over the treetops, ready to seize a lizard or snake from a branch.

Short-tailed hawks are Florida specialty, although nowhere common. They are usually found in central Florida in the summer and south of Lake Okeechobee in the winter. They may be as far north as Highland County in the winter. Both light and dark color phases may occasionally be seen soaring in thermals with vultures, and they may be found in pinelands or grasslands.

Fortunately, osprey populations have partially recovered since their perilous decline from the pesticide DDT in the 1950s and 1960s. Ospreys may be seen anywhere along the sea coast, Lake Okeechobee, other lakes, canals, and ponds. They often build their large stick nests atop utility poles. These permanent structures can be seen year-round, such as along US A1A on the east coast, although the nests are active only from December to May.

Bald eagles have also recovered since suffering the same fate as the ospreys and brown pelicans in the 1950s. In fact, their status was downgraded from endangered to threatened by the U.S. Fish and Wildlife Service in 1994. In Florida, there are more bald eagles than in any other state except Alaska, and the greatest concentration is in central Florida. About 600 pairs nest in Florida, with numbers swelling to 3,000 birds in the winter. Bald eagles can be seen year-round near large bodies of water where they hunt for fish or steal prey from ospreys. Bald eagles may be found around Lake Kissimmee State Park, Three Lakes Wildlife Management Area, Lake Okeechobee (a pair has been nesting along the Hoover Dike about 2 miles east of the Miami Canal in South Bay), and Myakka River State Park.

Crested caracaras are vulturelike members of the falcon family, with a range in the southeastern United States that is restricted to central Florida (they are also found in Texas and

American swallow-tailed kite (Wayne Hoffman)

Mexico). Specifically, most are found north and west of Lake Okeechobee. Caracaras prefer open grassland where they feed on carrion, especially if cabbage palms are present for them to nest on. There are only about 400 caracaras left in Florida because of habitat loss—citrus groves are taking over. As you drive along such roads as SR 70, SR 29, or US 441, watch the utility poles and fence posts for a perching bird. Check Lake Kissimmee State Park, Avon Park Air Force Range, Bull Creek Wildlife Management Area, and Three Lakes Wildlife Management Area for caracaras.

Burrowing owls prefer open, well-drained short grass fields, including fallow farm land, college campuses, and airports. A drive along an inland road, such as SR 70, SR 29, or CR 721 may produce the owls if you watch for levees or small mounds of dirt on which they like to stand.

WADING BIRDS

More than any other state, Florida is known for its large flocks of graceful and colorful egrets, ibises, herons, spoonbills, and storks, but they are fast becoming a memory. Prior to human intervention, approximately 100,000 pairs of wading birds nested in the Everglades region. Now it may be only 10,000 pairs in a good year, a reduction of 90 percent. Part of the decrease was caused by the practice, in the late 1800s to early 1900s, of killing the birds at the nesting sites to collect plumes for sale to the fashion moguls. Some species recovered, but some (like the reddish egret) have maintained low populations. The decrease was also caused by water management practices that altered the quality, quantity, and timing of water that flows into the Everglades. Those practices still continue and still affect wading birds.

One of the hardest-hit species is the white ibis, the most numerous wading bird in the state. Populations have plummeted so sharply from loss of habitat that the species was listed by the state in 1994 as a "species of special concern." This is an example of a wildlife agency trying to prevent a currently populous species from becoming endangered, when it is clear from the signs that it will. Remember the passenger pigeon, which numbered in the billions about a hundred years ago and is now extinct? It could happen again.

Another suffering species is the wood stork, which seems to be gradually pulling out of its population slump. Loss of wetlands contributed to its decline. Historically, the stronghold for wood stork nesting was south Florida. In the 1980s and 1990s, a new trend began emerging. Storks were shifting their nesting sites farther and farther north. Currently, central Florida holds the greatest concentration of stork colonies.

Another species in trouble is the snowy egret, which never quite recovered from the slaughter for its plumes in the early 1900s. Snowy egrets do not seem quite as resilient as tricolored and little blue herons, with which they share feeding and nesting habitats.

Roseate spoonbills nest primarily in Florida Bay, but a few nest at Pelican Island National Wildlife Refuge, near Sebastian. After the nesting season, the Florida Bay spoonbills disperse northward along the coasts (May through August). Then they may seen at Merritt Island National Wildlife Refuge, Jack Island

State Preserve, Myakka River State Park, and Fort DeSoto Park, for example.

Enough wading birds remain in Florida to make a thrilling sight. Species you are most likely to see are: great blue heron, great egret, snowy egret, little blue heron, tricolored heron, green heron, yellow-crowned night heron, white ibis, glossy ibis, roseate spoonbill, and wood stork. In general, the best time to see wading birds is from November to April, when decreasing water levels concentrate the birds around their aquatic prey and winter migrants are also present. The best places to look are Merritt Island National Wildlife Refuge, Fort DeSoto Park and adjacent mudflats, Pelican Island National Wildlife Refuge, and Myakka Lake at Myakka River State Park.

RED-COCKADED WOODPECKERS

Known in birding lingo as "RCWs," red-cockaded woodpeckers were once characteristic of mature, open pine forests of the southeastern United States. They are dependent on extensive stands of old loblolly and longleaf pines for foraging, 75- to 95-year-old pines for nesting cavities, a relatively dense population to accommodate their complex social structure, and fire to control understory growth. Due to commercial logging, RCWs were added to the endangered species list in 1970, but the species continues to decline. One reason is that timber companies prefer to harvest their stands in less time than it takes for the pines to mature. Another is that the RCWs' favorite tree, the longleaf pine, is not easily cultivated and is usually substituted with slash pines when stands are replanted.

RCWs depend on the presence of the red heart fungus (*Phellinus pini*), which is a heart rot found in older trees that makes the heartwood softer. These woodpeckers are unique because they excavate living trees for nesting cavities, as opposed to using dead trees as other woodpeckers do. It may take years to excavate enough for a nest, but the nest may be used for more than 50 years by succeeding generations.

Both sexes have white cheek patches and barred patterns on

their backs. Males have a small red spot (cockade) on each side of head, displayed only during courtship and threatening behaviors. Look for RCWs at DuPuis Forest, Avon Park Air Force Range, Lake Arbuckle area, Three Lakes and Bull Creek Wildlife Management Areas, and Withlacoochee State Forest.

Sandhill crane (Susan D. Jewell)

SANDHILL AND WHOOPING CRANES

Florida has a resident, nonmigratory race of sandhill cranes (Florida sandhill crane). Additionally, cranes from the Midwest (greater sandhill cranes) migrate to Florida for the winter. Both are found in shallow marshes and wet prairies around the state, but they particularly favor the Kissimmee prairies in central Florida. Sandhill cranes can be found at Lake Kissimmee State Park, Tosohatchee State Reserve, Rock Springs Run State Reserve, Myakka River State Park, Three Lakes Wildlife Management Area, and along SR 70 east and west of Lake Placid.

Whooping cranes were once extinct in Florida. In the entire world, only 15 whooping cranes were alive in 1941. The U.S. Fish and Wildlife Service launched an intensive captive breeding effort to recover the species. In 1993, the Service and the Florida Game and Fresh Water Fish Commission began reintroducing whooping cranes to Florida by releasing captive-raised young at Three Lakes Wildlife Management Area (see separate entry). Many of the first releases were killed by bobcats, but biologists eventually conditioned subsequent birds to avoid them. The goal is to establish a permanent population in central Florida. As more "whoopers" are released each year and some begin to reproduce, the chance of seeing one around Three Lakes will increase.

SCRUB JAYS

Many of the wildlife species that inhabit the scrub of Florida are also found in the desert areas of the western United States, but not in the states in between. The scrub jay is one of them. Climatic changes caused the split that isolated the Florida jays. Although both populations of jays look nearly identical (the Florida ones have a lighter forehead), the behaviors differ markedly. Florida birds have evolved a complex social structure with nest helpers, possibly because the amount of scrub habitat is so limited (even without development). With most other animal species that have territories, the young must leave their parents' territory and seek their own. The jays, however, would die if they had to leave, because there is nowhere for them to go that isn't already taken by another jay. Thus, they stay with their parents and siblings, helping to raise more young by bringing them food and watching for predators. When death causes a territory to become available, one of the sons (evidence suggests the eldest) takes over. This results in a higher survival rate for the whole family.

Scrub jays prefer oak habitats along ridges (such as Lake Wales Ridge and the Atlantic Coastal Ridge) where scrub oak, Chapman's oak, sand live oak, and myrtle oak provide their staple food, the acorn. The jays line their nests exclusively with the threadlike fibers from the leaf blades of the scrub palmetto. Territories cover about 20 acres each. Colonies of scrub jays may be found at Merritt Island National Wildlife Refuge, Archbold Biological Station, Oscar Scherer State Park, and Jonathan Dickinson State Park.

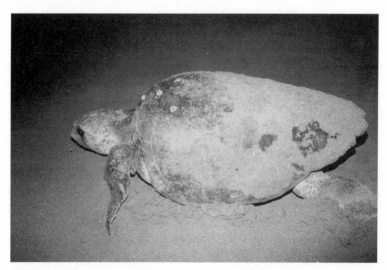

This loggerhead sea turtle, her back encrusted with barnacles, has come ashore to lay her eggs at Hobe Sound National Wildlife Refuge (Hobe Sound Nature Center)

IV
THE UNWANTED
PESTS

For several reasons, Florida is host to scores of plant and animal species that are not native to the area. Some of these live nearly innocuous lives, but the majority interfere with the natural ecological balance. A few are extreme pests that must be eliminated or we may face ecological disaster.

EXOTIC ANIMALS

One reason for the high concentration of exotic animals in Florida is that the mild climate allows many people to keep exotic pets outdoors year-round. Occasionally these escape or are released illegally when the owners tire of caring for them. Another reason is that Miami is a major U.S. port of entry from Central and South America and the West Indies. Animals intended for the pet trade occasionally escape while docked or are released by the shippers if the animals were illegally obtained and the authorities are closing in. Many of these animals can survive and even reproduce around the suburbs. Florida has the highest number of exotic fish species in the lower 48 states, partly because the numerous wetlands contain warm water year-round and the canal network makes a convenient vehicle for widespread dispersion. Fish from the aquarium trade have spread this way. Adding to the problem is that, occasionally, even the state wildlife agency has intentionally introduced exotic fish to promote sport fishing and birds (such as the white-winged dove beginning in 1975, which had not bred in Florida prior to introduction) to promote sport hunting.

Parrots, snakes, and lizards are three types of animals that seem to take to the Florida suburbs with ease. Great flocks of monk parrots, budgerigars, and canary-winged parakeets (some of which destroy fruit crops), can be found in the skies and trees of central and southern Florida. Also established are muscovy ducks and spot-breasted orioles. Established lizards include brown anoles, Mediterranean geckos, and Indopacific geckos. Other exotic herps found in the area include giant (marine) toads, Brahminy blind snakes, and assorted boas and pythons.

Muscovy ducks have become a nuisance around ponds near development. These ducks, native to Central and South America, are the only species of duck in the world besides mallards to be domesticated. Their black or white (or both) plumages and red warty faces are familiar around artificial ponds, which are abundant in central Florida. In this flat, low-lying terrain, builders must first dredge an area to provide the fill they need to build upon. This creates a depression that soon fills with water. As the new homeowners gaze across the barren pond, they yearn for something living to entertain them. They obtain one of the few animals that can survive in this artificial habitat—domesticated ducks. The muscovies and domesticated mallards do just fine, reproducing exponentially until the pond and all the surrounding lawns are filled with their droppings. Then neighbor confronts neighbor, tempers flare, and soon there are lawsuits over getting rid of the ducks!

Two introduced mammals that have become nuisances are the armadillo and feral hog. In 1943, a man brought a female nine-banded armadillo and six young from his native state of Texas to Wakulla, Florida. These spread, and probably others were introduced as well. Eventually, all the drier parts of the Florida (except the Keys) became home to this prehistoric-looking animal. Although inoffensive, the omnivorous armadillos are considered a nuisance species. Their primary food is insects and other invertebrates, but they will consume fruits and berries, seeds, mushrooms, and eggs. The eggs may be those of game birds, freshwater turtles, sea turtles, lizards, snakes, salamanders, or other animals that lay eggs on the ground. Their method of foraging by rooting around in the leaf litter destroys the integrity of that forest stratum. Armadillos do not appear to have good defenses against fires and often perish in them. However, they have few other enemies, since their armored skin protects them.

Feral hogs (a.k.a. wild hogs and feral pigs) have been established in the southeastern United States for 400 hundred years—so long that many people assume they are native. As descendants of the barnyard pigs that the Spanish explorers brought, they have thrived on the mast crops, ground-dwelling animals, and whatever other foods they can dig up. It is never difficult to tell when pigs have been around—the ground looks like a rototiller played hop-scotch in the woods. These telltale "rootings" may be all you see of these nocturnal animals. Feral hogs will eat almost anything edible they encounter. This includes eggs, snakes, and lizards, possibly including indigo snakes and other listed species. Such state parks as Myakka River, Lake Kissimmee, and Highlands Hammock have policies to eradicate the pigs from their lands. They cannot be trapped and released elsewhere without similar consequences. The carcasses are donated to state institutions for food. However, the pigs reproduce too fast for eradication efforts to keep pace. They will remain a pest for a long time to come. The only benefit that can be argued in their favor is that they are good prey for panthers. You can find feral hogs by walking at night wherever you see signs of recent rooting (such as the above-mentioned state parks, Dupuis Reserve State Forest, Withlacoochee State Forest, Lake Arbuckle area). Listen for gruntings and look with a flashlight, but keep your distance, for they are not domesticated anymore.

EXOTIC PLANTS

No animal has created as much turmoil as have some of the exotic plants in central Florida. More than a few biologists feel that they could be the ultimate destroyer of valuable habitat. Some of the plants are introduced from tropical and subtropical areas around the world and are cultivated in central Florida gardens. A number of plants were introduced for functions that were desirable at the time, such as coastal windbreaks and "swamp straws" (because they drink more than their share of water from the ground). These plants have now been classified as pests.

Not all exotic plants are pests. It is important to distinguish between "noninvasive" (which are not pests) and "invasive" plants (which are pests). A noninvasive plant will not reproduce or spread on its own—it needs horticultural help from humans. Many ornamental trees are noninvasive outside their home ranges. An invasive plant, however, can spread entirely on its own, either reproductively (through seeds or spores) or vegetatively (by runners or budding). The main reason the invasive plants spread so rapidly is that they have no natural enemies here as they do in their places of origin.

A word of caution is in order to those readers who feel safer now about planting noninvasive exotics in their yards. Biologists are finding that some exotic plants that were originally noninvasive have gradually adapted to local conditions and become invasive! Thus, the only truly safe plants for your garden are the native ones.

The U.S. Fish and Wildlife Service, National Park Service, U.S. Department of Agriculture, and state and county agencies have exotic plant removal programs aimed at the above-mentioned species plus many more. Programs include finding biological controls (such as insects, bacteria, or fungi) that will attack only the intended plant and not native ones. It's a never-ending battle to eliminate plants that spread faster than they can be removed.

Three exotic plants make the local conservationists' "most wanted to kill" list. They are melaleuca, Brazilian pepper, and Australian-pine. Several more are gaining momentum.

Melaleuca

Melaleuca (also called punk tree or cajeput) was introduced to Miami in 1906 during the early swamp-draining era. Seeds of this tree were allegedly broadcast-spread by air over the Everglades in the 1930s to facilitate draining the marsh. A striking tree with papery white bark, melaleuca uses several times more water than our native vegetation does. A large stand of melaleucas steals water from and crowds out native plants, thereby out-competing them. The phenomenal growth and reproductive rates, coupled with the variety of habitats it can grow in and the difficulty in killing it, make melaleuca one of the most formidable environmental enemies central Florida faces today. Currently, there are no known methods of large-scale eradication of these "swamp straws," except for pesticides. Stands of melaleuca can be seen along the Beeline Highway (SR 710) in Martin County.

Brazilian pepper

Brazilian pepper is a fast-growing, quick-spreading small tree that arrived from Brazil around 1941. Its clusters of bright red berries ripen around Christmas, and some people collect the branches (and encourage their growth) for Christmas wreaths. However, since Brazilian pepper is related to poison ivy (same family), touching it may cause dermatitis. The berries provide food for raccoons, robins, and other animals, but this benefit does not outweigh the detrimental properties. It grows as an extraordinarily dense understory tree, impenetrable by all but the smallest animals. Brazilian pepper is now one of the most common plants along the roads of central Florida, where it is also known as Florida holly. Once Brazilian pepper becomes established, it is virtually impossible to eradicate, since it is resistant to fires, floods, and droughts. Approximately one million acres of Florida are infested with it.

Australian-pine

Australian-pine, also known as Casuarina, is from Australia but is not a true pine. In fact, it's not even a conifer. Its wispy needles and small conelike fruits are reminiscent of pine trees. Australian-pines were introduced as soil retainers and windbreaks along the coast and canals. They outcompete native trees, but their weak branches make nesting risky for large birds, such as swallow-tailed kites, which prefer the native pines. As wind-breaks, they turned out to be worse than worthless when it really mattered. When Hurricane Andrew struck, the same Australian-pines that were planted along canals as windbreaks snapped in pieces and piled in the canals in a tangled mass. Hundreds of miles of canals were clogged. The resulting intensive and expensive debris removal prompted the South Florida Water Management District to cut the standing trees along the canals outside Andrew's path to prevent wind damage in the future.

Aquatic plants

Exotic aquatic plants have plagued Florida for decades by clogging waterways, interfering with fish reproduction, and reducing the dissolved oxygen. The latter effect has caused numerous fish kills. Three such plants are **water hyacinth** (from Venezuela), **hydrilla** (introduced from Sri Lanka for the aquarium trade), and **water lettuce**. All spread uncontrollably when dumped into canals. Water hyacinth was spread from *one plant*, by a woman who brought it back from an exposition in New Orleans. She thought it would look pretty in her backyard fish pond by the St. Johns River. Some waterways have been rendered useless to wildlife and humans by the plants forming a solid mat on the surface, which blocks access to the water and prevents sunlight from penetrating to the native submersed plants. Hydrilla, which spreads only vegetatively in Florida, covers more than 65,000 acres, or about half of the state's public waterways. Boaters inadvertently spread these plants when the plants hitch rides on their boats or on their trailers, which then travel to uninfested waters.

Climbing vines

Another group of plants, known as the climbing vines, is rapidly becoming the newest scourge in Florida. Most of these plants were introduced as house or garden plants, and they thrive in the warm humid climate. Examples are the **air-potato**, **Old World climbing fern**, and **kudzu**. Kudzu is from Japan and was introduced by a farmer in north Florida as cattle forage. The climbing vines have indeterminate growth, which means that they can keep growing as long as they have food and proper weather. In comparison, determinate growers never grow more than a certain genetically determined height. Thus, a climbing vine can grow up a tree trunk to the upper branches, resulting in a forest of blanketed trees killed by vines that shaded the sunlight from their leaves. Kudzu, air potato, and other climbing vines may grow a foot a day.

MAPS

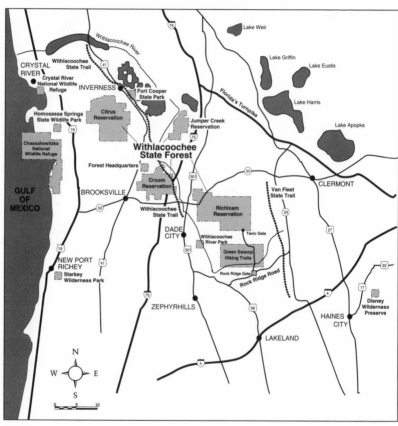

Northwestern central Florida—Crystal River to Haines City

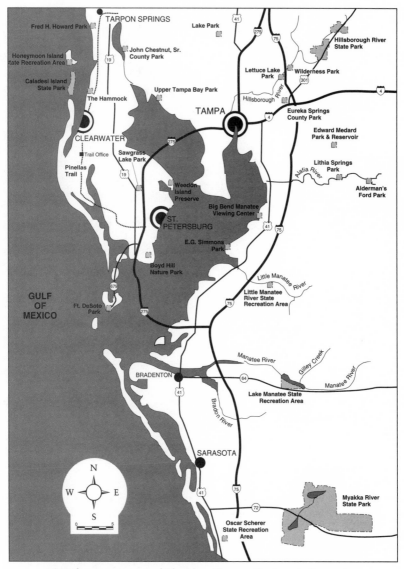

Southwestern central Florida—Tarpon Springs to Sarasota

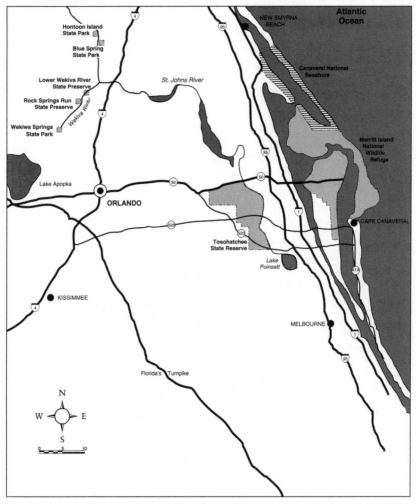

Northeastern central Florida—New Smyrna Beach to Melbourne

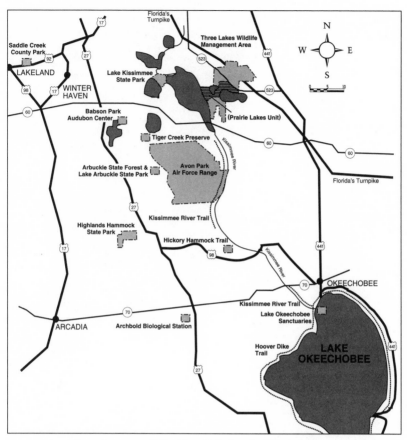

Interior central Florida—Lakeland to Okeechobee

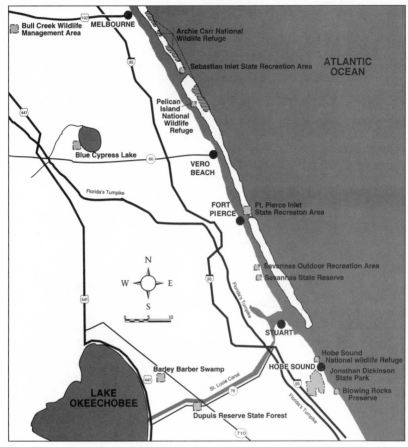

Southeastern central Florida—Melbourne to Hobe Sound

V
NATURAL AREAS— FEDERAL LANDS

ARCHIE CARR
NATIONAL WILDLIFE REFUGE

"America's only sea turtle refuge" is how this 20.5-mile stretch of oceanfront is billed. This length of beach along the Atlantic in Brevard and Indian counties lures more loggerhead sea turtles to nest than almost anywhere else in the world. More green turtles nest here than anywhere else in the United States, and occasionally leatherbacks appear as well. Densities of up to 1,000 turtle nests per mile have been counted. The beaches of Oman had the only higher densities in the world until the Persian Gulf War damaged them.

The refuge was established in 1990. About 6 miles of undeveloped beach remain targeted for purchase. The land is being purchased through the cooperation of state and county agencies and private conservation organizations. The refuge's namesake, the late Dr. Archie Carr, was one of the world's leading experts in the biological study of sea turtles. He wrote the famous sea turtle treatise *So Excellent a Fishe.*

The turtle nesting season extends from May to August. Often, 10,000 to 17,000 loggerhead nests may be made in a single season! The turtles require clean beaches, free from obstructions and free from nighttime artificial lights.

Other species benefit from the protection of the refuge. The refuge includes small parcels of coastal scrub, which support scrub jays, gopher tortoises, indigo snakes, and southeastern beach mice and such plant species as coastal vervain, Simpson's stopper, gallberry, sand holly, and beach creeper.

Location, Mailing Address, and Phone

On sections of beach on the Atlantic Ocean between Melbourne and Wabasso. Accessible from US A1A, mostly through small county parks along the road, such as Spessard Holland North Beach Park (somewhat developed for recreation; Brevard County) and Coconut Point and Bonsteel Parks (minimally developed; Brevard County); Treasure Shores, Golden Sands, and Wabasso Beach Parks (Indian River County); and Sebastian Inlet State Recreation Area (see separate entry).

c/o Merritt Island NWR, P.O. Box 6504, Titusville, FL 32782-6504; (407) 861-0667; (800) DIAL-FPL, ext. 79 for sea turtle information. For Brevard County Parks, call (407) 984-4852. For Indian River County Parks, call (407) 589-9223.

Facilities and Activities

Day-use beach, wildlife observation, public education programs (call for information). Open daily during daylight hours. No admission fee. A visitor center is being planned jointly with Pelican Island NWR, pending funding.

Best Time of Year

Summer for swimming and observing turtle tracks and nests.

Pets

Brevard County ordinance prohibits pets on Brevard beaches. Permitted on leash in Indian County.

AVON PARK AIR FORCE RANGE

Few military bases offer the public the recreational opportunities available at Avon Park. The base's primary mission is to train pilots. However, when military activities allow, sections of the base are open for outdoor recreation, including hiking, camping, bicycling, horseback riding, hunting, and fishing. Several trails were established specifically for recreation.

Narrow footbridge on Lake Arbuckle National Recreation Trail in Avon Park Air Force Range (Susan D. Jewell)

The base covers 106,000 acres and consists of pine flatwoods, oak hammocks, dry prairies, cypress swamps, and marshes. The western part sits on the Lake Wales Ridge and contains scrub habitat. The eastern boundary runs along the Kissimmee River and contains many square miles of bottomland. The four hiking trails vary in length from 0.5 to 16 miles. The longest trail is designated as a National Recreation Trail.

About 400 scrub jays inhabit this Air Force base, along with a dozen other threatened or endangered species. Look for caracaras and grasshopper sparrows.

Feral hogs are common, and the base allows hunting for these exotics during the hunting season. Cattle are permitted to graze in some areas (including around some of the trails) because they mimic some of the effects of fire.

Location, Mailing Address, and Phone

In Polk and Highland counties. From SR 17 in Avon Park, take CR 64 for 9.2 miles west to entrance gate. Proceed to Natural Resource Office by following main road for 1.5 miles, bearing left after the prison, to "Natural Resources - All Recreationists" sign and log cabin on left. Note: Visitors must go to the Natural Resources Office to obtain permit before going anywhere else on the base.

DET 1, 6th Support Group/CEN, 29 South Boulevard, Avon Park Air Force Range, FL 33825-5700; (941) 452-4119. Recorded message of trail closings: (941) 452-4223.

Facilities and Activities

Hiking, primitive backpack camping, campgrounds, boardwalk. Open most days, but may be closed for military activity on certain days (call recorded message above). Natural Resource Office open Thursday, noon to 6 PM; Friday to Sunday, 6:30 AM to 8 PM; Monday, 6 AM to 8 PM. Modest permit fee required for several trails (permit is good for all trails for whole weekend); several trails free; trails not handicapped-accessible.

Since this is a military base, all civilians must check in at the

Natural Resources office prior to going anywhere on the base. While it may seem like a nuisance, it is a simple procedure and should not discourage anyone from exploring this scenic area. Obtain trail maps at the office. Visitors are strongly recommended to call the recorded message a day or two prior to planning a hike, since the trails may be closed.

Hiking Trails

The shortest trail, Lake Arbuckle Nature Trail, is a boardwalk loop through a cypress swamp to the edge of Lake Arbuckle, where there is a 30-foot observation tower. It is located on Frostproof Road, 1.2 miles north of the Natural Resources office (permit required, small fee).

The Sandy Point Wildlife Refuge Trail is 6.5 miles long, with a few shortcut loops. The trailhead is located at the entrance of the Austin Hammock Campground, off of Ebersbach Road. The area is designated a wildlife refuge because it is closed to hunting at all times. The trail is a flat, narrow footpath.

The Florida National Scenic Trail (Kissimmee River section) parallels the Kissimmee River for 12 miles. It winds through oak hammocks, marshes, and pinelands. From the Air Force Range, it is accessible from the Fort Kissimmee Campground on Kissimmee Road. From outside the Air Force Range, it is accessible from SR 60 at the north end and S-65B Lock and Spillway at the south end (see **Kissimmee River Trail** under **FLORIDA TRAIL** section below). Permits, which are free, are required for trips originating from the Air Force Range.

The longest trail is the Lake Arbuckle National Recreation Trail (free). This 16-mile loop meanders through pine plantations, longleaf pine flatwoods, cypress lowlands, and sand pine-oak scrubs. A no-fee primitive campsite (a clearing on the ground) is located approximately 6 miles east of the Willingham Campground. Feral hogs and range cattle have made the trail very rough in many places. The trail begins at the Willingham Campground, on Frostproof Road, about 2 miles north of the Natural Resources office.

Campgrounds

There are three campgrounds (Willingham, Fort Kissimmee, and Morgan Hole), all nestled in live oak hammocks. They are used primarily by hunters during the hunting season but are available to nonhunters. They have minimal facilities (picnic tables, chemical toilets, fire grills, and water pumps; shower houses at Willingham and Morgan Hole).

Best Time of Year

Fall, winter, and spring have the best weather for hiking. However, the big game hunting season runs from mid-November to the beginning of January (the heaviest hunting and hunting with dogs until mid-December) and small game from January to mid-March. It is not recommended to hike during the hunting-with-dogs season. During any hunting season, hikers should wear fluorescent orange clothing. Call to confirm the hunting seasons.

Pets

Allowed except during spring turkey season.

CANAVERAL NATIONAL SEASHORE

So integrally connected to Merritt Island National Wildlife Refuge is Canaveral National Seashore that much of the information is redundant. The national seashore, established in 1975, and the refuge share nebulous boundaries, a visitor center, boat ramps, information brochure, and so on. The 59,300-acre seashore lies seaward of the refuge, protecting it with a 24-mile-long barrier beach. The beach shelters the nests of 3,000 to 4,000 sea turtles annually between May and September (primarily loggerheads, with some green turtles and an occasional leatherback). Park staff conduct weekly sea turtle nesting watches for visitors.

Other animals found at the seashore include bald eagles around deep water, wood storks around shallow water, gopher tortoises in the oak or pine scrub, manatees in the Indian River or Banana River, scrub jays in the oak scrub, and southeastern beach mice in the dunes. Feral hogs are a serious problem here as in most other natural areas in Florida. In one year, more than 2,500 hogs were removed from the park without any noticeable effect on the population.

Most visitors come to the seashore to enjoy the beach, preferring this to the more crowded beaches of Daytona.

Location, Mailing Address, and Phone

Located east of Titusville, adjacent to Merritt Island National Wildlife Refuge and Kennedy Space Center. To reach the North Beach area from I-95, take Exit 84 to SR 44, go east to SR A1A, then south 6 miles to Apollo Beach. To reach the South Beach area from I-95, take Exit 80 to SR 406 - Titusville. Go east on SR 406 over bridge, bear right onto SR 402, proceed to the end of the road, passing the joint Merritt Island NWR/Canaveral NS Visitor Center (about 5 miles from the intersection of US 1). NOTE: The South Beach area is closed to the public during space shuttle operations at Kennedy Space Center. Call before coming if near launch date (3 days before to 1 day after launch).

Headquarters: 308 Julia Street, Titusville, FL 32796; (407)267-1110

Information Center: 7611 South Atlantic Avenue, New Smyrna Beach, FL 32169; (904)428-3384

Facilities and Activities

Nature trails, beach, canoeing, backcountry camping, visitor center. No admission fee. Open 6 AM to 6 PM in winter, and 6 AM to 8 PM in summer.

Visitor Center

See entry for **Merritt Island National Wildlife Refuge.**

Nature trails

There are three relatively short nature trails: Turtle Mound, Castle Windy, and Eldora Hammock. Turtle Mound is a quarter-mile trail leading to a panoramic view from the top of a 50-foot

Timucuan Indian mound, believed to be a ceremonial burial mound. There are about 100 mounds in the area, since the Timucuan Indians lived in the vicinity for 2,000 years. Castle Windy (at Parking Area 3) is a 1-mile trail from the road to Mosquito Lagoon, with an Indian midden visible at the lagoon. Eldora Hammock, near the Information Center at Apollo Beach, is a half-mile loop through a coastal hammock.

Beach

The 24 miles of beach provide ample room for beachcombers, swimmers, birders, and so on, but the parking lots are the limiting factor. On fair-weather weekends, the lots may be filled, so arrive early.

Visitors may hike the entire length of the beach but should be aware that high tides may narrow the beach significantly. Hikers should also bring drinking water, since none is available along the beach. About half the length of the beach is accessible only by foot or canoe.

On the dunes, the sea oats stabilize the sand with long roots that may descend five feet. Other dune plants include yucca, sea ox-eye daisy, sea grape, and prickly-pear cactus. Gulls, terns, sandpipers, pelicans, and many other sea birds may be seen year-round.

Canoeing

See entry for Merritt Island National Wildlife Refuge for boat ramps. A 2-mile self-guided canoe trail starts at the boat ramp just north of Turtle Mound; it has two backcountry campsites.

Camping

Backcountry camping is permitted at certain seasons in certain areas along the beach and by canoe in Mosquito Lagoon. Camping along the beach is not permitted during sea turtle nesting season. Check with a ranger for acceptable areas and seasons and to obtain a permit. You must bring your own drinking water. The nearest potable water sources are at the information centers.

Best Time of Year
Summer for swimming, July to October for shorebird migrations, winter for hiking and backcountry camping, overwintering ducks. Expect insects in summer.

Pets
Allowed on leash. Not allowed on beach or in buildings.

CHASSAHOWITZKA NATIONAL WILDLIFE REFUGE

Many of the national wildlife refuges on the west coast of Florida are accessible only by boat. They exist to protect marine animals and nesting and migrating birds. Chassahowitzka (pronounced Chas-a-witz'-ka) is one of them. The refuge was established in 1941 to protect wintering waterfowl, but serves equally well in supporting manatees. The refuge includes the Homosassa and Chassahowitzka estuaries. The 30,500 acres of islands, estuaries, salt marshes, and swamps are pristine. A 7,600-acre wildlife sanctuary within the refuge is closed to all public use from October 15 to February 15.

In the winter, hundreds of ducks feed on the water milfoil, southern naiad, horned pondweed, and wigeon grass. In the summer, the manatees favor the shallow, calm waters where they may spend all day grazing up to 100 pounds of aquatic plants each. Sometimes in winter they seek the warm Chassahowitzka Springs water. Some 250 species of birds, 25 of mammals, and 40 of herps are documented for the refuge. White pelicans, magnificent frigatebirds, royal terns, bald eagles, wood storks and other wading birds, and painted buntings are a few of the birds you may see. Manatees and bottle-nosed dolphins may be seen in the shallow waters around the islands.

Canoeing is a great way to see the refuge. Endless coves and islands provide ample space and opportunity to quietly observe wildlife.

Part of the estuary at Chassahowitkza (Susan D. Jewell)

Location, Mailing Address, and Phone

Headquarters office at 1502 S.E. Kings Bay Drive, Crystal River (next to Port Paradise Resort Hotel). From the intersection of US 19 and SR 44 in the town of Crystal River, go north one block to S.E. Paradise Point Road. Turn left (west). Just past the curve to the right is the office on the left. (This is also the headquarters for Crystal River NWR.)

Boat launch

There are no boat launches in the refuge. A nearby launch is located at Chassahowitzka River Campground (904-382-2200) on SR 480, 1.7 miles west of US 19/98. The campground is privately owned. Other ramps may be found at dive shops.
1502 S.E. Kings Bay Drive, Crystal River, FL 34429; (904) 563-2088

Facilities and Activities

Canoeing, wildlife observation and photography, boating. No admission fee. If the headquarters office is closed, check the leaflet dispenser outside for refuge brochure, bird list, and hunting regulations.

Canoeing

The tides, river current, winds, and maze of islands in the refuge make it necessary to have some canoeing experience and to exercise caution. From the Chassahowitzka River Campground ramp, you'll be on the Chassahowitzka River, very near the springs, but not in the refuge. Novices will have no difficulty paddling around the springs and part of the way downstream. Experienced canoeists can proceed downstream the 4 miles to the refuge boundary, then paddle around the estuary inside the refuge. Note: the Wildlife Sanctuary is located at the north side of the river and is closed to the public from October 15 to February 15. Inquire about the tides at the campground office and plan to paddle with the tidal flow. Canoeists without marine charts should ask at the campground office for the canoe map (it's not a chart, but it's better than nothing). Exploring close to the campground will provide fascinating views in the clear water of the springs as they emerge from the earth. The campground office rents canoes.

Watch for manatees, bottle-nosed dolphins, and sea turtles in the water. Near the water's edge you may see the small ornate diamondback terrapins. Scout the air for magnificent frigatebirds, white pelicans, black-crowned and yellow-crowned night-herons, swallow-tailed kites, and black skimmers.

Best Time of Year

Year-round for canoeing, September-April for birding, April-September for manatees.

Pets

Allowed on leashes.

CRYSTAL RIVER NATIONAL WILDLIFE REFUGE

Crystal River National Wildlife Refuge is unique because it is the only national wildlife refuge established to protect the West Indian manatee. Thus it is primarily a marine refuge and includes Kings Bay, Crystal River, plus nine small islands that total 46 acres. The four largest are Banana Island, Buzzard Island, Parker Island, and Warden Key.

Since the refuge was established in 1983, it has been harboring up to 200 manatees at a time in the winters. In September or October, the manatees begin congregating to bask in the constant 72°F waters that flow from the springs. The numbers peak in Kings Bay late in December each year. Some manatees stay all year. It is one of the densest concentrations of manatees in the state.

Unfortunately, the manatees may be contributing to their own demise. Local dive shops have capitalized on the easy manatee viewing and sponsor regular diving and snorkeling trips into Kings Bay in the winter. Private boats comprise another faction. Hundreds of boats may visit the area on a single weekend day in winter. The result is excessive disturbance and life-threatening risk to the manatees by spinning boat propellers and moving hulls. Manatee sanctuary areas and speed zones were created by refuge personnel to ensure that activities on the refuge are compatible with the refuge's objectives.

Location, Mailing address, and Phone

Headquarters office at 1502 Southeast Kings Bay Drive, Crystal River (next to Port Paradise Resort Hotel). From the intersection of US 19 and SR 44 in the town of Crystal River, go north one block to S.E. Paradise Point Road. Turn left (west). Just past the curve to the right is the office on the left. (This is also the headquarters for Chassahowitzka NWR.)

The refuge's waters may be accessed by public boat ramps at Pete's Pier and Knox Bait House and by numerous private ramps at dive shops located throughout Crystal River. There are no boat rentals or boat ramps at the headquarters office.

1502 Southeast Kings Bay Drive, Crystal River, FL 34429. (904) 563-2088.

Facilities and Activities

Boating, wildlife observation and photography, snorkeling, scuba diving, swimming. Headquarters office open weekdays (except federal holidays) during business hours. No admission fee.

There are no land activities here and no equipment rentals. Diving and snorkeling equipment may be rented at dive shops located throughout the Crystal River area.

Best Time of Year

December to February is the best time to see the manatees (greatest concentrations).

Pets

Allowed on leashes.

HOBE SOUND NATIONAL WILDLIFE REFUGE

Florida has a number of refuges that are managed to protect specific animals, such as the Key deer, Florida panther, West Indian manatee, and American crocodile. Hobe Sound National Wildlife Refuge is one of these. Since it was established in 1969, it has protected the sea turtles that come to nest on the wide sandy beach. Initially, residents of Hobe Sound donated 229 acres to the U.S. Fish and Wildlife Service, and later donations brought the amount to 968. Refuge staff maintain an active exotic plant removal program, which includes removing Australian-pines from the beach so the turtles can nest.

Sand pines line the sandy trail on the coastal ridge at Hobe Sound NWR (Susan D. Jewell)

The northern section of the refuge is a 3.5-mile stretch of beach and dunes. It is one of the most productive loggerhead turtle nesting areas in the United States and may produce more than 100,000 hatchlings in one season. Green and leatherback turtles also nest here. Management for sea turtles includes controlling Australian-pines (whose roots prevent the turtles from digging nests) and predators (such as raccoons, which feast on the eggs). The beach also attracts human beach-goers who want a quiet, undeveloped setting.

The southern section of the refuge is situated on the coastal ridge. The sand pine scrub forest protects such wildlife species as scrub jays, gopher tortoises, and indigo snakes. A hiking trail provides access to this rare habitat. The refuge also protects manatees in the Intracoastal Waterway.

The Jobe (pronounced Hoe-bee) Indians inhabited the area when Jonathan Dickinson was shipwrecked on Jupiter Island near here in a hurricane in 1696. Assisted by steam-driven paddle boats, a community sprang up along Hobe Sound when the Jupiter Lighthouse was built in 1860; it has since disappeared.

Location, Mailing Address, and Phone

In coastal Martin County. Beach area: From the town of Hobe Sound, go east on CR 708 (Bridge Road) to the end. Turn left at Beach Road and go to end. Headquarters and nature center: 13640 SE Federal Highway, Hobe Sound. From the town of Hobe Sound, go south on US 1 for 2.2 miles to refuge on left.

Headquarters: P.O. Box 645, Hobe Sound, FL 33475; (407) 546-6141.

Hobe Sound Nature Center: P.O. Box 214, Hobe Sound, FL 33475; (407) 546-2067.

Facilities and Activities

Swimming beach, nature trail, nature center, nature programs, birding. Beach is federal fee area, hiking trail is free. Open sunrise to sunset daily (nature center has limited hours; call).

The beach offers a natural setting for swimming, snorkeling, and birding. Brown pelicans, ospreys, and many shorebirds frequent the water's edge. Winter brings northern gannets and common loons, plus such ducks as red-breasted mergansers, canvasbacks, and greater scaup. Look for sea turtle tracks in early morning sand from May to September.

The Sand Pine Scrub Nature Trail at the headquarters area is about a half mile long. Native vegetation includes sand pine, gopher apple, prickly-pear, rosemary, saw palmetto, and scrub oak. Signs along the way interpret the vegetation and terrain. Look for gopher tortoises, Florida scrub lizards, and scrub jays. Florida scrub lizards are found only in Florida and only in certain scrubs. They are similar in appearance to southern fence lizards but have a rusty horizontal stripe on their sides.

The nature center is operated by a cooperating association (Hobe Sound Nature Center, Inc.) and is located in the head-quarters area. The center includes exhibits on manatees, sea turtles, and other local wildlife. Environmental programs are offered throughout the year. During the summer and early fall, the center offers visitors the opportunity to watch sea turtles nesting at night (by reservation only).

Best Time of Year

Summer for beach activities, sea turtle nesting programs; winter for birding.

Pets

Allowed on beach on 6-foot hand-held leash, not allowed on trails.

MERRITT ISLAND NATIONAL WILDLIFE REFUGE

So, there was NASA (National Aeronautics and Space Adminis-tration) with all that land and nothing to do on it. Thousands of acres of healthy salt marsh, needed only as a buffer around its high-security activities. The solution? Let the U.S. Fish and Wildlife Service manage it for waterfowl. Thus, in 1963, over 140,000 acres of this internationally famous barrier island were reserved for tens of thousands of ducks, coots, shorebirds, and many other types of birds on the Eastern Migratory Flyway. At least 260 species of birds have been seen regularly, and many other accidentals are blown in from the sea by storms. One or two greater flamingos (most likely escapees from a nearby enter-tainment park) have been reliably seen year-round by boaters in the Mosquito Lagoon, causing the refuge to list the species as occasional on its bird list. Fifteen species of federally endan-

Freshwater marsh at Merritt Island National Wildlife Refuge (Susan D. Jewell

gered or threatened wildlife are found here, including manatees, scrub jays, piping plovers, indigo snakes, and sea turtles.

The shared responsibility of land management (which also includes the National Park Service's Canaveral National Seashore) is a unique arrangement. About half of the refuge is closed to the public all the time for security reasons associated with the Kennedy Space Center. Some additional parts of the refuge must be closed during a KSC launch or landing. From almost anywhere in the refuge, parts of KSC can be seen. Particularly visible is the Vehicle Assembly Building (where the tall rockets are assembled), a structure so large it creates its own weather inside! Moisture condenses under the roof to form rain clouds.

Over half of the refuge includes salt marshes and estuaries with mangroves. The rest is hardwood hammocks, palmetto flatwoods, and pine flatwoods. The mild coastal temperatures are favorable to subtropical flora. In the winter, up to 70,000 ducks and 100,000 coots from eastern and central North America feed and rest in the productive waters. Merritt Island has been a mecca for birders for generations. Over two million people visit the refuge each year.

A program initiated by the refuge in 1994 takes orphaned and rehabilitated manatees and prepares them for release into the wild by holding them in a large enclosed pen in the Banana River along the NASA Parkway. Biologists call it a "soft release site." Everyone else calls it a halfway house. It is not open to the public.

Location, Mailing Address, and Phone

Just east of Titusville. From I-95, take Exit 80 ("SR 406—Titusville"). Go east on SR 406 over bridge, bear right onto SR 402, proceed to the Visitor Center (about 5 miles from the intersection of US 1).

P.O. Box 6504, Titusville, FL 32782-6504; (407) 861-0667

Facilities and Activities

Nature trails, auto route, wildlife observation, canoeing, visitor center, boat ramps. No admission fee. Open sunrise to sunset daily. Note: parts of refuge may be closed during NASA launch activities.

Visitor Center 8-4 M-F 9-5 Sat-Sun

The Visitor Center serves as an information center for both the refuge and the adjacent Canaveral National Seashore. The central attraction is the life-sized bald eagle nest replica in a pine tree. Other exhibits of local wildlife and a large selection of natural history books for sale are also found here. Closed on federal holidays.

Boardwalk

The quarter-mile shady boardwalk behind the Visitor Center is handicapped-accessible. It penetrates a mesic hammock (having standing water during the rainy season) of oak and palmetto and has an overlook onto a marsh.

Oak Hammock Trail

(Located 1 mile east of Visitor Center.) This self-guided interpretive loop with boardwalks winds through a subtropical hammock for a half-mile. This seasonally-flooded forest consists of oaks, American elms, and red maples.

Palm Hammock Trail

(Located 1 mile east of Visitor Center.) For 2 miles this trail leads you through three shady cabbage palm-oak hammocks and over seasonally flooded marshes. The trail may be flooded in summer. Look for armadillos and feral hog rootings, as well as bromeliads and sawgrass.

Cruickshank Trail

(Located at Stop #8 of Black Point Wildlife Drive.) The 5-mile trail passes mangrove-rimmed ponds and salt marshes favored by waders and waterfowl. An observation tower and a photo blind are located along the trail.

Black Point Wildlife Drive *no gates - dawn to dusk*

(Located on SR 406, east of where it branches from SR 402.) An interpretive guide brochure is available at the beginning of this 7-mile drive. The speed limit on this dirt road is 25 mph. Early morning and late afternoon are best for wildlife viewing. Look for bald eagles, wood storks, reddish egrets, glossy ibises, and white pelicans in winter. Roseate spoonbills are common in summer. The impoundments were created for mosquito control in the 1950s. This, along with the spraying of DDT, led to the extinction of the dusky seaside sparrow by 1990. This was the only area in the world the species had ever been seen. Now the impoundments are managed with wildlife in mind, including using prescribed burns.

Canoeing

Private canoes can be launched at several public boat ramps on Mosquito Lagoon. To find the southern one, proceed east on SR 402 to the end (at Canaveral National Seashore) and the Eddy Creek parking lot, where the ramp is. The northern ramp is accessible via Canaveral National Seashore: from New Smyrna, take SR A1A south about 6 miles to just before Turtle Mound. This ramp is suggested for canoeists, because the maze of islands reduces motorboat traffic and provides excellent opportunities for exploring. Mosquito Lagoon is over 20 miles long, lined with mangroves and teeming with fish, birds, and (especially during the summer) its namesake—the mosquito. A boat ramp for the Indian River is on CR 3 at the Intracoastal Waterway by Haulover Canal. Another boat ramp for the Indian River is located along the causeway between Titusville and the refuge on SR 406.

Best Time of Year

November to March for birding (including waterfowl, shorebirds, songbirds, and raptors), January for nesting eagles and peak of waterfowl, April for manatees (peak month) and northbound shorebirds, August for southbound shorebirds. Expect insects in summer.

Pets

Allowed on leash.

PELICAN ISLAND NATIONAL WILDLIFE REFUGE

Brown pelicans have long cherished Pelican Island, with four to ten thousand birds formerly nesting year after year. Pelican Island, which is on the Indian River Lagoon, was one of the few high ground islands around that did not have raccoons to maraud the nests. The first account of the island appeared in 1859, when thousands of reddish, snowy, and great egrets, plus little blue and tricolored herons, roseate spoonbills, and brown pelicans nested annually. In the late 1800s, plume hunters ravaged the island by killing birds, collecting heron and egret plumes for the millinery market and pelican flight feathers for writing quills. In 1903, the Audubon Society and the American Ornithologists' Union lobbied to have Pelican Island set aside as a sanctuary. On March 14 of that year, President Theodore Roosevelt signed an executive order that established Pelican Island as the first national wildlife refuge in the country. Several expansions since then have enlarged the refuge to about 4,700 acres, including leased land. Sixteen mangrove islands, totalling 616 acres, now comprise the refuge. Most species never recovered their former population numbers. Pelican populations took another dive after 1945, when the pesticide DDT affected them. Now just several hundred brown pelican nests are counted each year. The refuge was designated a National Historic Landmark in 1963 and is also a wilderness area.

The birds nest only on the island called Pelican Island. While Pelican Island is less than three acres currently, it was about five acres a hundred years ago. Theories explaining the loss of land include sea level rise and erosion from boat wakes. The timing of nesting has also changed. A hundred years ago, most birds nested in the fall; now they nest in the spring. Besides brown pelicans, birds that nest on the island include wood storks, great blue herons, great egrets, snowy egrets, tricolored herons, little blue herons, white ibises, black-crowned night-herons, anhingas, and double-crested cormorants. Wood storks did not nest here prior to the 1960s. This new activity coincides with the species' general shift from nesting in south Florida to central and north Florida. Spoonbills and frigatebirds no longer nest here as they once did.

There are two nesting cycles: one starts in late November and the other starts in late March. The island is quiet for only about three months of the year, when there is no nesting activity. Tri-annual roost counts for one recent year showed the highest numbers in November (8,942 birds, 13 species) compared with April (2,135 birds, 15 species) and August (1,835 birds, 13 species).

Waterfowl are casual users of the refuge. Usually less than 3,000 individuals are found at the peak in winter, including lesser scaups, ring-necked ducks, pintails, widgeons, teals, mottled ducks, and red-breasted mergansers. Also in winter, white pelicans, ring-billed gulls, laughing gulls, Forster's terns, tree swallows, and common loons can be found.

Location, Mailing Address, and Phone

Accessible only by boat; landing on the islands is not permitted. Charter boat tours are available from River Queen Cruises (private concession at Captain Hiram's Restaurant at 1606 Indian River Drive in Sebastian; 407-589-6161). Local boat ramps may be found at the Wabasso Causeway (CR 510), Sebastian Yacht Club on Indian River Drive in Sebastian (2 blocks north of CR 512), City Boat Ramp on Indian River Drive at Main Street, and Sebastian Inlet State Recreation Area (see separate entry).

c/o Merritt Island NWR, P.O. Box 6504, Titusville, FL 32782-6504; (407) 861-0667.

Facilities and Activities

Birding and other wildlife observation. (No visitor facilities—a visitor center is being planned jointly with Archie Carr NWR, pending funding.)

Without a private boat, the only way a visitor can see the birds easily is from a charter tour boat such as the *River Queen*. This narrated tour leaves Captain Hiram's dock about 1.5 hours before sunset to observe birds flying in to roost on the island and returns around sunset. The 49-passenger boat runs daily in the winter and 3 to 4 times per week in the summer (reservations suggested). Boat ramps in the area are available for private boat owners. Watch for sea turtles (particularly juveniles), manatees, and dolphins feeding in the Indian River.

Best Time of Year

November to February for peak bird numbers (including white pelicans and other wintering species). Spring for majority of nesting birds. Great blue herons nest at nearly all times of the year. Roseate spoonbills and magnificent frigatebirds present in summer.

VI

NATURAL AREAS—
STATE LANDS

FLORIDA NATIONAL SCENIC TRAIL

What does Florida have in common with the Appalachians and the Cascades? It has a National Scenic Trail running through it! Congress authorized the trail in 1986, one of only eight in the country. The majority of the trail has been constructed, but new sections continue to be added by volunteers of the Florida Trail Association. The goal is a 1,300-mile trail that stretches from the Miami area to the Georgia border, where it would link with an extension of the Appalachian Trail. Thus, a person could hike from south Florida to Maine on one trail. Currently, the trail consists mostly of sections that are designated as "Florida Trail" and a few that are certified as part of the "National Scenic Trail" (a designation that gives more protection). The Florida Trails are marked with orange blazes and "FT" ("Florida Trail") signs.

About 1,000 miles of the National Scenic Trail and another 300 miles of side and loop trails are completed. The National Scenic Trail runs from Apalachicola National Forest in the north to Big Cypress Preserve in the south. Only one section in central Florida has been certified—the Kissimmee River Trail. A not-yet-certified 110-mile loop of the Florida National Scenic Trail rims Lake Okeechobee. All sections of the trail are open to foot traffic only (no bicycles, horses, or motorized vehicles).

Kissimmee River Trail

There are two stretches of the National Scenic Trail along the Kissimmee River. The northern stretch, 27 miles long, is located between SR 60 (northern terminus) and the S-65B Lock and Spillway (southern terminus). To find the northern trailhead, go to the west side of the bridge that crosses the Kissimmee on SR 60. Park at the public boat ramp parking lot on the south side of SR 60 (S-65 Lock and Spillway). Then walk west along the road 0.3 miles to a break in the guard rail and a small FT sign. The southern trailhead is near Hickory Hammock Trail (see separate entry). To find it, take US 98 to Bluff Hammock Road (12.9 miles west of CR 721, or 1.0 miles east of the post office in Lorida), then north on Bluff Hammock for 5.8 miles to the end. This is the S65-B Lock and Spillway, and there is a public boat ramp here. Walk back along the road about 0.2 miles to the trailhead on the right.

Heading north from S65-B, hikers will first encounter a section of the "real" river, which was the natural channel before the canal was built. The trail then proceeds north through sloughs and hammocks, occasionally wandering within sight of the river. Much of the southern half of the trail is within the Avon Park Air Force Range. If you are hiking through the Air Force Range (not originating from there), you may proceed without a permit. There is a campsite at Fort Kissimmee (closed to hikers during hunting season). **A minimum party of two people is required on the portion of the trail that goes through the Avon Park Air Force Range.**

At the north end of the Air Force Range is KICCO Wildlife Management Area. A settlement, the Kissimmee Island Cattle Company (KICCO, pronounced Kiss'-o), was located here from 1915 to the late 1920s. When the state purchased the land in 1985, a house and school were the only buildings left. They were badly deteriorated and a risk to the public. Before they were leveled, sketches were made for historical purposes. Some traces of the town, such as a sidewalk where the company headquarters was, can still be seen. The South Florida Water Management District is restoring parts of the area by recreating a natural marsh that had been drained for pasture, controlling exotic species, and conducting prescribed burns. The Wildlife Management Area has a backpack campsite at Camp Hammock (south end) and one at Long Hammock (north end).

Near the north end of the Kissimmee River Trail is the River

Ranch Resort (phone 800-866-6777). Hikers may contact the resort to arrange to park vehicles there. The River Ranch is located off SR 60, 1 mile west of the bridge over the Kissimmee River. The entrance to KICCO WMA is off the access road to River Ranch.

The Florida Trail Association conducts two 3-day group hikes on this section of trail, one in January and one in February. Half of the group starts from the north and the other half starts from the south. Somewhere in the middle, they meet and switch car keys, so all hikers can drive back to where they started!

The southern stretch of the trail along the Kissimmee River is a 9-mile length between SR 70 and SR 78. The northern terminus is located just east of the C-38 (Kissimmee River) Bridge on SR 70. To access the trail, drive down SW 144th Parkway to the 65-E Structure on the river. The southern terminus is on SR 78, just north of the C-38 Bridge at the Okee-Tantie Recreation Area. Since the southern terminus has an improved parking lot, and the northern one has only unimproved side-of-the-road parking, it may be better to park at the south end.

Hikers should bring ample potable water. Occasional opportunities exist to obtain water along the trail, but this should be purified first.

For more information, contact: South Florida Water Management District, Florida Trail Association, Florida Game and Fresh Water Fish Commission in Lakeland (see "For Additional Information" for addresses and phone numbers), or the Avon Park Air Force Range (see separate entry).

Lake Okeechobee Hoover Dike Trail

To some hikers, reaching the summit of a mountain is the ultimate challenge. For Floridians, who have no mountains in their state, the challenge is met by circum-hiking Lake Okeechobee. The 110-mile trail is situated on the Hoover Dike, the levee that encloses the 730-square-mile lake.

The dike was named for President Herbert Hoover, who ordered construction of the dike after the 1926 and 1928 hurricanes killed about 2,400 people. They drowned when a wind-driven wall of water overflowed the natural bank of the lake, flooding Belle Glade. Since then, the 38-foot-high dike and its associated water control structures have been used to control water levels in the lake, and the lake has been maintained at a lower level. Because of the reduced water levels, a once-familiar landmark to boaters, the "Lone Cypress," guides them no more. Its distinctive spreading crown now shades a roadside historic marker a half-mile from the lake!

The South Florida Water Management District maintains the dike and the control structures. The SFWMD continues to make improvements to the trail for hikers. For example, they provided a fenced walkway around a pump station near Belle Glade to save hikers a 9-mile detour.

Location

Several access points are: A) Moore Haven Recreation Area—Off US 27 in Moore Haven, one section west of the town and one section east of the Caloosahatchee River Canal bridge. B) Okee-Tantie Recreation Area—On SR 78, about 6 miles southwest of the town of Okeechobee. On the lake shore, north side of the Kissimmee River. C) Pahokee Recreation Area—Near the intersection of US 441 and SR 15/715 in Pahokee. D) Port Mayaca Recreation Area—Off US 441 in Port Mayaca, on the north side of the St. Lucie Canal. E) South Bay Access Area—From US 27/SR 80, go 1.2 miles west of the railroad tracks in South Bay, turn north onto Levee Road. F) Miami Canal—7 miles west of South Bay (look for "Hoover Dike Public Access" or "John Stretch Memorial Park."

For More Information:

Florida Trail Association, Inc.
P.O. Box 13708
Gainesville, FL 32604
(904) 378-8823
(800) 343-1882 (Florida only)

South Florida Water Mgt. Dist.
P.O. Box 24680
W. Palm Beach, FL 33416
(407) 686-8800
(800) 432-2045

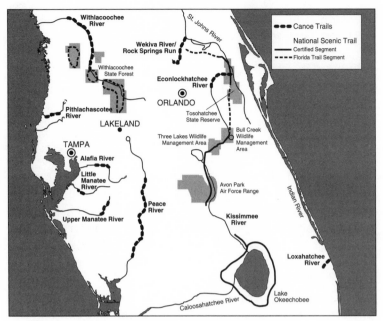

Central Florida canoe and hiking trails

Facilities and Activities

Hiking, bicycling, camping, wildlife observation.

Veterans of this loop hike comment that it shows an interesting side of Florida, a blend of nature and Cracker culture. Of the approximately 50 access areas, half are listed in the SFWMD recreational guide. Primitive camping is permitted along the levee or hikers may stay at fish camps. The mostly treeless trail is 20 feet above the surrounding land, offering dry footing and wide vistas. If the trail hasn't been mowed in a while, the grasses may be tall and hindering. The lake, marshes, cattle ranches, and citrus groves comprise parts of the view. On the south shore, 2.2 miles east of the Miami Canal and 3.8 miles west of the railroad tracks in South Bay, is a bald eagle nest in an Australian-pine that is visible from the dike.

The lack of shade necessitates a warning to all trail users: bring plenty of drinking water and sun protection, even in the winter. In winter, it's difficult to predict whether the temperature will be 80 degrees or 40, so be prepared for both.

Hiking

Before going on a long dike hike, hikers should acquire the "South Florida Water Management District Recreation Guide to Lake Okeechobee" brochure/map from SFWMD in West Palm Beach (call or write). It lists the camping sites and facilities, water and grocery stops, and access points and parks.

The Florida Trail Association sponsors an annual trek around the lake, dubbed the "Big O Dike Hike." It's held the week of Thanksgiving to allow for the eight days the trip takes, at a pace of 10 to 15 miles per day. The FTA makes all the necessary arrangements. Contact them in Gainesville for more information.

Bicycling

Bicycling is also permitted on the entire trail and is an excellent alternative to hiking. Mountain bikes would be appropriate, since the levee may be rough. With a bicycle, you can easily leave the trail and wander into one of the small lakeside towns for food, lodging, or just exploring. Plan about three days for a comfortable trip.

Best Time of Year

Winter, because of the cooler weather and lack of thunderstorms.

Pets

Permitted if under control.

FLORIDA CANOE TRAILS

The Florida Recreational Trails Act of 1979 authorized the state to establish recreational, scenic, and historic trails for the public. One network of trails is for canoeing. There are 36 such trails in the state trail system. The rivers and creeks were chosen for their scenic quality, variety of habitats, and distribution around the state. Almost 950 miles of these recreational water-ways lace the state. Nine of the trails are in the geographic area covered by this book.

The state trail designation does not mean that they are the only waterways worth canoeing. For example, lakes and larger rivers are not included but may be excellent for canoeing. Nor does it mean that they are only for canoeing—for example, motorboats are permitted on the Florida Canoe Trails. The waterways are publicly owned but often flow through private property, meaning that the stream banks are privately owned. Canoeists are responsible for making sure that they don't tres-pass. Some boat launches require fees.

Five of the nine trails in our area are described in the state or county park sections: Wekiva River/Rock Springs Run is described in "Wekiwa Springs State Park," Withlacoochee River is in "Withlacoochee State Forest," Alafia River is in "Alderman's Ford Park," Little Manatee River is in "Little Manatee River State Recreation Area," and Loxahatchee River is in "Jonathan Dick-inson State Park."

The following descriptions are for the remaining four trails, none of which flow through any park described in this book. The access points listed have parking areas. There may be other access points available which do not have parking. For more information and a trail map, contact the Department of Envi-ronmental Protection, Greenways Management and Trails, Mail Station 795, 3900 Commonwealth Blvd., Tallahassee, FL 32399-3000 (phone 904-487-4784) and specify the name of the trail.

Water conditions vary with weather and season. After heavy rains, current flow may increase dramatically. During the dry season, water levels may be low enough to cause short portages. In general, rivers that arise from springs have clearer water and more consistent flows than rivers that emerge from lakes or wetlands.

Econlockhatchee River

This shallow, winding river near Orlando, known locally as the "Econ," runs northeast through hardwood forests and sandhills to empty into the St. Johns River. The first half is narrow and shaded by oak-palm hammocks. Then it widens and exposes sandbars that can be used for camping (except those that are posted). The gentle current makes it attractive to novices. The Econ ends at the St. Johns River about a mile south of the bridge at SR 46.

To access the start of this 19-mile stretch of the river, take SR 50 east from Orlando to CR 419. Head north for 8.2 miles to the bridge. To access the river 8 miles farther downstream, take CR 426 east from Olviedo for 6.8 miles to Snow Hill Road. Turn south and go 2 miles to the bridge. To access the downstream end, take SR 46 east from Geneva for 4.8 miles to the bridge on the St. Johns River. The Econ is about a mile south of the bridge.

Pithlachascotee River

Part of the Pithlachascotee River flows through the town of New Port Richey, then into the Gulf of Mexico. This urban canoe trail requires some canoeing skill because of the tight turns and, near the Gulf, the waves. It's about 5 miles from the Rowan Road Bridge to the bridge at US 19.

One access is the Rowan Road Bridge: From SR 54, turn north onto Rowan Road (about 2 miles east of CR 595) and go about 1.5 miles to the Rowan Road Bridge. Another access is at Francis Avenue City Park. From Main Street in New Port Richey, take CR 595 south to Louisiana Ave., then turn east and proceed to park entrance.

Upper Manatee River

This 5-mile section is downstream of Lake Manatee State Recreation Area. It is easily accessible from Bradenton, only a few miles away, where the river empties into Tampa Bay. The slow current facilitates a return paddle and makes it suitable for beginners. Wading birds feed along the shallow banks. Allow a day for the round-trip. The Lake Manatee Dam is 3.5 miles southeast of the Rye Road bridge. The gates release water from the dam after heavy rainfalls upstream. This may cause problems for novice canoeists when the current increases, especially near the dam. Just prior to the gates opening, several blasts of a siren will warn you. You may also call the operator of the dam at (941) 746-3020 for release information.

To access from the upstream end, take Rye Road (a graded dirt road) south from CR 675 or northeast from SR 64 to the bridge by Upper Manatee River Road. To access the mid-point, go to the Rye Road Bridge, then west for 1 mile on Upper Manatee River Road to Hagle Park Road NE, then north to the river. This is a private canoe outfit which charges a small launch fee, but is more secure for parking than the Rye Road bridge. To access the end point (5 miles downstream), go to the Rye Road Bridge, then west for 2 miles on Upper Manatee River Road to Aquatel Road, then north to Aquatel Lodge. Another optional access point, about 2 miles downstream of Aquatel Lodge, is Fort Hamer, where there is a county boat ramp. To find Fort Hamer, take US 301 to Fort Hamer Road, about a mile south of Parrish. Go south on Fort Hamer Road to the end. Canoeists may want to avoid this ramp because of the heavy motorboat use.

Peace River

Long considered one of the most scenic rivers in Florida, the Peace River is a favorite among canoeists around the state. The state canoe trail covers 67 miles of the river, which originates at Lake Hancock. Very little development can be seen along the banks. The current is generally slow, increasing slightly in speed where the water passes between narrow banks. The many sandy beaches and shallow banks provide numerous camping sites. Sift through the sand for small, black fossil sharks' teeth. Look for turkeys, deer, otters, bears, and alligators.

There are many access points at the river. Here are ten, starting from the north (mileages are approximate):

- the bridge at US 98 (Fort Meade Recreational Park, 1 mile east of US 17); 3 miles downstream to next access
- the bridge at SR 657 (Mt. Pisgah Road); 7 miles downstream
- the bridge at SR 664 (Payne's Creek State Historic Site entrance is just west of the bridge); 4 miles downstream
- the bridge at SR 664-A (Lake Branch Road); 4 miles downstream

- the bridge at SR 664-A (Rea Road in Wauchula); 2 miles downstream
- the bridge at SR 64A/CR 636; 1 mile downstream
- the bridge at SR 652; 4 miles downstream
- the bridge at SR 64 (Pioneer City Park, west of US 17); 20 miles downstream
- the Gardner Boat Ramp (on River Road, 1.5 miles west of US 17); 12 miles downstream
- the bridge at SR 70; the river continues to Ft. Ogden and Charlotte Harbor

The 20-mile stretch from Pioneer City Park to the Gardner Boat Ramp is rated as the most scenic and having the most camping opportunities.

Two private local canoe outfits can assist you with your Peace River trip: Canoe Safari (3020 NW CR 661, Arcadia, FL 33821; 941-494-7865) and Canoe Outpost (2816 NW CR 661, Arcadia, FL 33821; 941-494-1215).

ARBUCKLE STATE FOREST AND LAKE ARBUCKLE STATE PARK

The Lake Arbuckle area has much to offer hikers and wildlife observers—to the east is the Avon Park Air Force Range (see separate entry), to the west is a state forest and a state park. A slightly confusing situation exists here: the state forest and state park share a boundary and common accesses. They both have hiking trails, primitive camping sites, and canoeing, but no visitor facilities. They are separated only by an unfenced dirt road. What's the difference? The rules for hunting differ and the forest allows logging. Other than that, hiking in one is much like hiking in the other.

The cause of this unusual situation is the origin of the funds used to purchase the land. They came from the Conservation and Recreation Lands program, so some of it had to go for a state park. Because of the controversies over the land, little development other than hiking trails (built and maintained by the Florida Trail Association) is planned.

On the forest's 10,697 acres and the park's 2,816 acres are the rare plant communities of Florida scrub and cutthroat grass. Pine flatwood, sandhill, seepage slopes, and bottomland forest communities are also found here. Twenty-two plant and 15 animal species are listed as endangered or threatened. Sand skinks, Florida panthers, red-cockaded woodpeckers, and Florida scrub jays are several listed animals known to occur here. State park personnel maintain bluebird nesting boxes, three of which have had evening bats in them. Some federally endangered plants found here include pygmy fringe tree, scrub plum, Carter's mustard, scrub blazing star, and Florida beargrass. A 20-acre parcel was added in 1994 to protect a patch of Florida ziziphus.

Canoeists can enjoy Reedy Creek, Lake Arbuckle (4,300 acres; 4.5 miles long), or Lake Godwin (20 acres). About 20 miles of hiking trails in the forest and six in the park pass through the various habitat types. Visitors can easily spend a weekend hiking and canoeing in this wild part of the Lake Wales Ridge.

Location, Mailing Address, and Phone

On the western side of Avon Park Air Force Range. North access: From intersection of CR 630 and US 27 Alt. (just north of Frostproof), go east 0.5 miles to N. Lake Reedy Blvd. Turn right and go 5.0 miles to Lake Arbuckle Road, then left for 1.5 miles to dirt road at state forest on right. Drive south on Rucks Dairy Road 0.8 miles to School Bus Road for hiking trails. South access: From US 17 in Avon Park, go east on CR 64 for 8.1 miles to forest/park on left (just before entrance to APAFR); hiking trails here. NOTE: School Bus Road is open to vehicles only from the north end, since the gate at the south end is closed. It is 4.8 miles from the north end of School Bus Road to the south gate.

State Forest—Division of Forestry, Lakeland District, 5745 S. Florida Ave., Lakeland, FL 33813; (941) 648-3163

State Park—c/o Lake Kissimmee State Park (941) 696-1112 or 452-1642

Hunting and fishing regulations—Florida Game and Fresh Water Fish Commission, 3900 Drane Field Road, Lakeland, FL 33811; (941) 648-3203

Facilities and Activities

Hiking, canoeing, primitive backpack camping. No admission fee. Open sunrise to sunset daily (hikers, beware of hunting season in November).

Hiking

Look for a box with trail map brochures at the north end of School Bus Road. Also look for the orange Florida Trail blazes. Take sufficient drinking water, for there is none along the way. From the north and the south accesses at School Bus Road, you can hike east or west and take the main trail all the way around both the forest and the park in a big loop (about 20 miles). The trail passes through forested wetlands, pine flatwoods, and scrub.

From the north, you can make several shorter trips. For example, you can hike east to Lake Arbuckle (3 miles). Or you can take the trail west for about 3 miles, then turn east at the trail junction and go to Lake Godwin. From the lake, you can take the road toward the east to School Bus Road, and then turn left and head back to your car (total trip about 6-7 miles). From the south, a 10-mile loop can be made through the state forest side; it also goes to Lake Godwin.

Canoeing

You can launch a canoe from School Bus Road where it crosses Reedy Creek, although the creek is very narrow here. From there, you can paddle east along the creek about 2 miles to Lake Arbuckle. Alternatively, you can head west along Reedy Creek for several miles, through forested wetlands. Canoeists can also drive their vehicles south on School Bus Road to the turnoff for Lake Godwin, and launch at the lake.

Another choice is to launch directly into Lake Arbuckle from the public boat ramp outside the park. This ramp is at the lake's south end and is reached via SR 64. Go east of the state forest/park entrance to a cluster of houses just before the Avon Park Air Force Range entrance. Follow a sign on the north side for a fish camp that points down a short drive to the ramp. (See also Lake Arbuckle Park under "Camping" below.) Lake Arbuckle has an undeveloped shoreline and can easily bestow a pleasant day of canoeing.

Camping

Campers must use one of the two designated primitive back-packing campsites. One is located less than 2 miles from the north access on the trail going west. The other is about a half mile from the south access on the trail going east to Lake Arbuckle.

A public campground is located at Lake Arbuckle Park, a Polk County park located near the north forest/park access (941-534-4341). To find the campground, keep going east on Lake Arbuckle Road for 2 miles past the turnoff for the state forest at Ruck's Dairy Road. The park is on the lake and has a boat ramp. It is open from 7 AM to 9 PM.

Best Time of Year

Winter is better for hiking (scrub habitat is hot in summer); best to avoid late October and the first two weeks of November due to hunting. Canoeing all year.

BLUE CYPRESS LAKE

One of the most beautiful lakes in central Florida (and with some of the cleanest water) is found in a remote area of Indian River County. Only one road leads to it. Were it not for the abundance of anglers in motorboats, this would be a wonderfully wild place. However, one may find quiet places and times to enjoy Blue Cypress Lake by canoe.

The lake acquired its name from the bluish reflection that the water casts on the cypress trees edging the lake in early morning. The lake is approximately 3 miles wide and 7 miles long (about 6,550 acres). Its average depth is 8 feet. Aside from the boat ramp area, there is no development around the lake. Around the perimeter, the cypresses march partway into the lake. Much of the area surrounding the lake is considered a marsh conservation area. This is because a levee east of the lake separates the agricultural runoff to the east from the clean waters of the lake's watershed. Agricultural waters, therefore, flow into canals and then to treatment areas, while the marsh water flows into the lake. The lake and surrounding area is owned by the St. Johns River Water Management District.

It would be easy to spend part or all of a day canoeing along the edges, exploring the back waters and the sloughs that feed the lake. Such marsh plants as white waterlilies flourish in the shallower areas. Watch for the bald eagles and ospreys that nest in the cypresses. Also watch for river otters, fox squirrels, alligators, and wading birds. Along Blue Cypress Lake Road are cattle pastures that may support caracaras.

Location, Mailing Address, and Phone

In Indian River County, about 25 miles west of Vero Beach. From I-95, take Exit 68 to SR 60. Go west for 18.4 miles to Blue Cypress Lake Road. Turn right and proceed north for 4.6 miles to the end. Or from Florida's Turnpike, take Exit 193 to SR 60. Go east for 6.6 miles and turn left at Blue Cypress Lake Road. Go 4.6 miles to end.

St. Johns River Water Management District, P.O. Box 1429, Palatka, FL 32178-1429. (904) 329-4500

Facilities and Activities

Canoeing, wildlife observation, limited facility camping, motorboat rentals, boat ramp. No admission fee. Open daily, all hours.

Canoeists may launch at the public boat ramp on the west side of the lake. A map with basic landmarks is available at the privately owned Bait & Tackle Shop for a small charge. No rental canoes are available. Camping is permitted near the small parking area around the store. It is county land (Blue Cypress County Park), and there is a bathroom with showers. Campers are asked to keep their sites clean in lieu of a camping fee. Despite the lack of a fee, camping should be considered only as a last resort because there is little room or privacy (no grills, either).

Best Time of Year
No preference.

Pets

Allowed on leash.

BLUE SPRING STATE PARK

Blue Spring's claim to fame is the large group of manatees that concentrate here every winter. The phenomenon is due to the warm spring waters that surface here and flow into the St. Johns River at the rate of 100 million gallons a day. The water of this first-magnitude spring is a constant 72° year-round, while the river will be 60° or colder in the winter. The manatees congregate to warm themselves in the vicinity of the spring, where they are easily observed. However, because there is little food for them near the spring, they must venture into the river to feed, where it is difficult to observe them without a boat or canoe. It is not unusual to see 40, 50, or even 60 manatees lolling in the observation area on a cool winter day.

Botanist John Bartram left the first written account of the area when he encountered the spring in his search for the source of the St. Johns River. It is known to be the largest spring on the river and is an official "State Natural Feature." The variety of wildlife includes 137 species of birds, 71 of fishes, 42 of reptiles, 21 of mammals, and 16 of amphibians.

On the last weekend in January, the Orange City Chamber of Commerce hosts a Manatee Festival at a local fairground. The event is too big for the park to host, but buses shuttle festivalgoers over to the park for manatee exhibits.

Location, Mailing Address, and Phone

In Orange City, about 30 miles north of Orlando. Take US 92/US 17 north from Orlando or south from Daytona to Orange City. In

Orange City, turn west onto West French Avenue (at the Blue Spring State Park sign) and go 2 miles to the park entrance.

2100 West French Ave, Orange City, FL 32763; (904)775-3663

Public Boat Ramp - continue on French past park entrance

Facilities and Activities

Hiking, campground, primitive backpack camping, cabins, interpretive boardwalk, interpretive center, swimming, canoeing, boating, fishing, concession. Admission fee charged. Open 8 AM to sunset daily.

Nature Trails

The Pine Island Hiking Trail is a 4-mile-long trail through sand pine scrub, pine flatwoods, marsh, and hammock. At the end of the trail is a primitive camping area (see "Camping" below). Hikers must return the same way, making an 8-mile trip. A tract acquired in 1994 (Stark Tract) added another hiking trail, about 1.5 miles long, that passes through hardwood hammocks. Bicycles are not permitted on either trail.

The boardwalk, about a half mile long, runs parallel to the Blue Spring Run (the section of water between the spring and where it empties into the river). The spring is a fissure in the rocks where the water appears to be boiling up. There are natural history interpretive signs along the way and several observation platforms for viewing the manatees.

Interpretive Center

A small museum houses information on manatees and local natural history. Rangers present slide shows on manatees daily from November 15 to April 15.

Swimming

The clear warm waters of Blue Spring are inviting even on chilly days. A roped-off swimming area is intended to keep humans from interfering with the manatees, but if a manatee should wander into the roped area, neither species is made to leave. The swimmers can stay and swim with them, as long as they don't bother the manatees.

Canoeing and Boating

Canoeing is popular on the St. Johns River and Blue Spring Run. A ramp on the river is available for private canoes. Rental canoes are available for day use from the concession. Motorboats can also be launched from the ramp, and there are short-term docks. Motorboats must remain in the river area (not permitted in Blue Spring Run).

Camping

The 45-site campground has both electric hook-up and non-electric sites. The sites are private and quiet (except when a train passes nearby). Reservations are suggested in the winter and on holidays. The less adventurous can rent one of the six fully equipped cabins, with central air-conditioning and heat plus a fireplace.

The more adventurous may prefer to backpack 4 miles to the primitive campsite on the Pine Island Trail. There are no facilities except a fire ring. The fee is less for the primitive site than the campground; backpackers must register first.

Concession

The concession sells snacks (including hot dogs, burgers, and pizza), film, manatee souvenirs, tee-shirts and sweatshirts, and some camping supplies and groceries.

Tour Boat

A private concession operates a two-hour tour boat cruise on the *John Bartram*. The boat runs from the Hontoon Landing Marina (outside of the park) to Blue Spring S.P. and passes Hontoon Island. The *Bartram* seats about 40 people and makes one run a day in the summer and two in the winter. For reservations (required) or more information, call the Marina at (800) 248-2474 or locally at (904) 734-2474.

Best Time of Year

November to March to see the manatees. The colder the river water, the more likely you'll see the manatees in the clear spring water.

BULL CREEK WILDLIFE MANAGEMENT AREA

The St. Johns River Water Management District owns the 22,206-acre Wildlife Management Area (WMA) but leases it to the Florida Game and Fresh Water Fish Commission for hunting and recreation. Its varied history includes timber harvesting, turpentine and resin production, and cattle grazing. Some of the crossroads are actually old railroad beds and tram roads from the cypress logging era. Hiking trails and an auto interpretive route traverse pine flatwoods, cypresses, live oak hammocks, oak scrubs, and freshwater marshes. The rural land surrounding the WMA adds to the possibility of seeing many types of wildlife, such as wild turkeys, limpkins, sandhill cranes, white-tailed deer, and bobcats.

Location, Mailing Address, and Phone

28 miles west of Melbourne. From I-95, take Exit 71 ("Melbourne - 192") to US 192. Go west on 192 for 19.5 miles to Crabgrass Road (see sign for Bull Creek WMA). Turn left onto Crabgrass and follow this dirt road for 6 miles.

St. Johns River Water Management District, P.O. Box 1429, Palatka, FL 32178-1429; (904) 329-4404.

Florida Game and Fresh Water Fish Commission, 1239 SW 10th Street, Ocala, FL 32674; (904) 732-1225.

Facilities and Activities

Hiking, wildlife drive, wildlife observation, primitive camping. No admission fee for hikers. May be closed during hunting season.

Wildlife Drive

The Wildlife Drive is a self-guided 8.6-mile loop that goes through all the habitat types in the WMA. The road starts at the hunt check station, where you can pick up the guide booklet from the dispenser box. Limpkins, mottled ducks, wild turkeys, and sandhill cranes are a few of the birds that may be seen, while bobcats, otters, white-tailed deer, and feral hogs are common mammals. In the hammocks, whisk ferns, shoestring ferns, and bromeliads grow on the trees. The road is rough and may be flooded in the wet season. Most hunting occurs in November and December.

Florida Trail

A section of the Florida Trail is accessible from the Wildlife Drive (see above). It is a 17.8-mile loop and starts from the hunt check station. It also visits all habitat types present in the WMA. The eastern side of the loop is part of the contiguous Florida National Scenic Trail. The trail may be flooded in the summer.

Camping

Primitive camping is allowed at designated campsites only, and a permit is not necessary if access is by through-hikers on the Florida Trail. The campsites along the trail are open all year, including during the hunting season (but only to nonhunters at that time). If access originates from the Bull Creek WMA, a camping permit must be obtained in advance from FGFWFC.

Best Time of Year

Fall, winter, and spring for migrant/overwintering birds; year-round for other wildlife. May be flooded in summer. Use caution and wear fluorescent orange clothing if hiking during hunting season.

Pets

Permitted on leash.

CALADESI ISLAND STATE PARK

A sparkling gem set in the Gulf of Mexico, Caladesi Island is a quiet place to relax or go birding. The state park actually contains six islands. Most of the 650 upland acres are on Caladesi Island, and over 1,000 acres are mangroves and seagrass beds. The lack of vehicles and development on the island make it a safer place for wildlife. The park service has obviously been hard at work controlling exotic plants, since Caladesi is the only island around without Australian-pine. Brazilian pepper is currently a target of the park service.

This barrier island was separated from Honeymoon Island in a hurricane in 1921. The resulting gap is now known as Hurricane Pass. Its location on the Gulf makes the beach good for shelling. The inland side of the island is a maze of mangroves where pelicans, herons, and egrets roost.

The proximity to Honeymoon Island State Recreation Area creates an excellent opportunity to explore two natural areas in one day. A logical route would be to take the ferry to Caladesi from Honeymoon Island, return within the 4-hour limit, then spend a few hours on the Honeymoon Island trails.

Location, Mailing Address, and Phone

On the Gulf of Mexico, near Clearwater. Accessible only by public ferry or private boat. Public ferries leave from two access points. One is from Honeymoon Island State Recreation Area (see separate entry) at the end of the Dunedin Causeway (SR 586; 12-minute ferry ride). The other is from the mainland in downtown Clearwater (Drew Street Dock, across from Coachman Park; 30-minute ferry ride). Call Clearwater Ferry Service for times, rates, and other information. Ferry runs weather permitting. Maximum 4-hour stay on island by ferry; no limit by private boat during daylight hours.

State Park Headquarters: #1 Causeway Blvd., Dunedin, FL 34698; (813) 469-5918

Clearwater Ferry Service: P.O. Box 3335, Clearwater, FL 34630; (813) 442-7433

Pine scrub in the coastal uplands of Caladesi Island State Park (Susan D. Jewell)

Facilities and Activities

Nature trail, swimming and shelling beach, snack bar/gift shop; marina. Admission and ferry fees charged. Open 8 AM to sunset daily.

The Island Nature Trail covers many habitats over its 3-mile length, including hammock, pine flatwoods and pine scrub, freshwater pond, mangroves, dunes, and beach. Ask at the office for the trail guide, or pick one up from the box on the trail. The pine scrub has very loose sandy soil, hence gopher tortoises and prickly-pear cactus can be seen. The gopher tortoises were probably present before the island was separated from the mainland. In the pines, the pair of barred owls seems out of place. The oak-palmetto hammocks and pines are on the highest elevations. These areas get washed by the tide only in extreme storms. The small freshwater pond is the only source of drinking water for wildlife on the refuge, so it is a good place to observe quietly. The trail empties onto the beach, from which it is an easy walk along the shore to the concession area. Mosquitoes can be a problem during all but the coldest months. Allow at least 1½ hours for the hike.

Along the 3-mile stretch of beach are dunes with sea oats. Loggerhead sea turtles nest from May to September. Shelling, shorebirding, and sunbathing are popular activities.

The marina's 99 slips are available for overnight docking, as long as the boats are registered at the office by sunset (first come, first served). The snack bar serves sandwiches, snacks, and drinks. The modest gift shop contains a small selection of tee-shirts and souvenirs.

Best Time of Year

April to November for beach; July to October for shorebird migrations; September to October for raptors, warblers, and other passerines; year-round for nature trail; winter for shelling.

DUPUIS RESERVE STATE FOREST

The 21,875 acres of Dupuis Reserve State Forest contain a variety of habitats: pine flatwoods, wet prairies, cypress domes, and marshes. Bald eagles, wood storks, limpkins, bobcats, deer, armadillos, and many other kinds of wildlife may be seen.

The reserve, straddling Martin and Palm Beach counties, was purchased in 1986 with funds from "Save Our Rivers," a program maintained by the South Florida Water Management District to protect water resources. It is managed as a limited multi-use area, allowing hiking, hunting, and horseback riding. The Florida Trail Association created and still maintains the hiking trails. The DuPuis Horsemen's Association developed and maintains the equestrian trails.

Cattle and sheep ranching operations by former owner John H. DuPuis (pronounced doo-pwee') are evident by the parklike understory and the drainage ditches and fences still crossing the land. The SFWMD is gradually filling ditches to restore the natural hydrology of the land.

Location, Mailing Address, and Phone

Near Port Mayaca. Take the Beeline Highway (SR 710) to SR 76. Go west on 76 about 6 miles. Look for Gate #2 on your left; this is the hikers' trailhead parking lot. Gate #3 is for horseback riders. Alternate route: take SR 441 to Port Mayaca, turn east onto SR 76 and go about 5 miles to gates (on right).

Public Lands Office, South Florida Water Management District, P.O. Box 24680, 3301 Gun Club Road, West Palm Beach, FL 33416-4680; (407) 686-8800 or 800-432-2045

Florida Division of Forestry (407) 924-8021

Facilities and Activities

Hiking, wildlife observation, primitive backpack camping, horse trails. Admission fee charged; extra fee for camping. Gate open dawn to dusk. Reserve may be closed on weekends during hunting season in the fall and winter; call the Division of Forestry in advance for the hunt schedule.

Hiking

Four loop trails give hikers a choice of four distances: 4.3, 6.8, 11.5, and 15.5 miles. You can easily plan an all-day hike. These trails are for hiking only; the horse trails are separate. The trails are flat, grassy, occasionally wet (especially in the summer and fall), and can be bumpy because of feral hog rootings. The canopy is open slash pines and live oaks (offering little shade) with frequent sabal palmettos. The understory is an open grassy parkland with saw palmetto clumps. Some plants you may encounter are round-leaved sundew, bog bachelor-button, gallberry, white sabatia, celestial lily (endangered), glades lobelia, and spider orchid.

Wildlife abounds for the observant hiker. Bobwhites, wild turkeys, raptors, gray foxes, deer, and bobcats are common. Bald eagles, sandhill cranes, alligators, and indigo snakes may also be seen. Waterfowl and wading birds feed in the marshes.

Camping

The distance from the trailhead to the West Route campsite is 5.7 miles and from the trailhead to the East Route campsite is 9.7 miles. Campers must obtain a permit from the Division of Forestry. When you get your camping permit, ask if there is water available (all water should be treated or boiled).

Horse Trails

There are three loop trails, with the shortest at 7.2 miles long and the longest at 16.5 miles long. These trails are located in the same general area as the hiking trails (which they occasionally cross), so the habitats are similar. However, the horse trails are placed on the more upland places within the area. A permit is required and can be obtained by calling the SFWMD. Camping is allowed by permit at the Equestrian Center (by the parking lot).

Best Time of Year

From December to April for the driest trail conditions.

Pets

Allowed on leash.

FORT COOPER STATE PARK

Fort Cooper is a reminder of the bitter Second Seminole War. The persecuted Seminoles, about to be forced off their adopted lands in Florida, began to attack military posts in the 1830s. Their tactics were so successful that it left the U.S. military with many wounded men. The fort was a waypoint where some of the wounded remained, in hoped-for safety, until reinforcements came.

The fort was located here because the spring-fed Lake Holathlikaha provided the men with ample clean water and food. The lake now serves visitors with recreational opportunities, including fishing, canoeing, swimming, and wildlife observation. Surrounding the lake are hardwood hammocks and sandhill habitats with hiking trails.

Location, Mailing Address, and Phone

Just east of Withlacoochee State Forest, about 55 miles northwest of Orlando. From US 41 in Inverness, go south 1 mile to East Eden

124

Drive, then left for a few blocks to Old Floral City Road (crossing Withlacoochee State Trail), then right, and go 1.1 miles to park entrance.

3100 South Old Floral City Road, Inverness, FL 34450; (904) 726-0315

Facilities and Activities

Nature trails, canoeing, wildlife observation, primitive camping, fishing. Admission fee charged. Open 8 AM to sunset daily.

Not long ago, a long horse trail (about 5 miles) looped through the sandhills of the park. When it became apparent that the presence of horses was detrimental to the habitat, the trails were restricted to foot traffic only. Thus, there are about 10 miles of hiking trails. Much of the sandhill section is loose sand with little shade. Several short interpretive trails near the lake pass through hardwood hammock, which is heavily wooded with more solid footing. Pits in the ground reveal former phosphate prospecting sites near the lake. Look for barred owls, ospreys, river otters, bobcats, fox squirrels, and gopher tortoises.

Two tent sites are available for primitive camping; reservations are recommended.

Best Time of Year

Winter for hiking, summer for swimming.

FORT PIERCE INLET STATE RECREATION AREA AND JACK ISLAND STATE PRESERVE

When is one park really two parks? When they're as different as this recreation area and preserve. The main section of the park is the 340-acre recreation area on the inlet and Atlantic Ocean. The swimming beach, short nature trail, and picnic area attract the majority of visitors. People who want to get away for some hiking and wildlife observation can go to the 631-acre Jack

Island Preserve on the Indian River. Jack Island is maintained for mosquito control by dikes and impoundments. Salt water is pumped into the impoundments in the summer to prevent mosquitoes from laying eggs. Miles of hiking trails and vistas of salt marshes and mud flats make this a great place for birding.

Development is rampant on other parts of this barrier island. The coastal hammock near the beach is a remnant of the maritime forests that formerly covered much of the subtropical barrier islands in Florida. This rare hammock is one of the state's northernmost pockets of subtropical plants. Gopher tortoises ramble around the sandy scrub near the entrance station. Mangroves comprise the Indian River side of the area (Jack Island), providing a rich nursery ground for crustaceans and fish. In summer, roseate spoonbills, gray kingbirds, and black-whiskered vireos can be found, while reddish egrets and smooth-billed anis are year-round residents. Because migrating birds often follow coastlines and seek undeveloped places to rest, both sections of this park are prime birding spots in the fall and spring. The picnic area at Dynamite Point (named for World War II military activities) is often a good birding spot at twilight, during storms, and in winter. Black skimmers, royal terns, and brown pelicans may be there at any time of the year, while plovers, sanderlings, and other shorebirds appear in winter (including hundreds of royal terns, sandwich terns, Forster's terns, and black skimmers). About 200 species of birds have been recorded at the park.

Location, Mailing Address, and Phone

Four miles east of Fort Pierce on Hutchinson Island. Recreation Area—From US 1 just north of Fort Pierce, take US A1A (North Beach Causeway) east across the Indian River for 2.5 miles. Jack Island State Preserve—Follow directions to recreation area above, but go north on A1A for 1.5 miles past the entrance to the recreation area on left.

905 Shorewinds Drive, Fort Pierce, FL 34949; (407) 468-3985.

Facilities and Activities
Hiking, swimming, picnicking, observation tower. Open 8 AM to ⸱
sunset daily. Admission fee charged at recreation area (no fee at
Jack Island).

Hiking

Coastal Hammock Trail—This half-mile trail is located at the
recreation area. Trail guide brochures are found in a box at the
trailhead. The dense, shady hammock of subtropical trees is
liked by black-whiskered vireos. Paradise-tree, gumbo-limbo,
strangler fig, beauty berry, and wild coffee are some of the
plants you're likely to see. Not handicapped-accessible.

Marsh Rabbit Trail—This is one of two self-guided interpretive trails at Jack Island Preserve. Trail guides can be acquired at
the recreation area or at the trailhead. True to its name, marsh
rabbits are commonly seen. To get to the trails on the island, you
will cross a cement bridge over the Fort Pierce Cut that is popular with anglers. The trail is about a mile long one-way and
runs across the top of a dike to the observation tower. Along the
way, you'll see four species of mangroves: white, red, black, and
buttonwood. The 20-foot-tall observation tower affords a view
of the mangrove lagoon. Look for wading birds and shorebirds.
In summer, look for spoonbills and reddish egrets. Yellow-
crowned night-herons are common residents.

Buttonwood Loop—This 0.1-mile trail is located near the beginning of the Marsh Rabbit Trail at Jack Island Preserve (see
above). The trail has signs along the way identifying various
native plants and trees, such as randia, salt bush, white stopper,
buttonwood, and black ironwood.

Mangrove and Marsh Trail—These trails are on the dike that
runs along the perimeter of Jack Island Preserve. The entire
perimeter is a 4.3-mile walk; this can be divided in half by cut-
ting across the island on the Marsh Rabbit Trail. The perimeter

dike overlooks mangrove lagoons and mud flats. Many shore-birds use the mud flats when the tide is low.

Beach

The beach (at the recreation area) is popular with human swimmers, and sea turtles lay their eggs here in the summer. The dune protects the coastal hammock by its covering of sea oats, railroad vines, and sea grapes. Songbirds rest here during migration. There are showers for the bathers.

Best Time of Year

Fall, winter, and spring for birding; summer for swimming; any time for hiking (some mosquitoes in summer).

GREEN SWAMP

One of the last large wildernesses in central Florida is also one of the most valuable. The Green Swamp is an amorphous region of 870 square miles and a lot more than swamp. This mostly state-owned land contains pine flatwoods, open prairies, and palmetto flats, besides the dense cypress and red maple swamps. However, it's because it is the heart of central Florida's water supply that it is so precious. The Green Swamp is a high, flat basin that holds, filters, and gradually releases water to the Floridan Aquifer, from which most Floridians obtain their water.

Topographically, the area is shaped like a saucer. It holds water at a higher elevation (125 feet) than the surrounding land. Much of the Green Swamp is underlain by porous limestone rock, which may come within 30 inches of the surface in the east. Water is stored in the rock, and when the aquifer is full, the water springs from it into the lower elevations. Thus, the swamp is the headwaters of five rivers: Withlacoochee, Little Withlacoochee, Oklawaha, Hillsborough, and Peace.

To the east, the Lake Wales Ridge holds water back. To the west, the Brooksville Ridge accomplishes this. To the south are the Winter Haven and Lakeland ridges.

Scenic Overlook at Green Swamp (Susan D. Jewell)

The Green Swamp has been a victim of pine and cypress logging and development schemes since the early 20th century. At that time, cypress trees at least 2,000 years old were felled. The state began acquiring land as part of a flood control project. Now the Southwest Florida Water Management District (SWFWMD) buys land for clean water supply. Under the Conservation and Recreation Lands program, development rights are being purchased to prevent further land degradation while allowing current owners to keep their property. While this seems like a win-win solution, it is not perfect. For example, farming is not an exempt activity. A landowner may not bulldoze his woods to build a house, but he may do so to grow sugarcane. In 1974, the Florida legislature designated the Green Swamp as an Area of Critical State Concern.

SWFWMD has been restoring the habitat by using prescribed burns and planting longleaf pines similar to the way they grow naturally. Bobcats, deer, turkeys, and bobwhites are common, as are the shy black bears. April is great for birding, when the spring insectivorous birds are migrating through or returning (such as vireos, warblers, orioles, swallow-tailed kites, yellow-billed cuckoos, and nighthawks). Hunting for deer, feral hogs, and small game occurs in the fall, so hikers should wear fluorescent orange clothing.

(See also **Van Fleet State Trail**)

Location, Mailing Address, and Phone

In Lake, Pasco, Polk, and Sumter counties. The accesses are fairly obscure. To access the southern area (Rock Ridge): Take SR 33 to Green Pond Road (about 4 miles south of the Lake/Polk county line, or about 8 miles north of Polk City). Turn west and proceed 6 miles (Green Pond becomes Rock Ridge Road) to a gate on the right (Rock Ridge Gate; hunter check station is through the gate). To access the Green Swamp Connector Trail from Withlacoochee State Forest area: take SR 471 south from SR 50 for 7.3 miles (2.2 miles south of Fish Hatchery). Or, take SR 471 north from US 98 for 13.9 miles. Look for an unimproved road on both sides of 471

*marked with orange blazes. The Green Swamp Connector Trail
goes east through the State Forest to the Green Swamp.*

*For camping permit: Southwest Florida Water Management
District (800) 343-1882 in Florida or (904) 796-7211, x4464 (see
"Other Sources of Information").*

*For trail information: Florida Trail Association (see "Other
Sources of Information").*

*For hunting information: FGFWFC in Lakeland, (941) 648-
3203 (see "Other Sources of Information").*

Facilities and Activities

*Hiking, primitive backpack camping, wildlife observation, bicy-
cling, hunting. No admission fee. Hiking trails open during
hunting season.*

Hiking

More than 20 miles of hiking trails are carved through this
wilderness and are maintained by the Florida Trail Association
(orange blazes mark the main trail, blue blazes mark the side
trails). Most of the habitat is pine flatwoods, including longleaf
pine, or cypress swamp with bromeliads. Also, live oaks, sweet-
gums, and red maples may be found.

A day hike suggestion is the 7.7-mile loop that starts from the
Rock Ridge Gate. Hike north for 2.3 miles on the Main Grade to
the Withlacoochee River, cross the river, then take the first left
("To scenic overlook" sign) and go straight to overlook, following
the old railroad grade that you started on; take it to the end, even
though the sign tells you to turn right near the trailhead. The
scenic overlook is merely the place where the railroad bed ends
and the land drops around you, so you are a *little* above the surrounding swamp. Even in winter, the red maples, cypresses, and
elms may harbor many types of small birds. Try "pishing" (a
birders' call) to attract black-and-white, pine, and yellow-
throated warblers, phoebes, blue-gray gnatcatchers, ruby-
crowned kinglets, Carolina and house wrens, white-eyed and
solitary vireos, and robins. Bobcat scats are commonly found

along the trail. After finishing at the overlook, backtrack to the first left, then right at the next junction and straight back to the Main Grade.

During the hunting season, the Rock Ridge Gate is open. Hikers may then drive the first 2.3 miles on the Main Grade to the trailheads. A permit is not required for day hiking.

Bicycling

Most of the roads are available for bicycling. These are all unimproved roads such as the Main Grade and Tannic Grade. Considering the many miles of roads that cover the Green Swamp, bicycling is a good way to explore (although it's easy to get lost if you take too many side roads). Bicycles are not permitted on the hiking trails. No permit is required for bicycling.

Camping

There are two primitive backpack campsites. Tillman Hammock Campsite is 4.1 miles from the Rock Ridge Gate and Mott Hammock Campsite is 5.0 miles from that gate. Both are situated in shady oak hammocks with open understories. The only improvements are fire pits; there is no drinking water. There is no fee, but campers must obtain a permit at least 10 days in advance by calling or writing the Southwest Florida Water Management District. *The backpack campsites are closed during hunting season.* During hunting season, the area around the Rock Ridge Gate is informally open to camping. It is intended for hunters but is open to anyone. There is no fee, and the only facilities are Port-o-lets. Space is limited and the ground may be wet.

Best Time of Year

Winter is best for hiking because of cooler weather and drier trails. Mosquitoes are abundant in summer and it is generally too wet to hike (except on unimproved roads). Check with FGFWFC in Lakeland for hunting season dates in fall-winter (October-early January). *When hiking during hunting season, wear fluorescent orange clothing, including an orange hat.* All things considered, the best conditions occur mid-January through April.

Pets

Allowed on leash.

HICKORY HAMMOCK TRAIL

Thanks to the realization that, to protect a waterway for the future, it is necessary to protect the surrounding watershed, many parcels of land have been preserved by Florida's Save Our Rivers program. One of them is a 9,487-acre section around the Kissimmee River in Highlands County. The South Florida Water Management District owns and manages the land as the Hickory Hammock Management Area, while the Florida Trail Association maintains the trail. The trail will eventually be part of the Florida National Scenic Trail. Live and laurel oaks form hammocks that provide shelter for songbirds. The understory is saw palmetto, which provides shelter for snakes and lizards. The land was once used for cattle ranching.

Location, Mailing Address, and Phone

About halfway between Sebring and Okeechobee along the Kissimmee River. To southeastern end of trail: From Okeechobee, take US 98 west past CR 721 for 7.9 miles (0.4 miles west of Istokpoga Canal) or 1.0 miles east from the post office in Lorida) and look for small sign on right; or from Sebring, take US 98 east through Lorida, then 5 miles past Bluff Hammock Road (railroad track crosses here) and look for small sign on left. To northwestern end of trail: From Okeechobee, take US 98 west past CR 721 for 12.9 miles to Bluff Hammock Road, then right for 1.6 miles; or from Sebring, go east on US 98 through Lorida to Bluff Hammock Road, then left for 1.6 miles. Note: The southeastern end of the trail is recommended, since it has a parking lot and there is no place to park at the northeastern end.

The Florida Trail as it passes through Hickory Hammock (Susan D. Jewell)

South Florida Water Management District, P.O. Box 24680, West Palm Beach, FL 33416-4680; (407) 687-6635

Facilities and Activities

Hiking, wildlife observation, primitive backpack camping, picnicking. No admission fee. Open sunrise to sunset daily.

The hiking trail is 7.9 miles long and is open to foot traffic only. From the parking lot on US 98, the trail goes north for 5.2 miles through a mature oak hammock. The trees attract warblers in the fall, winter, and spring. Slight changes in elevation cause depressions where small ponds form and slight hills where a small amount of scrub exists. Past the oak hammock area, the trail turns west and follows pastures for 2.7 miles. Look for sandhill cranes, which may nest here. Crested caracaras and swallowtailed kites may also be seen.

The campsite is located approximately 3 miles from the parking lot. A special use license is required and may be obtained free of charge by contacting the South Florida Water Management District. Give sufficient time to have the license mailed to you. By contacting the SFWMD in advance, you can have them send you the trail map.

Best Time of Year

Winter and spring for cooler weather and drier trail.

Pets

Allowed on leash.

HIGHLANDS HAMMOCK STATE PARK

The enchantment begins as soon as you enter the park and drive the main road through the hammock. Slash pines with an understory of saw palmetto give way to dense stands of tall cabbage palms that create a lush, shady atmosphere. This stand once yielded the champion cabbage palm, which has since fallen. Live oaks laden with resurrection ferns and other epiphytes add a touch of a time long ago. In this park in the 1930s, Oscar Baynard found an ivory-billed woodpecker—one of the last ever seen in Florida.

Were it not for the foresight and efforts of local residents in the early 1930s, Highlands Hammock's trees would have been leveled and its soils plowed under for farming. Now visitors can enter the world of a virgin cabbage palm hammock, one of the few large ones left in Florida. This feature earned it the designation of a "State Natural Feature." The Civilian Conservation Corps aided by developing roads and structures in the 1930s.

The 3,800-acre park also encompasses a cypress swamp, pine flatwoods, sand pine scrub, flatwoods, and marshes. Of interest to botanists is the mixture of southeastern canopy trees and West Indian understory plants.

Many types of wildlife seek shelter in the dense and varied vegetation. Alligators are commonly seen, especially on the Cypress Swamp Trail. Deer are often seen grazing in the orange grove in the evening. Bobcats, gray foxes, otters, and raccoons are commonly seen and rarely a panther. Three or four nests of swallow-tailed kites are active in the park each year. The park's bird checklist records 177 species. As in so many Florida parks, feral hogs are numerous here and destructive to the habitat.

Location, Mailing Address, and Phone

West of Sebring on US 98. From the north on US 98, go south 8.7 miles past SR 64 to state park sign on 98. Turn right and go 2.7 miles to park entrance. From the south on US 98, go north 5.5 miles from SR 66 to sign on 98 and turn left, going 2.7 miles to park entrance.

5931 Hammock Road, Sebring, FL 33872; (941)386-6094

Facilities and Activities

Nature trails, birding and wildlife observation, campground, interpretive center, horse trails, concession, bicycling and bicycle rentals, tram ride. Admission fee charged. Open 8 AM to sunset daily.

Nine nature trails give the visitor a variety of habitats to experience. All are relatively short in length and will take about 15 to 20 minutes to stroll. The Cypress Swamp Trail (the most popular) penetrates a pristine cypress swamp, and most of its 2,355-foot length is a narrow boardwalk. A short distance of boardwalk is handicapped-accessible. The Big Oak Trail (975 feet long) highlights a laurel oak that is over 1,000 years old and several others that are 800 to 900 years old. The Young Hammock Trail and the Ancient Hammock Trail are about 3,000 feet, the Fern Garden Trail is 1,650 feet (handicapped-accessible; some boardwalk through a hardwood swamp), the Lieber Memorial Trail is 1,800 feet (some boardwalk), the Hickory Trail is 2,200 feet (some boardwalk), the Wild Orange Trail is 3,000 feet, and the Allen Altvater Trail is 2,200 feet.

Feral hog rootings can be seen all around the trails. You may see a feral hog if you hike at dusk on one of the trails. You may also see armadillos and deer. Deer especially like to feed in the open fields around the Orange Grove at twilight. The park bird list has 177 species and the butterfly list has 56 species.

Campground

Reservations may be made up to 60 days in advance. During the winter, this is recommended, because the campground is often full. It is a quiet place in a beautiful setting and centrally located for many Floridians. There are 138 sites with water and electricity available in one campground area. The other area has 16 primitive sites with an outhouse, but no water or electricity. Don't panic if you hear a rustling sound around your campsite after dark—it's probably an armadillo. See also "Horse Trails" for equestrian campers.

Interpretive Center

Slide programs are presented Saturday nights for the campers. From approximately mid-October to mid-May, rangers conduct guided walks and other programs. Inside the Center are exhibits of habitat types, native and exotic wildlife, and a giant fossil tortoise shell (about 4 feet long). The shell was uncovered in the park in the 1930s and is from a species that was once common here but died out with the last ice age.

Tram rides, operated by the park, are given around the 3.2-mile main park road daily except Mondays (buy tickets at entrance station and meet the tram in front of the Center).

Bicycling

Bicycles are permitted only on the paved roads. The main paved road is 3.2 miles round-trip from the entrance station and is a delightful shady ride. Bicycles may be rented from the ranger station.

Horse Trails

Eleven miles of trails are dedicated to visitors who bring their own horses. The trails are separate from the hiking trails and not shown on the park map. Ask for the horse trail map at the entrance. Five campsites are placed in the horse trail area, so that riders can camp in small groups.

Concession

Bailey's Camp Store sells camping supplies, firewood, and food. The phone number is (941) 471-6400 and the mailing address is the same as the park's.

Best Time of Year

For bird migrations: October and late February to early March. Summer is hot, hence fewer visitors.

HILLSBOROUGH RIVER STATE PARK

One of the oldest state parks, Hillsborough River encompasses 2,981 acres, although not all are contiguous to the main use area. The Civilian Conservation Corps established the park in the 1930s and reconstructed the fort. The Florida Park Service restores the natural resources by conducting prescribed burns in fire-adapted habitats and by removing exotic plants.

Sandhill cranes, ospreys, bald eagles, and brown-headed nuthatches are permanent residents. Bobcats, river otters, fox squirrels, and round-tailed muskrats are some of the mammals inhabiting the park. Reptiles include alligators, gopher tortoises, coral snakes, cottonmouths, indigo snakes, and eastern glass lizards. Some amphibians include eastern narrowmouth and eastern spadefoot toads, little grass frogs, barking treefrogs, and gopher frogs.

Location, Mailing Address, and Phone

12 miles north of Tampa. From north or south, take I-75 to Exit 54. Go a mile east on SR 582 to US 301. Turn left and go north 9 miles to park entrance.

14302 US 301 North, Thonotosassa, FL 33592; (813) 987-6771

Facilities and Activities

Hiking, canoeing, canoe and boat rentals, campground, swimming, fishing, historic tours of the fort, camp store concession. Admission fee charged; additional fee for camping, swimming, fort tour. Open 8 AM to sunset daily.

Hiking

The Baynard Trail winds through a hardwood hammock in the Hillsborough River floodplain. The trail is bumpy, with roots and small hills (not wheelchair accessible), and may be wet at times.

The Rapids Trail, a short self-guided interpretive trail through slash pine, oak, and cabbage palm, leads to the river. The first part (from the parking lot to the river) is wide, flat, and hard-packed, making it wheelchair-accessible. It pauses at an overlook of the rapids, then continues as a narrow rough trail along the river. The trail becomes a boardwalk where it crosses through floodplains into a cypress swamp. Armadillos are commonly seen rooting around in the leaf litter for insects.

The longest trail is a 3.2-mile loop (not on the park brochure) on the north side of the river. It is maintained by the Florida Trail Association and thus is known as the Florida Trail. It is accessible by crossing the bridge near the concession, starting out on the Baynard Nature Trail, then walking north on the Baynard a short distance to the trail junction. Feral hogs have damaged a lot of habitat here, as elsewhere in the park.

Canoeing

The gentle flow of this beautiful river makes for a few hours of peaceful canoeing. People may launch their own canoes at the dock by the concession (hand launch only) or they may rent canoes at the concession (starting at 10 AM). After floating about 4 miles downstream, you'll reach a place where the river spreads out—the "17-Runs" area. Then you must find the main channel from among the many side channels, which isn't obvious, or turn back. If you try upstream instead, you'll soon hit the rapids, formed by limestone outcroppings breaking the surface. There is a maximum of 5 hp for motors on any boat.

Swimming

Once the place to swim was in the river. Then agricultural runoff upstream contaminated the water, so the park built a 400,000-gallon swimming pool. It was intended to resemble a pond, but it falls short of that goal. The water is conserved by recirculating it. The pool is only open from Memorial Day through Labor Day.

Camping

Two camping areas provide a total of 118 campsites, not including the youth camping area. Many sites are well-vegetated, but some are somewhat open. The nearby concession sells sandwiches, snacks, limited camping supplies, ice, books, and tee-shirts.

Fort Foster

Built during the Second Seminole War (1836) by Lt. Col. William S. Foster, the fort and footbridge have been authentically reconstructed. Tours are given on weekend and holiday afternoons year-round. Soldiers dressed in period costumes present living history programs.

Best Time of Year

December-March for camping and hiking; hot and buggy in summer, but popular for swimming and canoeing.

HOMOSASSA SPRINGS STATE WILDLIFE PARK

A unique state park can be found within an hour or two drive from Tampa, Orlando, and Ocala. The site has a long history as a tourist attraction, often touted as a natural "fishbowl." Where the Homosassa Springs emerge, thousands of fish congregate and can be easily viewed in the clear water. An underwater viewing room allows a rare opportunity for spectacular views of 21 species of saltwater fish and 14 of freshwater fish as well as manatees. The presence of saltwater fish is due to the slight amount of salts in the water (oligohaline).

The state uses the spring and the Homosassa River for rehabilitating wildlife in natural conditions. Most of the captive animals are permanently injured or human-dependent and would not survive on their own. The semi-aquatic species live directly in the river in enclosures that closely resemble their natural habitats, and where the river can constantly flush the enclosures with clean water. The emphasis is on rehabilitating manatees, which may be seen at close range every day of the year. This is the best place for a guaranteed view of manatees in a natural setting.

Allow at least 3 hours to see the 150-acre park.

Location, Mailing Address, and Phone

About 50 miles north of Tampa. One of the entrances is on US 19/98, just south of CR 490A in Homosassa Springs.

Entrance to the "Fish Bowl," the underwater viewing room at Homosassa Springs State Wildlife Park (Susan D. Jewell)

9225 W. Fishbowl Drive, Homosassa Springs, FL 34448; (904) 628-2311 or (904) 628-5343 on weekdays.

Facilities and Activities

Live animal exhibits, interpretive programs, underwater viewing room, native plant garden, boat ride, snack bar, gift shop. Admission fee charged. Open 9 AM to 5:30 PM daily (ticket counter closes at 4:00).

Paved walkways along the water lead to each exhibit. Exhibits include outdoor enclosures for such animals as alligators, crocodiles, river otters, bobcats, western cougars, bald eagles and other raptors, black bears, and white-tailed deer. There is even a celebrity hippopotamus. A reptile building houses many native snakes.

The Fish Bowl is a glass-sided underwater room directly over the spring, which issues forth several million gallons of nearly fresh water every hour. Thus, freshwater fish can certainly be seen, but many saltwater species are attracted. Some of the saltwater fish include sheepshead, crevalle jack, snook, striped mullet, stingray, and redfish. Manatees can clearly be observed swimming underwater.

The Museum and Education Center has displays of nests, shells, animal skeletons, and so on. The Garden of the Springs is a small collection of labeled native plantings.

The gift shop contains a large selection of field guides, tee-shirts, jewelry, souvenirs, videos, and art. The snack bar serves sandwiches, drinks, ice cream, and other snacks.

Best Time of Year

All times of year are good.

Pets

Not allowed; kennels provided free of charge.

HONEYMOON ISLAND
STATE RECREATION AREA

The forces of wind and waves have shaped this young island since it emerged 7,000 years ago. A hurricane in 1921 split the island in two, creating Caladesi Island to the south. The long sandy beach attracts birders, swimmers, and beachcombers. Birders also find mudflats galore around the island and along the causeway leading to the island, providing excellent opportunities to search for shorebirds and wading birds, while ducks are found just offshore.

Several development schemes have threatened the island in the past. One included filling in with 1.5 million cubic yards of material dredged from the Gulf before diligent citizens were able to halt it and preserve the island. Although part of the island is developed, about 400 acres of upland and 2,400 submerged acres are protected in the park. An 80-acre slash pine tract is one of the few virgin stands of that species left in the state. Gopher tortoises may be found feeding on prickly-pear cactus here.

Look for frigatebirds, brown pelicans, ospreys, roseate spoonbills (spring-fall), American oystercatchers, black skimmers, reddish egrets, bald eagles, mangrove cuckoos, as well as gopher tortoises and rattlesnakes.

Spend a leisurely day hiking the trails, beachcombing, and birding along the mudflats, or combine a half day at Honeymoon with a half day at Caladesi Island State Park (see separate entry). The ferry for Caladesi departs from the dock just inside Honeymoon Island's entrance station.

Location, Mailing Address, and Phone

On the Gulf coast, near Clearwater. From Tampa, go west on SR 580 to SR 752, then SR 586 (Curlew Road) west to the end. From north or south, take US 19 to SR 586, then west to the end.

#1 Causeway Boulevard, Dunedin, Fl 34698; (813) 469-5942

Facilities and Activities

Nature trails, swimming beach, picnicking. Open 8 AM to sunset daily. Admission fee charged.

Nature Trails

Two trails, the Osprey and the Pelican Cove, provide about 3.5 miles of hiking. The Osprey Trail is a wide, hardpacked, self-guided trail (handicapped-accessible; look for trail guide at trailhead). At Stop #5 is an osprey nest in a dead pine. In 1993, there were six active osprey nests in the park. The trail enters a virgin slash pine stand, which park staff maintains by prescribed burns. Allow at least 1.5 hours.

For habitat variety, take the Pelican Cove Trail back from the Osprey Trail (not entirely handicapped-accessible). It parallels the beach, where you can find shorebirds, shells, urchins, and sea oats. Across the cove is a protected area, where waterbirds roost and nest (good for using a spotting scope). The trail ends in a salt marsh.

Mangrove cuckoos nest in the mangroves on the island in the spring and summer (this is about the farthest north they nest). The best way to find them is to listen for their calls during the breeding season, around April to June. There are red, black, and white mangroves along the Pelican Cove Trail. American oyster-catchers also nest in the park; look for their nest scrapes (depressions in the sand that hold the eggs) on sandbars from March to July. Beginning in June, black skimmer nest scrapes may also be found on the sandbars.

Shelling

The west coast barrier islands are excellent for finding a variety of shells in good condition, and Honeymoon Island is no exception. Conchs, whelks, scallops, clams, mussels, augers, ceriths, slippers, and many others are commonly found. Beachcombers may also find sand dollars, hermit crabs, sea urchins, sea stars, and horseshoe crabs.

Best Time of Year

July to November for migrations (shorebird, raptor, and passerine), October to April for wintering birds and hiking, May to October for swimming, year-round at low tide or after a storm for shelling.

HONTOON ISLAND STATE PARK

One of the pleasures of this park is that cars are not allowed. A narrow stretch of the St. Johns River separates the access road from the island. The small passenger ferry is handicapped-accessible and runs about every quarter hour. Many people choose to go by private boat, and there is ample dockage on the island to accommodate them.

The 1,650 acres on Hontoon Island are covered with three main habitat types: pine flatwoods, oak-palmetto hammock, and cypress swamps. Miles of hiking trails and old roads permit easy access all over the island. Bald eagles are frequently sighted. Alligators are common enough to prevent the park service from allowing swimming. Deer and armadillos have swum to the island. Manatees may be seen in the St. Johns River in the

Shells of a small freshwater snail species comprise this food midden made by Timucuan Indians about six hundred years ago (Susan D. Jewell)

warmer months. Abundant canoeing is available on the St. Johns and Huntoon Dead Rivers.

Location, Mailing Address, and Phone

Six miles southwest of DeLand. NOTE: This park is accessible only by boat. Private boats are permitted to dock. To get to the state passenger ferry (free)—take SR 44 west of DeLand for about 6 miles (7 miles west of I-4) to CR 4110 (small state park sign). Turn left and go 1.8 miles to CR 4125 (Hontoon Road). Turn left again and follow CR 4125 for 3.3 more miles to state park parking lot.
2309 River Ridge Road, DeLand, FL 32720; (904) 736-5309

Just beyond is Hontoon Landing Marina — boat ramp, restaurant, 2hr eco boat tour nice!

Facilities and Activities

Nature trails, campground, canoeing and canoe rentals, observation tower, overnight dockage, concession store, picnicking. Open 8 AM to sunset daily. Admission fee charged. Extra fee for camping and canoe rental. No fee for state park passenger ferry, which operates 9 AM to one hour before sundown.

Trails

The self-guided nature trail goes through an oak-palmetto hammock to the Timucuan Indian mounds about 1.5 miles from the campground. It is a narrow footpath (not handicapped-accessible) with interpretive signs along the way. The Indian mounds are middens of freshwater snails that were a staple food for the Timucuans who lived here about 600 years ago. Talk about working for your food—these snail shells are only a half inch long! The elevation is higher because of the mounds, and some oak trees on top of them grow quite large.

Miles of old roads are available for hiking. Some go through the pine flatwoods, some through the hammock, and some to the cypresses by the river's edge. Ask at the office for a map to the hiking trails.

Canoeing

The rivers surrounding the island are wonderful for canoeing—if the motorboaters are well-behaved. It's generally not recommended to canoe here on a weekend, particularly on a holiday. If you do, stay near shore and watch the boat wakes. From the boat dock area at the north end of the island, you can paddle around several branches of the St. Johns River or up the Huntoon Dead River all the way around the island. You can explore Lake Beresford or a house-lined canal or even paddle to Blue Spring State Park, about 3 miles to the south. Watch for manatees year-round, but particularly in summer. Campers may want to fish for their dinners.

Campground and Overnight Dock

The campground is small and quiet, with 12 tent sites shaded in the pines. Barred owls and squirrel treefrogs will lull you to sleep. Each site has water and the bathrooms have hot showers. A youth group site and six cabins are also available. The cabins are rustic, with electricity, ceiling fans, and screened porches elevating them a step above camping. Reservations are accepted for tent sites and cabins.

The campground is located about a quarter mile from the boat dock. A ranger will drive you to the campground from the dock, but you can only bring what you can carry comfortably onto the ferry and van.

The boat dock is located on the north side of the island, by the concession store and park office. The 48 boat camping slips are popular all year but are available only on a "first come" basis. The concession store sells basic camping supplies and snacks. It is open until the park closes in the evening.

Observation Tower

This has to out-class all other observation towers around. From the top of its 80-foot-high platform, you can see great distances in all directions. You are well above the tops of the trees and can see the St. Johns River in both directions. If you can stomach the climb, it is well worth it. Yes it was!

1. The gumbo limbo tree, which has red, peeling bark, grows on coastal hammocks from Brevard and Pinellas Counties southward.

2. Upper Tampa Bay Park's salt marshes and estuaries provide hours of scenic canoeing only minutes from Tampa.

3. The relatively pristine freshwater marsh at Savannas State Reserve is about 10 miles long. The trees on the far side are growing on the coastal ridge.

4. The previous season's stalks of sea oats stand tall above the new growth. Sea oats help to stabilize the dunes.

5. A worker at Homosassa Springs State Wildlife Park cares for a rehabilitating manatee.

6. The fragrant wool-bearing cereus, an endangered cactus, grows at Savannas State Reserve.

7. The trail at Tiger Creek Preserve shows the dramatic difference a few inches of elevation can make. Note the light sand at the far end of the trail, where the elevation is less than a foot higher than the near end, which is much wetter and richer.

8. The pristine Blue Cypress Lake is rimmed by cypress trees.

9. Limestone outcropping along the Atlantic Coast.

10. Small springs feed the headwaters of the Chassahow-itzka River.

11. Resurrection fern grows epiphytically on branches.

12. A variety of habitats, including pinelands and wetlands, can be found at Avon Park Air Force Range.

Rob Bennetts

13. With his hooked bill, this male snail kite has extracted an apple snail from its shell.

Wayne Hoffman

14. Smooth-billed anis are usually seen in shrubs near fresh water, often with grackles.

15. Zebra longwing butterflies are common in central Florida, where they may be seen in tropical hardwood hammocks. They often roost communally at night in small trees.

16. Fulvous whistling ducks nest in central and southern Florida, usually near agricultural land.

17. The eastern diamondback rattlesnake is one of four venomous snakes found in central Florida.

18. This red-cockaded woodpecker (endangered) has been leg-banded with U.S. Fish & Wildlife Service bands to study its family structure.

James Phillips

19. The Florida panther is one of the rarest mammals in the world. The USFWS is working to restore the panther to central Florida.

James Phillips

20. The crested caracara can be found around cattle pastures in central Florida.

21. Butterfly orchids are found in swamps and wet hammocks in central and south Florida.

James Phillips

Best Time of Year

Fall, winter, and spring for birding and cooler hiking. You may have the place to yourself in summer; some mosquitoes.

JONATHAN DICKINSON STATE PARK

Steeped in history, both human and natural, Jonathan Dickinson State Park is an all-around interesting place to visit. Its story began in 1696, when a shipwreck off the coast of Jupiter Island left Jonathan Dickinson, with his wife and baby and shipmates, stranded on the beach by Hobe Sound. They eventually made the perilous journey north to St. Augustine by foot and canoe, aided by the Jobe Indians who found them. It is Dickinson's journal that today sheds so much light on early Florida.

In spite of all the development on the southeastern Florida coast, the Loxahatchee River, which flows through the park, has remained relatively undisturbed. This led to its designation in

The Loxahatchee River, lined with cabbage palms and red mangroves, at Jonathan Dickinson State Park (Susan D. Jewell)

1985 as a "National Wild and Scenic River," the only one in the state. Many a canoeist has paddled these beautiful waters.

The park's nearly 11,500 acres includes sand pine scrub (the largest remnant in this part of Florida), slash pine flatwoods, and oaks that harbor such wildlife as sandhill cranes, scrub jays, white-tailed deer, gopher tortoises, and Florida scrub lizards. A pair of bald eagles has nested consistently at the park recently in an area that has been used by eagles since the 1960s. A relic sand dune called Hobe Mountain, which rises 85 feet above the surrounding land, adds unexpected topography in this part of the state. Visitors can drive partway up the mountain, walk the short trail to the top, and climb the 25-foot observation tower for a spectacular 360° view of the ocean, river, and park.

Over 25 miles of hiking trails lace the park. Between the hiking, canoeing, boat tour, and camping, this park is a great all-weekend destination.

Location, Mailing Address, and Phone

Just north of Jupiter. From the south via I-95, take Exit 59, go east on SR 706, turn left onto US 1, heading north to park entrance on left. From the north via I-95, take Exit 60, go east on SR 708, turn right onto US 1, heading south to park entrance on right.

Park Office: 16450 Southeast Federal Highway, Hobe Sound, FL 33455; (407) 546-2771.

Tour Boat Concession: (407) 746-1466

Facilities and Activities

Hiking, campgrounds, primitive backpack camping, cabin rentals, canoeing and canoe rentals, boat ramp, boat tour, observation tower, bicycling, concession store. Admission fee charged; fees for camping, boat rental, and boat tour extra. Open 8 AM to sunset daily.

Hiking

Two short hiking trails, the Kitching Creek and Wilson Creek Trails, are located by the picnic area near the river. They are not part of the Florida Trail, and one could probably guess that by the lack of trail markers. Ask for a trail brochure at the entrance station, but be prepared to be confused anyway.

Sand Pine Nature Trail—This is actually the beginning section of the Florida Trail (see next paragraph) and is located at the north end of the parking lot by the entrance station. It is 0.2 miles one way. There is a guide brochure box at the trailhead. The numbered stops point out common native plants in the area. Thus, it's a good first stop upon entering the park. Some of the plants are scrub mint, gopher apple, rosemary, and hog plum.

Florida Trail—For the serious hikers, there are over 20 miles of hiking trails. Most of the trails are part of the Florida Trail and are well-maintained by the Florida Trail Association. The East Loop (which includes the Scrub Jay Campsite, see Camping below) is 9.4 miles and the West Loop (which includes the Kitching Creek Campsite, see Camping below) is 17.7 miles. Aside from the first few miles, which parallel US 1, the trails are quiet and peaceful. They may be wet in some low-lying areas, particularly in summer and fall. Much of the habitat is sand pine scrub and oak scrub.

Canoeing

The Loxahatchee River is a National Wild and Scenic River that winds through subtropical cypress and mangrove swamps. Pond apple trees, orchids, and ferns also line the tannin-stained waters. The skeletal ghosts of the cypress trees and cabbage palms are evidence of the increase in the river's salinity. Red mangroves encroach farther upstream each year as the line of fresh water recedes and the salt water intrudes. The cause is channelization and diversion of fresh water upstream for drainage. Efforts are ongoing to restore the oxbows to the river, which were cut off by human-related activities. As people portage their canoes for shortcuts, the traveled ground becomes depressed and filled with water. Then, during high water, the river also takes a shortcut, choking off a bend in the river. The oxbows prevent river water from draining too quickly to the sea and prevent salt water from pushing farther upstream.

river was higher + faster than usual, still EZ to paddle upstream

Otters, raccoons, bobcats, ospreys, wading birds, and alligators live along the river. Turtles frequently bask on fallen logs in midstream, alluding to the source of the river's name Loxahatchee, which means "river of turtles" in the native tongue. Peninsula cooters, Florida softshells, Florida redbellies, and Florida snapping turtles are common, as are such fish as mangrove snappers and mullets. *mangroves downstream; cypress upstream*

Four miles upstream from the concession is the landmark destination of Trapper Nelson's cabin. Before he died in 1968, Trapper Nelson, known as the "Wild Man of Loxahatchee," lived off the land without electricity in a cabin he built himself. The cabin is perched on the highest land next to the river. He trapped otters and raccoons for pelts. He planted fruit trees and kept penned gopher tortoises for food. He earned money by housing and feeding river-going travelers. His homestead is now maintained by the park and is a popular stop by canoeists. A ranger is often present to give short tours.

One option for canoeists is to rent canoes at the park concession (or launch a private canoe) and go upstream toward Trapper Nelson's or downstream toward the ocean. Canoes may be rented by the hour.

Another option is to launch a canoe farther upstream at Riverbend County Park and paddle down to the park (approximately 8 miles, moderate difficulty). If you go to Riverbend, call the concession at Riverbend (407-746-7053) first to schedule a launch time, since a limited number of canoes are permitted each day to protect the river. To get to Riverbend Park, take SR 706 (Indiantown Road) 1.5 miles west of Florida's Turnpike and I-95 interchanges (Exit 48 from the Turnpike and Exit 59 from I-95). Two water control structures necessitate minor pull-throughs, depending on water levels.

opens 8 AM

Please heed this warning: the state park regulations prohibit people from feeding alligators and from stepping out of their canoes anywhere except at the main dock and at Trapper Nelson's. This is because there are alligators around. The alligators should not bother you while you are in the canoe.

concession is Canoe Outfitters of Jupiter. They'll pick you up in the park if others to pick up, too — so could call ahead

Camping

There are two full-facility campgrounds. The Pine Grove Camping Area is heavily shaded with Australian-pine. While the shade is welcomed even in winter, purist naturalists may feel uncomfortable in this unnatural setting. They may prefer the River Camping Area, with its open slash pine scrub habitat. The primitive Youth Camp is available by reservation. Cabins are available for rental by contacting the concession.

Two primitive campsites are available for backpackers on the Florida Trail. The Scrub Jay Campsite can be reached by a 3.8- or a 5.6-mile trail and linked with longer loops. The Kitching Creek Campsite can be reached by a very short hike or a 9.3-mile hike, also connecting with longer loops. Register at the entrance station.

Boat Tour

A trip up the Loxahatchee River is a treat for naturalists and outdoor enthusiasts. If you can't do it by canoe, take the tour boat. The 30-passenger pontoon boat *Loxahatchee Queen* takes a two-hour narrated trip to Trapper Nelson's Cabin. The passengers disembark for a guided walking tour of the buildings and gardens. It is an eerie place, full of fascinating history about the Wild Man and how he lived off the land. Call the concession for tour schedule; reservations not accepted.

Bicycling

There is a paved 10-foot-wide bicycle path starting near the entrance station and ending at the railroad tracks. Bicyclists may also ride the long main park road. The Florida Trails are closed to bicycles. A few unmarked trails may be ridden.

Concession Store

The store sells snacks, sandwiches, basic camping and picnic supplies, tee-shirts, gifts, local field guides, and historical books. Canoes and cabins are rented here and the tour boat is booked here. Open 9 AM to 5 PM.

Best Time of Year

Winter for most activities because of the cooler weather and lack of thunderstorms.

LAKE KISSIMMEE STATE PARK

The 35,000-acre lake that lends its name to the park is an important landmark in Florida. It is the state's third largest lake and part of a series of lakes that begets the Everglades. Most of the park is relatively pristine. Park staff assist natural processes by conducting prescribed burns. Habitats include scrubby pine flatwood, mesic pine flatwood, wet pine flatwood, wet prairie, hardwood swamp, and oak hammock.

The wet prairie around the shallow lake is a natural pasture that early settlers used for cattle and horses in the 1800s. At that time, efforts were made to drain the wet prairie by canals to create more pasture and cropland. The canals still exist and allow water to bypass the marshes which filter the water naturally.

White-tailed deer, gray foxes, bobcats, and fox squirrels are commonly seen. Fox squirrels do not adapt to human activity as well as gray squirrels and consequently are found farther from development. This is partly the cause of their gradual population decline.

Over 250 species of birds have been seen in the park. A few snail kites appear each year and nest on the lake. Scrub jays commune around the entrance station. Crested caracaras are uncommon but are a local specialty.

History buffs will appreciate the Cow Camp, a living history demonstration of life in an 1876 cow hunter's camp.

Location, Mailing Address, and Phone

About 15 miles east of Lake Wales. From the junction of SR 60 and US 27 in Lake Wales, go east on SR 60 for 9.4 miles to Boy Scout Road. Turn left and go 3.6 miles to Camp Mack Road, then pro-

ceed to park entrance. From Florida's Turnpike, exit at #193 and go west on SR 60 about 38 miles to Boy Scout Road, just past Hesperides. Turn right and follow above directions to park.

14248 Camp Mack Road, Lake Wales, FL 33853; (941) 696-1112

Facilities and Activities

Hiking, primitive backpack camping, campground, boat ramp and docks, "Cow Camp" historical site. Open 7 AM to sunset daily. Admission fee charged; extra fee for camping. nice kayaking here
(airboats noisy)

Hiking

Thirteen miles of hiking trails provide ample opportunity for wildlife viewing and photography. Walk the dirt roads in early morning to see white-tailed deer. The dirt roads (which serve as fire breaks) criss-cross the park and add many more miles of hiking potential. The trails are dry in winter but may be wet in summer.

The Buster Island Trail is a 6.7-mile loop through a shady pine and oak hammock. Look for eastern bluebirds, fox squirrels, deer, and armadillos.

Gobbler Ridge is a small ridge on the western shore of Lake Kissimmee. It can be accessed by hiking from a sunny trail near the campground or near the Youth Camp. Since turkeys (or "gobblers") are uncommon in the park, you are more likely to see a sandhill crane. You may also see bald eagles and snail kites.

The Flatwoods Pond Nature Trail is a self-guided loop, about a half mile long, that takes a leisurely 20 minutes. Pick up the trail guide at the trailhead. The trail passes through oak hammock and pine flatwoods communities. A bit of history transpired here in the 1800s when the pine tree trunks were slashed for their sap, which was made into turpentine (hence the name slash pine).

Camping

The campground has 60 sites, of which half have water and electricity. Reservations are not accepted. Most sites are surrounded by vegetation in this pine-oak community. The busiest season is from mid-November to Easter. The campground fills on weekends and especially on holiday weekends. The nearby Youth Camp has two sites that hold 25 people each.

The campground could easily be rated one of the nicest in Florida were it not for an outside disturbance beyond the control of the park management. All day the boaters on nearby Lake Kissimmee roar across the water. As darkness falls, the roar continues, later and later into the night, until you wonder why the rangers bother to have quiet time at 10 pm. Before dawn, the roar begins again. Pity the owls which are trying to hunt.

The two primitive campsites (one on the Buster Island Trail and one on the trail around the park road) are equipped with picnic tables and fire rings. The Buster Island campsite is about three miles from the trailhead, and the other site is about 2.4 miles. Primitive sites can be reserved.

As of this printing, there will be no concession store in the park indefinitely. Campers should come prepared with food and supplies.

Cow Camp

A highlight of the park is the living history Cow Camp. On weekends and holidays (9:30 AM to 4:30 PM), visitors can enter the bygone era of scrub ranching in central Florida. Forget the present! Once you enter through the gates, the year is 1876. The cow hunter (he objects to being called a cowboy) in the thatch chickee will tell you all about what he does for a living and how he does it. He'll show you his 15-foot-long leather cracker whip, which is "never used on a cow, only to scare it." He'll crack the air so fast it sounds like a gunshot. He'll show you his herd of scrub horses and longhorned cattle that live off the land (one of the few remaining such herds).

Best Time of Year

Winter is better for hiking because the trails are drier; overwintering birds are present.

LAKE MANATEE STATE RECREATION AREA

About fifty to sixty thousand people visit this small (556 acres), relatively quiet recreation area annually. The main attraction, Lake Manatee, is a reservoir that supplies drinking water to Manatee and Sarasota counties. The 2,400-acre reservoir was formed by damming the Upper Manatee River. The surrounding land is valuable for watershed protection.

Location, Mailing Address, and Phone

About 15 miles northeast of Sarasota. From north or south, take I-75 to Exit 42, then go east on SR 64 for 8 miles. From Bradenton, go east on SR 64 for about 15 miles.
  20007 SR 64, Bradenton, FL 34202; (941) 741-3028

Facilities and Activities

Hiking, campground, boating, fishing, swimming, horse trail. Open 8 AM to sunset daily. Admission fee charged; fees for camping, horseback riding, and boat rentals extra.

Hiking

Several hiking trails are not on the park brochure. Thus, be sure to ask a ranger about them if you want to hike. One is about 1.5 miles long and begins at the rangers' office. Hikers may also walk on the 5-mile horse trail by the shop area. This is not in the main part of the park, so you must check in with a ranger first and get directions. The terrain is flat, and the habitat is mostly pine flatwoods and sand pine scrub. Bobcats, red and gray foxes, deer, armadillos, raccoons, and alligators are commonly seen.

A patch of sand pines encompasses about 100 acres around the picnic area and beach. There is not much of this scrub habitat left in Florida. Several 5-minute, unmarked, confusing hiking trails wander through the sand pines and Spanish moss-draped live oaks, one going from the boat ramp to the swimming area.

Camping

The 60-site, full-facility campground doesn't get the crowds that some of the state parks get, but it often fills in the winter (particularly January to March). Reservations are not taken—all sites are first-come, first-served. The insects are rarely bothersome in the winter and not too bad in the summer, when it's the hour after dark that they are active.

Boating

A boat ramp onto the lake allows access for fishing and nature study. Boats are limited to 20 horsepower maximum. Bald eagles have occasionally been seen on the lake. Anglers may catch largemouth bass, bluegills, and catfish by boat or from the fishing pier. The rangers have two rental john boats, so get there early if you want one.

Swimming

The swimming area on Lake Manatee is a small grassy beach near the Sand Pine Picnic Area. The swimming area has a bathhouse with showers.

Horse Trail

A 5-mile trail for people bringing their own horses is in a separate area of the park. You must check in with a ranger first (small fee). No camping with horses is available.

Best Time of Year

Summer for swimming; winter for camping and hiking; boating year-round.

LITTLE MANATEE RIVER STATE RECREATION AREA

An unrecognized beauty of a park, Little Manatee River SRA is 1,638 acres of unspoiled oak and pine scrub. The river is worth a trip if you are looking for a half to a whole day canoe trip. A wilderness trail invites hikers and backpackers. The small, quiet campground is a welcome change from the heavily visited parks. The area's significance is supported by the fact that The Nature Conservancy acquired more than 228 acres at the northeast corner of the park, including hammock, scrub, scrubby flatwoods, and floodplain swamps.

Watch for gopher tortoises and Sherman's fox squirrels as you hike. The park's bird checklist records 148 species, including scrub jay, bald eagle, Bachman's sparrow, sandhill crane, and swallow-tailed kite.

Location, Mailing Address, and Phone

South of Tampa. From Tampa, take I-75 south to Exit 46. Go east on FL 674 (Ruskin-Wimauma Road) to US 301. Turn right and go south about 5 miles to Lightfoot Road. Turn right and follow signs to park. From Bradenton/Sarasota, go north on I-75 to Exit 45. Go east on Moccasin Wallow Road to US 301. Turn left and go north about 5 miles to Lightfoot Road. Turn left and follow signs to park.

215 Lightfoot Road, Wimauma, FL 33598; (813) 671-5005

Facilities and Activities

Hiking, campground, primitive backpack camping, canoeing, horse trails, fishing. Admission fee charged, additional fee for camping. Open 8 AM to sunset daily.

Hiking

A 6.5-mile hiking trail meanders along the Little Manatee River, through turkey oaks, thick hammock areas, slash and longleaf pines, and scrub. This flat trail, with its numerous bridges and two boardwalks, is maintained by the Florida Trail Association. Hikers must register for this trail, because it goes through a wilderness part of the park north of the river, accessed from US 301. Get specific directions when you register.

There is a primitive campsite 2.6 miles from the trailhead for backpackers. No water is available at the campsite. Rangers recommend that overnight backpackers carry four quarts of water per person per day.

Oxbow Nature Trail—This is a 20-minute loop trail around an oxbow lake that leads through sand pine scrub, hammock, and river floodplain communities. The trail is not handicapped-accessible. Interpretive signs along the trail explain the flood plains, oxbows, fire-adaptability of sand pines, and other interesting ecological facts.

Canoeing

The Little Manatee River has been designated by the state as an "Outstanding Florida Water," which protects it legally from pollution. Only 1 mile of the 40-mile length is developed, making this one of the most scenic rivers in Florida. It is one of the 36 canoe trails on the state's recreational trail system.

About 5 miles of the river flow within the park. A canoe launch onto the river is available for people with their own canoes. There are no rentals in the park. Canoes can also be launched upstream at the bridge at US 301 (about a mile north of Lightfoot Road) for a 5-mile run ending in the park.

The river is steep-sided and tidal. Tannins from oaks and other plants stain the water dark brown. You'll float over the sandy bottom through sand pine scrub, willow swamp, and hardwood forest. Watch for river otters, alligators, and turtles.

The trip can be extended about 10.5 miles upstream. To access the upstream end: from US 301, go east 4 miles to Leonard Lee Road (graded dirt road), turn right and go south 2.5 miles to the bridge.

A private canoe outfitter on the Little Manatee River just outside the park on US 301 rents canoes: Little Manatee River Canoe Outpost (813) 634-2228. They have a variety of trips where they will pick you up downstream or drop you off farther upstream.

Camping

A quiet 30-site campground with electric and water hookups is located in a sand pine scrub area. The sites are very private and shady, surrounded by pines and other vegetation. There is also a Youth Camping area and amphitheater.

For backpack camping, see "Hiking" above. Three sites are reserved for horseback riders. Equestrian campsites are not common in the state park system, so these sites are quite popular.

Horse Trails

Two trails (Dude Lake and Mustang), totaling 6 miles, are reserved for horseback riders. For camping with horses, see "Camping" above.

Best Time of Year

Mosquitoes bad in June, July, and August. Winter months are best for weather (October to December is good weather and campground not crowded; after December, campground gets full).

LOWER WEKIVA RIVER STATE PRESERVE

A 4,636-acre plot of pristine central Florida upland and bottom-land is protected in this preserve. Plant communities include sandhill, blackwater stream, pine flatwood, sand pine scrub, swamp, floodplain hardwood, marsh, and riverine. Black bears, river otters, alligators, indigo snakes, and sandhill cranes may be found. The Wekiva River, which flows through LWRSP, has been designated an Outstanding Florida Water.

Nonconsumptive recreational activities are permitted. Biologists and rangers manage the habitat by prescribed burns and removal of exotic plants.

Location, Mailing Address, and Phone

Nine miles west of Sanford on SR 46 (almost 1 mile east of the Wekiva River, which is also the Lake County/Seminole County boundary). A small brown preserve sign set back from the road on the north side (where the parking lot is) is the only clue you'll see. 8300 West SR 46, Sanford, FL 32771; (407) 330-6728

Facilities and Activities

There are no visitor facilities (no restrooms, water, etc.) and usually no attendant. Hiking trails, horse/bicycling trails. No admission fee. Open 8 AM to sunset daily.

Sandhill Nature Trail

This gentle 1-mile trail travels through a sandhill community, which consists of turkey oaks, longleaf pines, wiregrass, gopher apple, and other fire-adapted plants. The wiregrass flowers and sets seed only during the one or two years following a fire. Fox squirrels, bears, and turkeys may be seen here. A printed interpretive guide is available at the sign-in board.

Gopher tortoise burrows are evident if you're looking for the apron of sand at the entrance of each one. You may even see a tortoise if the weather is not too chilly or wet. In cooler weather, tortoises may come out only for a short time if they can forage in a sunny spot. Otherwise, the burrows are warmer.

The southeastern pocket gopher is common here, although you'll most likely see only signs of its presence—small mounds of light-colored sand dug from its tunnels. The small rodent lives in tunnels and feeds underground on roots and rhizomes. Pocket gophers can chew through plant fibers without "eating dirt" by closing their lips behind their large front incisors. Their prolific excavations are a valuable natural tool to recycle nutrients from underground. The southeastern species ranges from Georgia and Alabama to central Florida.

Horse (and Bicycling) Trails

There are two horse trails: Black Bear loop (3.2 miles) and Flatwoods loop (2.2 miles plus part of Black Bear loop). The Black Bear trail goes through upland habitats such as sandhill and pine flatwood. Bears commonly pass through here in the fall, but they are shy and not likely to be seen. The Flatwoods trail may be closed occasionally during the wet season. No water is available for horses on either trail.

Bicycles are permitted on the horse trails only. Bicyclists should yield the right-of-way to horses.

Canoeing

There are no canoe launch accesses in the preserve. Canoeists can launch at Wekiwa Springs State Park and paddle downstream through the Lower Wekiva River Preserve.

Best Time of Year

No preference.

MYAKKA RIVER STATE PARK

One of the oldest and largest of Florida's state parks, Myakka has been long recognized for its unspoiled beauty. Established in 1936, the 28,875-acre park was so wild and inaccessible that it was not open to the public until 1942, when the Civilian Conservation Corps built a few roads and structures. In 1994, the Southwest Florida Water Management District purchased more than 8,000 acres along the park's southern boundary with the intent to lease it to the park. The parcel includes dry prairies, mesic flatwoods, prairie hammocks, and wetlands.

Here is one of the few areas in central Florida where people can backpack a reasonable distance under very scenic and usually dry-footing conditions. About 240,000 people visit Myakka each year.

The variety of habitats includes dry prairie, pine flatwood, marsh, hammock, scrubby flatwood, swamp, sandhill, lake, and river. Wildlife is abundant. This is a likely place to see alligators, gopher tortoises, sandhill cranes, wood storks, and bald eagles. Purists can hike through the 7,500-acre Wilderness Preserve or canoe the wild and scenic Myakka River.

The Bird Walk boardwalk on the edge of Upper Myakka Lake is a reliable place to find a variety of water birds (Susan D. Jewell)

Location, Mailing Address, and Phone

Just east of Sarasota. From north or south, take I-75 to exit 37. Then go 9 miles east on SR 72 to main park entrance.

For park information, write Myakka River State Park, 13207 SR 72, Sarasota, FL 34241-9585. For tram and boat tour information, write Myakka Wildlife Tours, Inc., 3715 Jaffa Drive, Sarasota, FL 34239.

For park information, call (941) 361-6511. For tram and boat tour information, call Myakka Wildlife Tours at (941) 365-0100. For concession store information, call Myakka River Outpost at (941) 923-1120.

Facilities and Activities

Hiking, primitive backpack camping, birding and wildlife observation, canoeing, bicycling, boating, fishing, horse trails, interpretive center, campground, boat and tram tours, concession; rentals of cabins, bicycles, boats, and canoes. No swimming allowed. Admission fee and camping fee charged. Open 8 AM to sunset.

Hiking

A 0.6-mile loop nature trail (with interpretive signs) along the Main Park Drive goes through oaks and cabbage palms; it is handicapped-accessible. For the more energetic hikers, there are 38 miles of hiking trails in the main part of the park. The trailhead is located about 2 miles past the Big Flat Campground. Service roads (unpaved) are also usable by hikers, and there are many more miles of these. The trails cover many different habitats, such as oak and palm hammocks, dry prairies, and pine flatwoods. In the wet season, approximately June to October, the trails may be wet, making hiking uncomfortable.

Wilderness Preserve

The 7,500-acre preserve, located south of SR 72, is a limited access area. Entrance into the preserve is by permit only (free), obtained at the entrance station. Only 30 visitors are permitted in the preserve each day. Visitors can hike along a service road to Lower Myakka Lake, about 1 mile, where roseate spoonbills, wood storks, otters, and deer may be seen. Another mile farther is the Deep Hole.

Camping
Campgrounds

There are two full-facility campgrounds for tents and trailers. The Old Prairie Campground has 24 sites and the Big Flats Campground has 37 sites. The sites are generally small and not very private. Reservations are recommended for winter camping (December to March).

Five rustic cabins with electricity are available for rent at the Old Prairie Campground.

Backpacking

Serious hikers may prefer to backpack to one or more of the five remote designated campsites. The nearest site is about 5 miles from the trailhead and the farthest one is about 12 miles. The service roads can be used as shortcuts. They are not shown on the trail guide, but you can ask a ranger to draw them in.

Backpack campers must register with a ranger before setting out on a hike. There are no facilities at any of the primitive sites except wells with water pumps. The water should be purified by boiling or chemical treatment, and in the dry season, the wells may dry up.

Birding and Wildlife Viewing

Birding is good all over the park, but any birding trip to the park should include a visit to the Bird Walk. This is a 400-foot-long boardwalk that juts out over Upper Myakka Lake. In the winter, waterfowl, wading birds, shorebirds, swallows, rails, terns, and many other birds can be seen here. Sandhill cranes, wood storks, and bald eagles are often seen in the winter. Swallow-tailed kites are spring migrants and roseate spoonbills are summer residents. The Bird Walk is located 1.5 miles past the Big Flat Campground on the Main Park Drive and is handicapped-accessible.

The park provides such a variety of habitats that birds of all types can be found. Park staff have documented 238 species. Ospreys, turkeys, bobwhites, limpkins, owls, woodpeckers, and many songbirds can be seen. Caracaras are beginning to nest again in the park. The trails can provide views of such mammals as deer, gray and red foxes, bobcats, raccoons, river otters, opossums, armadillos, feral hogs, and very rarely, a Florida panther. Many species of sunfish and catfish tempt the angler, as does the occasional snook or tarpon. Alligators are abundant in the lakes and rivers, but pose no threat to canoeists. The alligators are, however, the reason that swimming by humans is not permitted. Much wildlife can be seen on the park's 7-mile Main Park Drive.

Seven species of turtles, 7 of lizards, 23 of snakes, 4 of salamanders, 13 of toads and frogs, and 25 of mammals have been documented in the park. The park's bird checklist and annotated vertebrate list are available at the entrance station.

Canoeing and Boating

In 1985, the state designated the Myakka River a "Wild and Scenic River" to protect and enhance its resources. Twelve miles of the river flow through the park, including through the Upper and Lower Myakka Lakes and the Wilderness Preserve. Rivergoers can continue out of the park to Charlotte Harbor, about 20 more miles. Canoes and boats may be launched at the Upper Myakka Lake Boat Ramp or at the "Wild and Scenic River Access" on the Main Park Drive, where the road crosses the river. Camping is not allowed along the way within the park.

Canoes and boats may be rented at the concession. Because of the exotic aquatic weed hydrilla and the shallow conditions, motorboats may have a difficult time navigating through the lakes and the river. After heavy rains in summer (such as around August to September), the weeds may be flushed down the river from the lake, causing jams which canoeists must portage around. During the winter, low water may also necessitate occasional portaging. However, the canoeing is usually excellent. Look for alligators and softshell turtles, bald eagles, and river otters.

Bicycling

The 7 miles of paved road are available for bicycling. Cyclists may also use the many miles of unpaved service roads (wide tires recommended). Bicycles may be rented at the concession.

Horse Trails

Visitors who bring their own horses have 15 miles of trails to enjoy. The trails wind through flatwoods, with hammocks and marshes interspersed. This section is separate from the other hiking trails, and riders must register at the entrance station.

Interpretive Center

Originally this was a horse barn when the park was established, because there weren't roads sufficient for motor vehicles. It was converted in 1972 to house several large habitat displays, with examples of many of the species of wild animals found in the park, including a stuffed panther. An unusual display is the soil exhibit, prompted by the fact that a soil type found at the park, called Myakka Fine Sand, is the state soil. It is the most extensive soil found in Florida and is associated with flatwoods. As its name implies, it is sandy-textured. It is also low in organic matter and poorly drained.

Concession

The Myakka River Outpost concession store sells snacks, sandwiches and burgers, drinks, film, firewood, field guides, and other nature books. Canoes, boats, and bicycles can be rented here by the hour, half-day, or day.

Boat and Tram Tours

The Myakka Wildlife Tours, Inc., a private concession, runs the tours within the park. One-hour boat and tram rides can be taken. The boat seats 70 passengers, making it one of the world's largest airboats. It tours Upper Myakka Lake. The tram travels on unpaved roads in search of upland and marsh wildlife. Boat and tram tours are handicapped-accessible.

Best Time of Year

October to April for best weather; October to December for migrating birds; November to May for hiking (trails are drier); May and June for plants in flower. Christmas to Easter is the busy season (make reservations for camping).

OSCAR SCHERER STATE PARK

If you are in the Sarasota area, and you're looking for scrub jays, Oscar Scherer is the place to go. Scrub jays are well-established here and can be observed regularly at the Lake Osprey picnic area. After an absence of 20 years, the jays returned to nest when the park staff conducted prescribed burns to reduce heavy undergrowth. Fire is a natural part of this scrub habitat but was suppressed previously. Many other species, such as gopher tortoises and indigo snakes, benefit from the burns.

Two major habitat types comprise this 1,384-acre park: scrubby flatwoods (where the jays, gopher tortoises, gopher frogs, and indigo snakes prefer) and pine flatwoods. Bald eagles are common in winter, when they nest near the lake.

This park has come a long way from the small, unnatural

recreation area it used to be. It is becoming a local hot spot for naturalists as intensive efforts are being made to restore its natural resources. Besides added acreage, removal of exotic plants, and use of prescribed burns, recent park improvements include a 5-mile hiking trail (made with aid of high school volunteers).

Location, Mailing Address, and Phone

On US 41 between the towns of Osprey and Laurel. Park entrance is 1.5 miles north of the intersection of 41 with the Venice Connector (SR 681). Note: Exit 36 of I-75 is one-way only (you can't get off there—you can only enter). From I-75, you must exit at Exit 35 coming from the south or Exit 37 from the north and go to US 41.
   1843 S. Tamiami Trail, Osprey, FL 34229; (941) 483-5956

Facilities and Activities

Hiking, self-guided nature trail, canoeing, canoe rentals, swimming, campground. Admission fee charged. Open 8 AM to sunset daily.

Hiking

A wonderful addition to the park is the 5-mile marked hiking trail completed in 1993 that passes through the scrubby flatwoods and pine flatwoods. Ask at the entrance station for the park's animal checklist. It lists 142 bird, 26 reptile, 9 amphibian, and 17 mammal species. Look for gopher tortoises, bald eagles, indigo snakes, bobcats, deer, and skinks. The scrub jays may be seen regularly at the Lake Osprey picnic area. The self-guided Nature Trail is a leisurely 30-minute trail through a scrub community along South Creek. Some plants you'll see are Chapman's oak, slash pine, coontie, beauty berry, leather fern, and coral bean. Alligators and otters may be seen in the creek. The trail has interpretive signs; not handicapped-accessible.

Rangers and volunteers conduct bird, plant, and general nature walks, mostly in the winter. A local club, The Friends of Oscar Scherer, holds meetings at 7:30 PM on the first Wednesday of each month at the Recreation Hall at Lake Osprey. Program subjects include scrub jays, panthers, and other local natural history. The public is welcome.

Canoeing

Canoes can be rented from the ranger station and used on the tidal South Creek. Private canoes may be launched from the canoe launch at the South Creek Picnic Area. From there, you can paddle upstream in brackish water a mile to the dam, about an hour round-trip. The swamp along the creek is undeveloped and there's a good chance to see some wildlife. Anglers catch saltwater species here. Above the dam is freshwater, but it is too overgrown to make paddling worthwhile. Downstream from the picnic area, the creek empties into the Gulf of Mexico just outside the park. However, paddlers can't get past the bridge at US 41. Rangers conduct guided canoe trips year-round.

Camping

The 104-site full-facility campground is so popular from December to April that it's often full even on weekdays. Reservations are highly recommended for that period and can be made by phone up to 60 days in advance. There is no concession at the park, but supplies may be purchased in the town of Osprey.

Best Time of Year

The scrub jays are year-round residents.

ROCK SPRINGS RUN STATE RESERVE

Bordered by the Wekiva River and Rock Springs Run is the 13,910-acre tract of Rock Springs Run State Reserve. A variety of habitats is found here: sand pine scrubs, pine flatwoods, bayheads, hammocks, and hardwood swamps. The land was purchased in 1983 through the Conservation and Recreation Lands Program and is managed for multiple use. Originally, it was logged, farmed, and grazed extensively, but restoration is underway. Prior to European interference, the Indians used this area regularly, evidenced by the nine middens scattered along the Wekiva River and Rock Springs Run.

The uplands support black bears, indigo snakes, scrub jays, deer, turkeys, and much more. In fact, so many black bears are struck by cars in this area that the State Department of Transportation built an underpass for bears in 1994 along SR 46, near the entrance to the reserve. An immense chain-link fence guides the bears toward the underpass. Although bears are relatively common in this part of the state, only about 1,500 (or 12 percent of the historic population) currently exist in Florida. Adult male bears require 66 square miles of habitat. In modern Florida, this means that they have to cross roads to travel within their own territories. Acorns attract the bears to the reserve in the fall (although the shy omnivores are present year-round), so look for their tracks around the oaks.

The wetlands are home to many species, including sandhill cranes, wood storks, and river otters. The cranes may be seen in open, wet fields, such as near the entrance gate.

Location

16 miles west of Sanford and 3.5 miles east of Mt. Plymouth, off SR 46 on CR 433. From I-4, take Exit 51 to SR 46. Go west on SR 46 and note where the bridge crosses the Wekiva River, which is also the Seminole County - Lake County border. Go 1.75 miles from the bridge to CR 433, where the gap in the fence is.

Mailing Address and Phone

Route 1, Box 365D, Sorrento, FL 32776; (904) 884-2009 (Wekiva Springs State Park)

Facilities and Activities

Hiking, primitive backpack camping, wildlife observation, primitive youth camping, horse trails; hunting during season with Wildlife Management Area stamp. No visitor facilities. No

*admission fee. Open 8 AM to sunset daily. See also "Canoeing"
and "Camping" sections under "Wekiwa River State Park" entry.*

Hiking and Backpack Camping

There are at least 20 miles of hiking trails. Most of the trails are on
former logging roads called "trams." The Indian Mound Primitive Campsite is near the river and is a short hike from a parking
lot on the Back Tram. Call ahead to reserve the campsite.
Canoeists using Rock Springs Run may also use the campsite.
The trails wander through all the reserve's habitats. A short spur
trail leads to the river. Lizards and snakes abound in the sand
pine scrub, where scrub jays and gopher tortoises are also found.
The trails and campsite are closed to hikers for about nine weekends in October, November, and December for special hunts
(call ahead for hunting schedule).

Horseback Riding

About 9 miles of trails are available to equestrians. They coincide
with some of the hiking trails, and thus go through the same
habitats. The trails are closed for hunting on certain weekends in
the fall (call for schedule). Water is available at one location for
the horses but is not potable for humans.

Best Time of Year

Winter is more comfortable weather for hiking. Avoid hunting
season in fall.

SAVANNAS STATE RESERVE

One of the more unusual natural areas in central Florida is also
one of the least publicized. This undeveloped reserve (recently
acquired by the Florida Park Service) includes a long, narrow
coastal freshwater wetland and part of the Atlantic Coastal
Ridge. The 4,600 acres extend 10 miles from north to south with
an average width of 1 mile. The pristine marsh is nestled
between the Indian River Lagoon and the North Fork of the St.

Lucie River. It is a remnant of a coastal wetland system that formerly extended along much of the southeastern Florida shore.

Along the eastern boundary is a 287-acre section of coastal ridge. This elevated area (30 to 50 feet above sea level) with sandy, well-drained soil, supports a sand pine scrub community. The understory contains myrtle, Chapman's, and sand live oaks, with a ground cover of wiregrass, *Cladonia* lichens, and annuals. Florida scrub lizards, gopher tortoises, and a few scrub jays reside here. An endangered cactus, the fragrant wool-bearing cereus (or fragrant prickly apple) can be found by the headquarters area, a few hundred yards past the gate at the south end (ask the ranger to show it to you). This cactus has a bromeliad, the ball moss, growing on it—a most unusual sight. Bromeliads also grow on the open branches of the stunted oaks on the scrub ridge. The water table recharge that occurs along the ridge benefits by preventing saltwater intrusion into the aquifer.

Much of the reserve lies just west of the ridge, in depressions that are 12 to 17 feet above sea level and are perched on a less permeable substrate. The resulting marshes, lakes, and wet prairies together are known locally as savannas. They may hold water for a few months or the whole year. Sawgrass and other sedges, bladderwort, St. John's-wort, wax myrtle, pickerel-weed, and spadderdock are a few typical species comprising these wetlands. Farther west, the pine flatwoods sit on poorly drained soil. Slash pines comprise the overstory, while gallberry, saw palmetto, and wiregrass grow beneath.

Although there are no hiking trails available to the public yet, a tour on one of the unimproved roads can be arranged by a volunteer. Anyone with a strong interest in botany should try to get a guided tour of the Savannas. Little exotic plant growth can be found.

Canoeing is excellent along the savannas. Except during droughty winters when the water is low, there is ample surface area to explore. Wading birds, eagles, sandhill cranes, river otters, turtles, and an occasional alligator may be seen feeding and resting.

As you drive along Walton Road, notice the proximity of the wetland to the Atlantic Coastal Ridge (where the railroad tracks run). The ridge drops off immediately into the wetland, which is an unusual ecological situation.

The reserve has been greatly aided by a group of local volunteers, called the Citizen Support Organization, that has accomplished maintenance, litter clean-up, plant identification, and a multitude of other indispensable tasks. The CSO volunteers also provide most of the guided tours for the reserve.

(See also **SAVANNAS OUTDOOR RECREATION AREA** in St. Lucie County)

Location

Between Fort Pierce and Stuart. Take US 1 north from Stuart or south from Fort Pierce to Walton Road (about 2.5 miles north of the Martin County–St. Lucie County line). Turn east and go 1.5 miles to Sandhill Crane Park for one access. For another access, continue another 4 miles to the end at CR 707 (Indian River Drive). Turn right and go 0.4 miles to Riverview Drive. Turn right and go over railroad tracks, then the first left (Gumbo Limbo Drive), and go 500-600 yards to the grassy area and canoe launch. The headquarters area is located straight past the railroad tracks, but the gate is only open for guided tours.

Mailing Address, and Phone

Savannas State Reserve, c/o Fort Pierce Inlet, 905 Shorewinds Drive, Fort Pierce, FL 34949; (407) 468-3985 (information on guided walks, canoe trips, and so on).

Savannas State Reserve (407) 340-7530.

Facilities and Activities

Canoeing, hiking, guided trips. No admission fee. Open 8 AM to sunset daily.

Guided walks and canoe trips are announced in the local newspaper. In addition, visitors can arrange for a guided tour by a staff member or volunteer by calling ahead.

Hiking

Aside from the guided walks, visitors can hike from the Sandhill Crane Park access any time during daylight hours. Drive down the turnoff road to the park for a quarter mile and look for the blue blazes. This trail is about 5.5 miles one way and goes through pine flatwoods.

Canoeing

The public may launch a canoe from the access off Gumbo Limbo Road, head south, and explore the southern end of the preserve. The water around the headquarters area is not part of the original savannas. This section was dredged by a former owner to connect it with the savannas. The fill was used for the building sites and for an airstrip, the remnants of which can be seen just north of the dock by the headquarters.

As you canoe around the savannas, you'll see sawgrass, which is a light grayish green, grasslike sedge. This is an indication that the water is relatively pristine. The more the cattails begin to outcompete the sawgrass, the more disturbed the system is becoming. This is because sawgrass thrives in a low-nutrient system, which is what the savannas is supposed to be. Few nutrients naturally wash down from the sandy, scrubby coastal ridge. If sewage is added anywhere along the savannas watershed, it will throw the low-nutrient system out of balance.

Look for anhingas and great blue herons nesting from January through March. Bald eagles also nest here. Watch for wood storks and sandhill cranes all year and migrating songbirds from fall through the spring.

Best Time of Year

Winter for hiking (trails may be wet in summer). Year-round for canoeing. Mosquitoes not a problem in summer.

Pets

Allowed on a leash.

SEBASTIAN INLET STATE RECREATION AREA

The man-made Sebastian Inlet splits the park in two—part is on the north side of the bridge and part is on the south side. Furthermore, part is east of SR A1A on the ocean and part is west, along the Indian River. Although most people appear to visit this park to fish, there are other treasures to seek. The 3-mile-long beach is prime nesting grounds for loggerhead, green, and occasionally leatherback sea turtles. A variety of water birds may be found along the beach, just offshore, and in the Indian River. Mangroves, lagoons, and coastal hammocks are some of the other habitats within the 587-acre park.

Location, Mailing Address, and Phone

On SR A1A in Melbourne Beach, about 40 miles south of Merritt Island. From the north (US 192 in Indiatlantic), take SR A1A south for 17.4 miles. From the south (CR 510 in Wabasso), take SR A1A north for 7 miles.

9700 South A1A, Melbourne Beach, FL 32951. (407) 984-4852. For sea turtle walks, phone Sea Turtle Preservation Society (407) 676-1701.

Facilities and Activities

Swimming beach, snorkeling, campground, picnicking, fishing, boating, snack bar, Museum/Visitor Center. Admission fee (extra fee for camping and museum). Open daily.

On the ocean side is the beach, relatively pristine with occasional bath houses along the dune line. During fall and spring migrations, look for shorebirds and waterfowl. Ospreys and brown pelicans are present all year. Look for osprey nests atop isolated trees or poles. Manatees and young sea turtles are common in the Indian River, although not always easy to spot. In June and July, rangers take visitors to the beach at night to watch the turtles lay their eggs (reservations necessary).

The campground, which has 51 small sites, is located at the park's south end on the Intracoastal Waterway. The habitat is open and privacy is scarce. Water and electricity are available. Many campers have fishing boats with them.

At the north end is the restaurant concession, which serves breakfast and lunch. Also available for sale are bait and tackle, snacks, camping supplies, and gifts. Boat rentals are available.

The McLarty Treasure Museum and Visitor Center, located on A1A south of the South Entrance, houses exhibits of a shipwreck in 1715. A slide show on the local natural and cultural history is presented.

Best Time of Year

Winter for birding, summer for beach activities.

THREE LAKES WILDLIFE MANAGEMENT AREA AND PRAIRIE LAKES UNIT

History is being made at Three Lakes with the reintroduction of whooping cranes, formerly extinct in Florida. The cranes are hatched and raised elsewhere, then brought here as juveniles for a "soft release." The young cranes have been shielded from seeing humans. The pens at Three Lakes gives them a way to adapt to their new surroundings slowly. When they are old enough to fend for themselves, the pen doors are opened, and the cranes are free to leave when they choose. The pens are off-limits to visitors, but the released cranes may be seen in the area.

Many old woods roads can be driven or hiked in a search for red-cockaded woodpeckers, sandhill and whooping cranes, burrowing owls, swallow-tailed kites, bald eagles, and crested caracaras. A section of the Florida National Scenic Trail runs through the 45,303-acre management area. The Prairie Lakes Unit (8,900 acres) of Three Lakes WMA has restricted hunting, and the possibilities for seeing wildlife may be slightly better during the hunting season than in other parts of Three Lakes. The highest concentrations of bald eagles in the continental United States are in this area. There is a good chance of seeing one at any time of the year.

The many habitats encompassing the management area include dry prairie, live oak hammocks, pine flatwoods, cypress domes and strands, and hardwood swamps.

Location

Prairie Lakes Unit—One entrance is from CR 523 (Canoe Creek Road), 9.5 miles northwest of US 441 in Kenansville. Florida Trail—One terminus is from SR 60, 5 miles east of the Kissimmee River (or 14.8 miles west of US 441).

Mailing Address, and Phone

Florida Game and Fresh Water Fish Commission, 1239 SW 10th Street, Ocala, FL 34474; (904) 732-1225

Facilities and Activities

Hiking, primitive camping, bicycling, wildlife observation. No admission fee for hikers. Open 8 AM to sunset daily.

Motorized vehicles are permitted on any numbered road. Contact the FGFWFC in Ocala for a map of the area, because the numerous dirt roads may become confusing (there is a separate hunting-regulations-and-map brochure for Three Lakes and for the Prairie Lakes Unit). Roads may be flooded in the wet season. Several campsites are available by permit but may be closed during hunting season.

One driving route for wildlife observation could start at the Prairie Lakes entrance given above, at Road 16. Go west on 16, turn right at Road 19, follow to Road 5, turn right at the T-intersection (left goes to Lake Jackson Boat Ramp) to Canoe Creek Road, and end back on CR 523, 2 miles north of where you started. This 5-mile drive covers most of the habitat types. The whooping cranes were released near the south end of Lake Jackson.

Three primitive campgrounds are located in the Prairie Lakes Unit. A permit is required (free), and may be obtained by contacting the FGFWFC. Camping is year-round, except during designated hunting seasons.

Best Time of Year

Winter for drier roads and concentrations of wildlife (most wildlife species are present all year). Avoid during hunting season (call FGFWFC for dates).

Pets

Allowed on leash.

TOSOHATCHEE STATE RESERVE

Relegated to that introverted category of 'state reserve' (as opposed to the extroverted state parks that boldly advertise their presence), Tosohatchee is a shy place, not given to broadcasting its natural merits. Its 34,000 acres of nearly pristine Florida flank the banks of a 19-mile stretch of the St. Johns River and is one of Florida's most outstanding natural areas. Its marshes, swamps, hammocks, and pine flatwoods have been preserved by the state since 1977 to protect the water supply to the river. The cypress trees along Jim Creek comprise one of the few remaining virgin cypress swamps in the country. Also within the reserve is a rare virgin stand of slash pine, with some trees over 250 years old. Mounds left by the indigenous people are a sign that they occupied the area for many years.

During the winter months, the marshes nurture thousands of migrating ducks. In the uplands, turkeys, bobcats, gray foxes, fox squirrels, indigo snakes, and gopher tortoises may be found. Bald eagles, white-tailed deer, river otters, and black bears may also be seen. Limited hunting is permitted.

In 1994, the state began restoration of 6,000-8,000 acres of marsh that had been drained prior to state ownership. Over 14 miles of canals were backfilled and adjacent levees were leveled.

The reserve is managed by a multi-agency agreement by the Division of Recreation and Parks, the Florida Game and Fresh Water Fish Commission, the St. Johns River Water Management District, the Division of Forestry, and the Division of Archives and History.

Location, Mailing Address, and Phone

From Orlando, go east on SR 50 to Christmas. Turn right on Taylor Creek Road and head south for 3 miles to the State Reserve entrance (look for sandhill cranes in the pastures along this road). Or from Titusville, go west on SR 50, past the St. Johns River. At Christmas, turn left onto Taylor Creek Road and go south for 3 miles to the entrance.

3365 Taylor Creek Road, Christmas, FL 32709; (407) 568-5893.

Facilities and Activities

Hiking, primitive backpack camping, wildlife observation, horse trails, fishing, bicycling, limited hunting by special permit. Admission fee charged. Fee charged for camping. Open 8 AM to sunset daily.

Hiking

Hikers may enjoy over 60 miles of trails and dirt roads. Loops from a few miles to 17 miles are available. Trails marked with white blazes are for hikers only. Orange-blazed trails are multi-use. The trails pass through floodplain marshes and swamps, hydric hammocks near the river, and pine flatwoods. Look for the endangered hand fern (which grows as an epiphyte high on the trunks of cabbage palms), as well as pitcherplants, butterworts, terrestrial and epiphytic orchids, bromeliads, and strap ferns. Gopher frogs live in the gopher tortoise burrows found here.

During hunting season, hikers should wear fluorescent orange clothing.

Camping

Camping is arranged by telephone reservation only, made at least two weeks in advance (call the office between 8 AM and 12 noon). The Tiger Branch Campsite is a 3-mile hike from the Youth Camp parking lot, and the Whet Rock Campsite is a 7.5-mile hike. Portable toilets are the only facilities. The Taylor Creek Campsite is a 17-mile hike from the trailhead. For horse-packers, there is a campsite by the Horseback Trailhead.

Bicycling

Bicycles are permitted on all park roads, orange-blazed trails, service roads, fire lines, and horseback trails. The trail sections that are part of the National Scenic Trail System are open to multiple use and allow bicycles as well as horses and hikers.

Horse Trails

Riders can enjoy about 23 miles of horse trails (marked with fluorescent orange diamonds), most of which are in the northern part of the reserve.

Best Time of Year

November to May for dry trails. Note: Hunting seasons from late September to mid-April; hunts not continuous. Call the Reserve or Florida Game and Fresh Water Fish Commission for dates.

VAN FLEET STATE TRAIL

The old Seaboard Coast Line Railroad has been transformed by a rails-to-trails project into a linear state park. The trail extends for 29 miles from Mabel to Polk City. Although it skirts the corner of Withlacoochee State Forest, it penetrates the Green Swamp's interior. Most of this trail goes through relatively remote areas, including uplands and wetlands, with few paved road crossings. Bicyclists looking for a scenic route on a good trail should give this priority.

Location, Mailing Address, and Phone

North terminus located on SR 50 in Mabel, about 30 miles west of Orlando; south terminus in Polk City, about 10 miles north of Lakeland and Winter Haven. North end (from Orlando): Take SR 50 west for 0.8 miles past CR 469. North end (from I-75 and west): Take SR 50 east for 5.3 miles. South end: Go to Polk City via I-4 and SR 559, then left onto SR 33. Go short distance to 655, then look for old railroad track and trail signs.

Florida Department of Natural Resources, Division of Recreation and Parks, Region 3 Administration, 12549 State Park Drive, Clermont, FL 34711; (904) 394-2280. Ask for trail map.

Facilities and Activities

Walking/jogging, bicycling, horseback riding. No admission fee. Open sunrise to sunset daily. Handicapped-accessible. No motorized vehicles.

The trail is excellent for pedestrians and bicyclists (scenic, can't get lost). Horseback riders are permitted on the parallel bridle path.

Best Time of Year

No preference.

Pets

Allowed on leash.

WEKIWA SPRINGS STATE PARK

Wekiwa Springs State Park is blessed with two springs, one in the park and one just outside it, which contribute to the clear water and the diversity of wildlife and habitats. The 8,136-acre park is located on the eastern part of the Mount Dora Ridge and contains 12 plant communities from the wetland swamps to the upland sandhills. Observant hikers and horseback riders will spot sinkholes off the trail. These were formed when the lime-stone substrate dissolved from rainwater and collapsed.

The name "Wekiwa" comes from the Creek Indian word meaning "spring of water" and it is the source of the Wekiva River. The name "Wekiva," also Creek, means "flowing water," as in a river. Once you understand the difference, it will be easy to keep the names straight.

If you camp here, you can easily fill a weekend with hiking and canoeing.

Location, Mailing Address, and Phone

Northeast of Apopka. From I-4, take Exit 49 to SR 434 going west. Go about 0.75 mile to Wekiva Springs Road, turn right, and follow signs to the park (about 4 miles). From Apopka, go east on SR 436 to N. Wekiwa Springs Road (about 2 miles). Turn left and head north about 2.5 miles; follow signs to park.

Wekiwa Springs State Park, 1800 Wekiwa Circle, Apopka, FL 32712; (407) 884-2009

Facilities and Activities

Hiking, primitive backpack camping, wildlife observation, canoeing, canoe rentals, swimming, campground, horse trails, bicycling, picnic shelters, fishing, concession. Admission fee charged. Open 8 AM to sunset daily.

Hiking Trails

There are about 13 miles of hiking trails, developed and main-tained with the help of the Florida Trail Association. The trails cover many habitats, including lowlands by the springs and uplands along the sandy ridge. The lowland swamps support cypress, black tupelo, red maple, Carolina ash, and sweetgum trees. Alligators, limpkins, otters, raccoons, herons and egrets, and turtles can be commonly seen. On the highest, driest ground grow longleaf pines and turkey oaks. On the slope in between grow trees and shrubs like pond pine, slash pine, saw palmetto, and gallberry. Black bears, gopher tortoises, fox

Visitors can see the water bubbling up from the springs that gives the park its name (Susan D. Jewell)

squirrels, and pocket gophers can be found. There is also a sandhill pine community, which is quite xeric. The dryness is a result of the porous nature of the sandy soil, which does not retain water. Some animals which have adapted to this condition are Florida worm lizard, sand skink, gopher frog, and crowned snake. Look for this habitat type around the Sand Lake Picnic area.

A 5.3-mile loop trail "Volksmarch Trail" (with orange blazes) begins at the spring. Participants in the Volksmarch program can register at the ranger station for hiking credit. Along the section of trail that runs west from Wekiwa Spring once lived a champion sand pine tree. Typically, sand pines are short scrubby trees, often only 15-20 feet tall. Although this particular tree was 103 feet tall, it was a champion in crown width—43 feet wide—not in height. The tree blew down in the "Storm of the Century," known outside of Florida as the "Blizzard of '93" (March 1993), which packed hurricane-force gusts. That is the price the tree paid for having such a wind-catching crown. It can still be seen along the trail in its prostrate obscurity.

A wheelchair-accessible boardwalk connects the parking lot to the spring. From the edge of the spring, you can see the water seething up from a fissure in the limestone.

Horse Trails

The 8.5-mile day-use horse trail has two loops. There is a fenced parking lot for horse trailers. The only horseback camping site is at Camp Big Fork along the trail (see "Camping" below).

Bicycling

Bicyclists may use any of the paved roads, service roads, and horse trails. Bicycles are not permitted on the hiking trails.

Canoeing

Canoeists may bring their own canoes or they can rent one at the concession.

Wekiva River/Rock Springs Run Canoe Trail—This is part of the Florida Recreational Trails System. The canoe trail actually begins at Kelly Park, where Rock Springs is (outside Wekiwa Springs State Park), but the closest access is at King's Landing. You can access the canoe trail farther downstream at the canoe landing by the concession in the state park. The trail will then start for you at the Wekiwa Spring and flow into the tannin-stained Wekiva River. You can drift downstream along the Rock

Springs Run and Lower Wekiva River state reserves for about 17 miles to the St. Johns River. Ask for a canoe map at the park entrance station. Some of the access points have nearby private canoe rental operations (such as King's Landing and Katie's Landing). The access points, starting near the river's source, are:

- King's Landing (from Apopka, go north 6 miles on CR 435 to Kelly Park Road, then east for 0.3 miles to Baptist Camp Road, and north 0.7 miles to Kings Landing); 9 miles downstream to next access
- Wekiwa Springs State Park; 1 mile downstream
- Wekiwa Marina (go east from park entrance on Wekiva Springs Road 1.1 miles to Miami Springs Road, then north 1 mile to marina); 10 miles downstream
- Wekiva Falls (take SR 46 for 5.2 miles west of I-4, cross the river, go south on Wekiva River Road 1.4 miles to Wekiva Falls Resort); 1 mile downstream
- Katie's Landing (take SR 46 for 4.6 miles west of I-4 to Wekiva Park Road, turn north and go 1 mile to landing; 1 mile downstream
- Wekiva Haven (pass Katie's Landing above, going north about a half mile more); 5 miles downstream
- High Banks Road Landing (from US 17/92 in DeBary, take High Banks Road west for 2.9 miles to landing); just upstream from here, the St. Johns River flows into the Wekiva and the Wekiva ceases to exist on its own.

The current is usually 2-3 mph, but may be greater after heavy rains. Look for otters and black bears. The Big Buck Canoe Campsite is located on Rock Springs Run and is available for canoeists (see "Camping" below).

Swimming

The swimming area is at the natural spring, where the water is always 68°-72°and clear. Summer is the most popular time for this, and lifeguards are on duty then.

Camping

A 60-site family campground, located in the upland sandhill habitat, offers full facilities. More adventurous campers may backpack to two primitive sites (Camp Cozy and Live Oak Camp) on the main hiking trail, which is a 9-mile loop. These can be reserved in advance for groups. Otherwise, they are on a first-come, first-served basis.

Canoeists may camp at the Big Buck Canoe Campsite, about 75 yards from Rock Springs Run. This primitive site has no facilities. Reservations can be made up to 60 days in advance. Canoe-campers must check in at the ranger station before embarking.

Horseback riders may camp (by reservation only) at the trail-side Camp Big Fork site. This is the only place where water is available for your horse. Horseback campers must check in at the ranger station before starting on the trail.

There is a fee for camping at any of the camping areas in the park.

Concession

The concession sells snacks, sandwiches, tee-shirts, basic camping supplies, and souvenirs. Canoes can be rented here.

Best Time of Year

Winter for hiking, canoeing; summer for swimming, canoeing

WITHLACOOCHEE STATE FOREST

Here is a forest treasure in the backyards of Tampa (45 miles away) and Orlando (67 miles away). Withlacoochee State Forest consists of 123,240 acres of varied habitats managed for multiple uses such as timber harvest, recreation, and hunting. Within the vast acreage is room for everyone. Areas are set aside for the different activities, making each a quality experience. During November and December, some areas may be set aside for

EXPLORING WILD CENTRAL FLORIDA

hunting. The forest is named for the Withlacoochee River that flows through it. "Withlacoochee" means "crooked river" in the native Indian language.

The forest is divided into five disjunct main tracts: Citrus (42,613 acres), Croom (21,359 acres), Headquarters (1,230 acres), Jumper Creek (10,068 acres), and Richloam (49,200 acres). Jumper Creek is the newest addition, and it protects bottomland communities along the Withlacoochee River (which borders it) and Jumper Creek (which bisects it). This tract does not yet have a system of hiking trails. The primary management activity for the Citrus tract is game management, particularly for white-tailed deer. Croom is managed primarily for recreation (hiking, camping, canoeing, motorcycle trails) and is easily accessible from exits 61 and 62 off I-75. Some timber harvest occurs on Croom. The motorcycle trails are in a separate area that is a reclaimed phosphate mine. Citrus, Croom, and Richloam offer hiking and camping. Citrus offers horse trails and equestrian campground. Access to the Withlacoochee River for canoes is at Croom and Richloam.

Wildlife is plentiful and diverse. Such mammals as white-tailed deer, fox squirrels, bobcats, wild hogs, and armadillos are common. Reptiles such as gopher tortoises, indigo snakes, diamondback rattlesnakes, and ground skinks thrive here. Bald eagles and red-cockaded woodpeckers are also found here.

Due to the size and locations of the tracts and the variety of activities, it is strongly recommended that prospective visitors obtain the "mapguide" or the hiking trail maps from the Headquarters Office weekdays from 8 AM to 5 PM. There are too many trails and accesses to describe below. It is easy to spend many days hiking, camping, and canoeing here.

Location

Forestry Headquarters Office—On SR 41, 8 miles northeast of Brooksville (just north of CR 476).

Citrus Tract: Holder Mine Recreation Area—(From the north) From SR 44, go south on CR 581 for 2.6 miles to

"Trail 10." Turn right and go 1.9 miles to Holder Mine Campground; trailhead nearby. Mutual Mine Recreation Area—from SR 44, go south on CR 581 5.3 miles to "Mutual Mine" sign on right. Turn right and go 0.1 mile to campground; trailhead nearby. (From the south) From CR 480, go north 4.2 miles to "Mutual Mine" sign on left. Tillis Hills Recreation Area—From CR 581 go west on CR 480 about 3.5 miles to Trail 13. Turn right and head north almost 2 miles, bearing right at the road to the recreation area.

Croom Tract: To trails—(From the north) From corner of CR 481/581 and CR 476, go east on 476 for 7.2 miles to Edgewater Ave. on right (may not be marked). Turn right and go south. Road turns to unpaved Croom-Nobleton Road. Continue to junction of Croom Road. Turn right onto Croom; trailhead seen almost immediately. (From the south) From SR 50, go north on Croom-Rital Road (which is less than a mile east of Exit 61 from I-75), go under I-75 overpass, and turn left onto Croom Road where it meets Croom-Nobleton Road; trailhead seen almost immediately. To Silver Lake Recreation Area—(From the north) Take CR 476 to Edgewater Ave./Croom-Nobleton Road; stay on Croom-Nobleton Road just past I–75 overpass; look for Silver Lake Recreation Area sign on left. (From the south) Follow directions above to trails, taking Croom-Rital Road north from SR 50, but turn right at 3.5 miles (before I-75 overpass).

Richloam Tract: From I-75, take Exit 61 and go east on SR 50, past US 301 to state forest boundaries. Watch for orange blazes on both sides of the road, marking the trails.

Mailing Address, and Phone

Withlacoochee Forestry Center, 15019 Broad Street, Brooksville, FL 34601; (904) 796-5650

Facilities and Activities

Hiking, wildlife observation, primitive backpacking, camp-grounds, canoeing, bicycling, fishing, horse trails. No admission fee. Fee charged for campgrounds.

Hiking

Besides the marked hiking trails, you may hike on any of the dirt roads. This cuts down to manageable size some of those long hiking trail loops, since you can take a short-cut road back. The hiking and nature trails are for foot travel only. The Florida Trail Association works cooperatively with the Forest Service in establishing and maintaining the hiking trails.

The Withlacoochee State Trail passes through the Croom Tract in several places. One of them is accessible from Croom-Rital Road, about 2.5 miles north of SR 50 (where there is an east-west jog in the road). Hike north from there, and you can go about 6 miles through the state forest.

Headquarters Tract

McKethan Lake Nature Trail—This 2-mile loop trail encircles McKethan Lake, which provides forage for wading birds, turtles, and other wetland animals. The trail has numbered posts corresponding to a printed interpretive guide available at the start of the trail and at Forestry Headquarters. Four species of native pines grow along the trail: loblolly, longleaf, sand, and slash. Bottomland hardwoods also grow here. To find the trail, head north on US 41 from the Forestry Headquarters Office 0.2 mile to the McKethan Lake Recreation Area on the left. Open 8 AM to sunset.

Colonel Robins Nature Trail—This 110-acre area has a self-guided interpretive trail totaling 2.5 miles (trail guide available from Forestry Headquarters). Three loops of up to a mile each make for easy hiking. Pines, oaks, dogwoods, palmettos, hickories, and magnolias are typical trees on this trail. To find this trail, go south on US 41 from the Forestry Headquarters Office 2 miles to the Colonel Robins Recreation Area on the left. Open 8 AM to sunset.

Citrus Tract

The Citrus tract contains the upland habitats of sandhill scrub, sand and longleaf pine, and oak. Limestone outcroppings occasionally break the rolling terrain. The trails are dry all year. The Citrus Hiking Trail is 46 miles in total length, with many shorter loops. The shortest, Loop A by Holder Mine Recreation Area, is 8.5 miles.

Croom Tract

The Croom Hiking Trail totals 31 miles, consisting of several loops. The terrain is rolling hills with prairies and hardwood hammocks. Chapman's and turkey oaks and longleaf pines are trees commonly seen here in relatively natural (unlogged) states. The tract is managed primarily for recreation, but most activities not compatible with each other are in separate areas. The shortest hiking trail loop is 4 miles and starts at the Silver Lake Recreation Area.

Richloam Tract

The rich soil gives this tract its name. It's not as sandy as the other tracts and the understory is more lush. It grows trees well and makes timber harvesting of pines the primary management goal. Cypress and water oaks grow naturally here. The Richloam Hiking Trail is 31.5 miles, with a loop of 24.9 miles and a 6.6-mile side trail that connects to the Green Swamp to the southeast. Look for indigo snakes, fox squirrels, deer, bobcats, turkeys, migrating birds, and red-cockaded woodpeckers.

Driving and Bicycling

There are hundreds of miles of unpaved fire roads in Citrus, Croom, and Richloam tracts. Visitors may drive and bicycle on any *named* or *numbered* road to look for wildlife. For example, you can take Trail 10 west from Holder Mine Recreation Area in the Citrus tract, then go south on Trail 13 all the way to CR 480. It's possible to see a lot of wildlife by driving slowly on these roads. Keep in mind that some roads may not be graded and some may be impassable during rainy periods.

Canoeing

There are two Withlacoochee Rivers in Florida—the northern one on the Georgia line and the southern one, west of Ocala and Orlando. This description is for the Withlacoochee River (South) trail, which flows through 13 miles of Withlacoochee State Forest. The river originates in the Green Swamp region of Lake County, then flows for 70 miles north through Polk, Pasco, Hernando, Sumter, Citrus, Marion, and Levy counties before emptying into the Gulf of Mexico. The state recreational trail covers an 83-mile section of the river. The access points are spaced at 2- to 15-mile intervals, described here from south to north (some mileages are approximate):

- Coulter Hammock Recreation Area (from US 301, take SR 575 east to Coit Road, go south on Coulter Hammock Road 2.5 miles to river); this is in the Richloam Tract of WSF; 2 miles downstream to next access

- bridge at CR 575 (1.2 miles northeast of Lacoochee); 2 miles downstream

- bridge at US 301 (1.2 miles north of Trilacoochee); 2 miles downstream

- bridge at US 98 (0.7 miles north of Trilby); 6 miles downstream

- bridge at SR 50 (12 miles east of Brooksville); 7 miles downstream

- Silver Lake Recreation Area (see "Camping" below); this is in Croom Tract of WSF; 9 miles downstream

- bridge at SR 476 (0.25 miles east of Nobleton; 9 miles downstream

- bridge at SR 48 (west of Bushnell); fee for private boat ramp; 11 miles downstream

- Carlson Landing (from SR 44 west of Wildwood, take 470 south for 2 miles, turn right, go less than a half mile to Gator Lodge, turn right and go to ramp; 4 miles downstream

- bridge at SR 44 (just west of Rutland); 6 miles downstream

- ramp at SR 581 (from US 41 in Inverness, take CR 581 northwest for 7 miles to ramp; 10 miles downstream

- bridge at SR 200 (take SR 200 north from Hernando for 6.5 miles to wayside park; 15 miles downstream
- bridge at US 41 (wayside park at Dunellon)

There are other accesses besides those listed. A primitive canoe camping site is located about a mile north of the Silver Lake Recreation Area, on the west bank of the river. This large open area can fit many small tents.

The Canoe Outpost, a private outfit in Nobleton, will supply you with rental canoes, transportation, and everything you need for canoe camping. You can write to them at P.O. Box 188, Nobleton, FL 34661 or phone (904) 796-4343.

Camping

Many camping opportunities exist throughout the state forest. There are fee campgrounds and no-fee primitive sites. The campgrounds offer very basic facilities: small open-air bathrooms, hot showers (no showers at Mutual Mine), some sites with electric hookups; no place to buy supplies. The individual sites are fairly open and not private.The primitive sites are along the hiking trails in Citrus, Croom, and Richloam tracts; some are very short hikes from roads. They are cleared areas with no facilities. You will likely have to share a primitive site on a weekend.

Citrus Tract has campgrounds at Holder Mine, Mutual Mine, and Tillis Hills Recreation Areas. Croom has three campgrounds at Silver Lake Recreation Area (Silver Lakes camping area has only electric hookup sites; Cypress Glen camping area has only nonelectric sites and is cheaper). Richloam does not have any campgrounds.

Horse Trails and Camping

The Citrus Tract has a 14-mile "One Day" trail and a 24-mile "Two Day" trail. Both trails start at the Tillis Hill Recreation Area, where riders can camp with their mounts. There is a stable and corral there. Riders on the "Two Day" trail can camp at the primitive site at Perryman Place Plantation, about halfway around the trail. A guide to the Citrus Horse Trails is available from the Forestry Headquarters Office.

Best Time of Year

Hiking in winter for cooler temperatures; canoeing in late summer and fall for higher water; camping in winter (cooler weather).

Pets

Not allowed.

WITHLACOOCHEE STATE TRAIL

A "rails-to-trails" achievement, this 47-mile trail straddles the former Atlantic Coast Line railroad bed. The trail is a linear state park, and therefore, many of the state park rules apply. For example, all plants and animals are protected and firearms are prohibited. The trail passes mixed forest, sandhill, and wetland communities, as well as some human development. Part of the trail bisects Withlacoochee State Forest (see "Hiking" for **WITH-LACOOCHEE STATE FOREST**) and Croom Wildlife Management Area.

Most of the trail is not paved. The paved section starts 1,000 feet north of the US 41 overpass in Inverness and goes south about 5 miles to Fort Cooper Road.

Currently, 40 miles of the trail are open for use. The remaining 7-mile stretch (south of SR 50/US 98), is currently closed but is expected to be the southern terminus some day.

Location

In Citrus, Hernando, and Pasco counties. The northern terminus is at Haitian Avenue north of Citrus Springs. The southern terminus is currently at Croom-Rital Road, near SR 50/US 98 in Ridge Manor. Parking for vehicles is provided at the Haitian Avenue and Ridge Manor trailheads, as well as Croom-Rital Road, near the Istachatta Post Office, Fort Cooper Road (near south end of Fort Cooper State Park), Wallace Brooks Park, and North Apopka Avenue.

Mailing Address, and Phone

Florida Department of Natural Resources, Division of Recreation and Parks, Region 3 Administration, 12549 State Park Drive, Clermont, FL 34711; (904) 394-2280. Ask for trail map.

Facilities and Activities

Walking/jogging, bicycling, horseback riding. No admission fee. Open sunrise to sunset daily. Handicapped accessible. No motorized vehicles.

As with the Van Fleet State Trail, this trail is excellent for pedestrians and bicyclists (scenic, can't get lost). Horseback riders are permitted on the parallel bridle path.

Road crossing along the Withlacoochee State Trail (Susan D. Jewell)

Best Time of Year

No preference. During hunting season at Croom Wildlife Management Area (October to March), use caution and wear fluorescent orange clothing.

Pets

Allowed on 6-foot hand-held leash.

VII
NATURAL AREAS—
COUNTY, CITY,
PRIVATE, AND LOCAL
PARKS

ALDERMAN'S FORD PARK

It may be hard for us to realize now, but it once was a major effort to travel through Florida's land of rivers. When James Alderman modified the steep banks on this part of the Alafia River in 1848 so that people could ford it, it became a popular convergence place and remained so for 100 years. Hillsborough County purchased 360 acres in 1950 and later expanded this county park to 1,141 acres. The steep sides of the floodplain are sprinkled with numerous small springs and creeks. Above the floodplain, the terrain is flat, and the longleaf pines and scrub oaks are xeric– and fire-adapted. The relatively pristine river is a draw for canoeists.

Location, Mailing Address, and Phone

About 15 miles east of Tampa. From Tampa, take SR 60 east to CR 39, turn right and head south to the park, which is on Thompson Road. Or, from I-75 (north or south), take Exit 51 and go east on SR 60, then south on CR 39 to Thompson Road.

9625 Canoe Launch Loop, Lithia, FL 33547; (813) 757-3801.

Facilities and Activities

Nature trails, canoeing and canoe launch, primitive camping, biking/jogging trail, boardwalk, visitor center, picnicking. No admission fee. Handicapped-accessible. Open 8 AM to sunset daily.

A hiking trail less than a mile long leads to two primitive campsites in the uplands. Backpackers must reserve in advance by calling to obtain a permit. There are several other shorter nature trails for 10- to 20-minute walks. The 1,875-foot-long boardwalk makes a loop within the convergence zone of two forks of the river. The scenic biking/jogging trail is over 2 miles long. The Visitor Center, which is open limited hours, has interpretive displays. This is a popular weekend picnic park, particularly in summer.

A highlight of this park is canoeing on the Alafia River, one of the 36 state canoe trails. The launch is on the west side of SR 39 by the park office (no rentals available). You can paddle downstream about 10 miles to Lithia Springs Park (see separate entry below; optional exit). The next 3 miles to Bell Shoals Road bridge (no parking at bridge) has some of the nicest scenery on the river. Camping places occur along the river where there are no property signs posted. The twisting river flows swiftly (up to 4 mph) after heavy rains and forms rapids over limestone, which become small shoals at low water. Some portaging may be necessary, especially in summer. The river is shaded by cypress, cedar, and oak trees. The water is higher in winter. Some experience is recommended for this trip.

Best Time of Year

Canoeing is popular in summer (but may be crowded on weekends).

Pets

Allowed on a 6-foot hand-held leash.

ARCHBOLD BIOLOGICAL STATION

One person can make a difference. In this case, one man's simple dream snowballed into a major nonprofit, ecological research center and an outstanding natural-area preserve. It began with Richard Archbold, a renowned scientific explorer born in 1907 to a Standard Oil Company fortune. His dream was to establish an independent biological research station where staff and visiting scientists were provided housing, laboratory space, equipment, a library, and a preserve, so they could devote themselves to serious field studies of native plants and animals. In 1941, he established such a station on 1,050 acres in Lake Placid. Archbold died in 1976, but his estate remained to provide core funding for the station's continued operation. Extensive research on the scrub flora and fauna convinced the staff of the imminent need to preserve the remaining xeric uplands of the Lake Wales Ridge. The station's scientists played a significant role in working with the U.S. Fish and Wildlife Service to develop plans for the Lake Wales Ridge National Wildlife Refuge and with The Nature Conservancy and the state of Florida to develop plans for a state network of scrub preserves.

The 5,000-acre preserve that the station now owns and manages is at the southern end of the Lake Wales Ridge. Elevations on this narrow north-south ridge range from 100 to 300 feet. The sandy substrate is a silent reminder that the ocean's waves once pounded an emerging Florida here. Modern habitats on the ridge are sand hills, sand pine and oak scrubs, scrubby flatwoods, rosemary scrubs, seasonal ponds, bayheads, and many sinkhole lakes. The flatlands bordering the ridge are dominated by pine flatwoods, wet and dry prairies, live oak/cabbage palm hammocks, and smaller areas of swamps dominated by cypresses, bays, and red maples. Watch for sandhill cranes, crested caracaras, and burrowing owls in the area.

The station has been designated as a National Natural Landmark by the U.S. Department of the Interior. Because of the multitude of scrub-related ecological research projects the staff is involved in, and because the staff is restoring the habitat through prescribed burns, much of this extraordinary tract is

Scrub palmetto along the nature trail at Archbold Biological Station (Susan D. Jewell)

off-limits to the general public. The station's long-term population study of Florida scrub jays, begun in 1968, is one of the most comprehensive ever undertaken on any bird species.

There are still a few precious tracts of scrub on the Lake Wales Ridge that need to be protected. Archbold is actively involved in buying adjacent tracts of natural land to be protected as part of the station. Since the station is able to operate almost entirely on endowment income and fees from visiting scientists, its current policy is to seek and use donations strictly to acquire scrub. Visitors to the Nature Trail are encouraged to make a donation and are assured that all donations are matched equally by Archbold, with every dollar used for acquisition of scrub.

Location, Mailing Address, and Phone

8 miles south of the town of Lake Placid. From the junction of SR 70 and US 27, go west on 70 for 1 mile to Old SR 8. Turn left and go 1.8 miles south to entrance on right. Nature trail starts near office. P.O. Box 2057, Lake Placid, FL 33862; (941) 465-2571

Facilities and Activities

Nature trail, butterfly garden, scrub video and exhibits in auditorium. Trail open to public Monday to Friday 8 AM to 5 PM, except holidays. No admission fee (donation encouraged to help acquire habitat). Visitors should register in the office (south end of Main Building), obtain a trail brochure, and sign a release.

The Self-Guiding Nature Trail is only about 2,000 feet long, but it is so distinctive that you may want to stroll slowly, studying the plants and animals carefully. Many endangered or threatened plants can be found along the trail. Botanists will appreciate the plant labels, since many of the plants are endemic to Florida's scrub. Four species of scrub oaks grow along this trail, as well as silk bay, scrub hickory, scrub palmetto, and scrub blazing star. Prescribed burns were conducted along part of the trail in 1990 and 1992. Before that, deer were rare along the trail. Since the burn, deer are common. All but one Florida species of woodpeckers (red-headed, red-bellied, yellow-bellied sapsucker, downy, hairy, northern flicker, and pileated; RCWs extirpated from the station about 50 years ago) may be seen along the trail. Also present are gopher tortoises, most of which carry harmless notches on their carapaces as part of a study of individual movements and life spans. The butterfly garden is near the beginning of the Nature Trail.

Best Time of Year

Winter for cooler hiking temperatures (the sparsely shaded trail can get quite hot in summer) and wintering birds.

Pets

Not allowed on Station premises.

BABSON PARK AUDUBON CENTER

On the Lake Wales Ridge, a 50-acre sanctuary has been established by the appropriately named Ridge Audubon Society. Since 1964, the small nature center has offered educational programs on the scrub habitat. A short nature trail gives visitors a good introduction to scrub habitat and plants.

Location

About 13 miles north of Avon Park and a half mile north of Babson Park. From SR 60, go south on US 27 for 4 miles. Turn left onto CR 640, go east for 0.9 mile, bear right onto US 27-A, then 2.2 miles east/south to N. Crooked Lake Drive.

Mailing Address, and Phone

Ridge Audubon Society, P.O. Box 148, Babson Park, FL 33827; Nature Center (941) 638-1355

Facilities and Activities

Nature center, nature trail, educational programs. No admission fee. Caloosa Trail open sunrise to sunset daily. Nature Center open limited hours, usually only weekdays in winter.

Nature Center

The modest nature center houses dioramas, rocks, fossils, stuffed birds and animals, and other educational displays of the local natural history. The shop sells field guides, Florida guidebooks, feeders, and other nature items. A volunteer may be available to open the nature center if requested in advance.

Caloosa Trail

This sandy, mile-long trail goes through typical Lake Wales Ridge scrub to Crooked Lake. Thirty posts mark locations that correspond to the printed trail guide (available from the nature center) that describes the habitats. Many plant names are labeled with metal tags. Plants include scrub oak, scrub hickory, scrub beargrass, gopher apple, and staggerbush. Look for scrub jays, gopher tortoises, and bluetail mole skinks. Allow at least an hour for the trail.

Best Time of Year

Winter for cooler hiking weather. Nature center may be closed May-September.

Pets

Not allowed.

BARLEY BARBER SWAMP

The 450-acre swamp is part of the 12,000-acre Martin Site of Florida Power & Light Company (FPL). Fortunately, it has been recognized as a special area for a long time and has been protected from draining and logging. On one side, however, is the 6,600-acre cooling pond for the power plant. On the other side are sugarcane fields.

FPL built the original boardwalk in 1980 and replaced it in 1993 with a wider one. The mile-long boardwalk traverses a cypress-red maple swamp. Many cabbage palms get their feet wet here, but the live oaks keep theirs dry on the higher ground of the Indian midden, where bones and artifacts dating back to 1000 A.D. have been recovered. One of the oldest cypresses in the state can be seen from the boardwalk. It is estimated to be 900-1000 years old. Most of the cypresses are 200-400 years old. The branches are carpeted with ferns and bromeliads.

Since you must be accompanied by a guide who has a schedule to keep, the opportunity for spending time observing wildlife is limited. If your goal is to bird, botanize, or photograph, let the FPL staff know that when you make the reservation, so that they can plan it into the schedule. Also when you call, you may want to request that the guide bring the bird, mammal, herp, insect, and plant lists for you.

Location, Mailing Address, and Phone

7 miles northwest of Indiantown. From West Palm Beach, take SR 710 (Bee Line Highway) west for 7 miles past the St. Lucie Canal at

Cypress trees along Barley Barber Swamp boardwalk (Susan D. Jewell)

Indiantown; from Okeechobee, take SR 710 east for 20 miles. Turn at the flashing yellow light into the FPL property. (Note: FPL will send complete directions when you call to reserve.)

Florida Power & Light Company, P.O. Box 1080, Indiantown, FL 34956-1080; (800) 257-9267

Facilities and Activities

Boardwalk trail, wildlife observation. BY RESERVATION ONLY. No admission fee. Open daily except Thursdays. Tours at 8:30 AM and 12:30 PM. Call at least a week in advance.

The tour starts near the entrance to the FPL property. After a 5-mile drive to the far side of the cooling pond, the guide stops at a chickee built by Seminole Indians. The boardwalk starts here and goes through shady cypresses covered with Spanish moss, giant wild pines, needle-leaved wild pines, and other bromeliads. Animals find food in the pond apple, live oak, strangler fig, and wax myrtle trees. Alligators, otters, raccoons, and many butterflies can be seen. The boardwalk is handicapped-accessible. Allow 2-2 1/2 hours for the tour.

Best Time of Year

Winter for birding; summer is nice, also (trail shady, few mosquitoes, few people).

Pets

Not allowed.

BIG BEND MANATEE VIEWING CENTER

Manatees can be quite predictable. When the ambient temperature drops in winter, they'll head for the nearest warm water. Around Tampa, that would be the power plant of the Tampa Electric Company at Apollo Beach. Manatees are attracted to the warm water flowing out of the plant, which is always warmer than the surrounding Gulf of Mexico waters when the plant is operating. As many as 120 manatees have been seen in the canal at one time during very cold weather. The artificial concentration of this endangered species prompted Tampa Electric to provide the public with an opportunity for viewing and learning about these giant marine mammals.

A canal leads from the power plant to the Gulf, and since boat traffic is prohibited in the canal, the state designated it a manatee sanctuary in 1986. The canal is surrounded by a 20-acre mangrove forest that nourishes the surrounding estuary and the seagrasses that feed the manatees. A boardwalk parallels the canal, offering a close view for the 84,000 people that gather each year to watch the manatees lolling in the warm water. Also look for wading birds, fiddler crabs, oysters, and many types of fish in the water.

The Visitor Center houses educational exhibits. The gift shop, operated by the Lowry Park Zoo, benefits the zoo's manatee recovery facility.

Location

About 10 miles south of Tampa. From north or south, take I-75 to Exit 47 (Apollo Beach exit). Go west on CR 672 (Big Bend Road), go 1.0 mile past US 41 to "Manatee Viewing Center" on right.

Mailing Address, and Phone

Corporate Relations, Tampa Electric Company, P.O. Box 111, Tampa, FL 33601; (813) 228-4111. Viewing Center information recording: (813) 228-4289

Facilities and Activities

Visitor Center, manatee observation boardwalk, educational programs, picnic area, gift shop. No admission fee. Open 10 AM to 5 PM from December to March including holidays, closed Mondays. Closed April to November.

Several opportunities are available to place yourself in a good position to view the manatees. Tampa Electric has built a boardwalk along the canal and observation decks near the warm water outflow. While you're waiting for a manatee to grace the water, you can view the educational video in the Visitor Center and study the other manatee-related exhibits (including a manatee skeleton). A large selection of manatee-related gifts is available at the shop.

Best Time of Year

Colder weather during the four-month season, especially when Tampa Bay water temperature is less than 68°F (check local newspaper).

Pets

Not allowed on boardwalk or in building.

BLOWING ROCKS PRESERVE

The strange name of this Nature Conservancy preserve comes from an ancient natural feature. A 4,000-foot-long outcrop of Anastasia limestone, the largest on the Atlantic coast, parallels the shore. When the tide is particularly high, such as in winter and during storms, tons of water are forced through small fissures and solution holes eroded in the Pleistocene-aged rock. This forces a geyserlike plume of water as much as 50 feet skyward.

While the blowing rocks are an important geological feature, they are not the only reason The Nature Conservancy was interested in protecting the area. The mile-long beach is one of the densest nesting areas for sea turtles on the Atlantic coast. About 500 loggerhead, green, and leatherback turtles haul themselves over the rocks from April to September to bury their eggs in the clean, warm sand.

The 113-acre preserve includes a mile of shoreline along the Intracoastal Waterway. This mangrove and seagrass habitat is important for the manatees that occasionally visit. Other habitats in the preserve are tropical hammock, coastal strand, and beach dune. About 150,000 people a year visit the preserve.

The Nature Conservancy is building a $500,000 multipurpose

education center on the Intracoastal Waterway, scheduled for completion by late 1995.

Location, Mailing Address, and Phone

On Jupiter Island in Martin County, close to Jonathan Dickinson State Park. From I-95 take Exit 59 or from Florida's Turnpike take Exit 116 to SR 706 (Indiantown Road) and go east to US 1. Turn north onto US 1, cross the Jupiter Inlet bridge, then turn right onto CR 707. Go 1.9 miles north after crossing Jupiter Sound bridge to preserve parking on right.

P.O. Box 3795, Tequesta, FL 33469-2766; Office (407) 575-2297, Preserve (407) 747-3113

Facilities and Activities

Swimming beach, snorkeling, dune nature trail, guided walks. No admission fee but donation requested. Open 6 AM to 5 PM (last car in at 4:30) daily. No food or smoking allowed.

The uncrowded, pristine beach is attractive for swimming and snorkeling (at one's own risk) and sunbathing. There are some shallow submerged limestone rocks very near shore that shelter such fish as ocean surgeons, sergeant majors, foureye butterflyfish, mangrove snappers, and margates.

Along the ridge of the dune is a walking trail (about a quarter-mile long) lined with sea grape trees. There are more than 100 species of trees in the tropical hammock. Since 1985, The Nature Conservancy has made an intensive effort to eradicate exotic plants, such as Australian-pine, and to plant native species. The organization maintains its own on-site native plant nursery to provide the stock. Some native plants you can expect to see are wild coffee, gumbo limbo, wild-lime, coco-plum, and sea oats.

Guided programs are offered by volunteers. Every Sunday all year an introductory walk is given along the dune trail. Call for other programs.

Best Time of Year

Summer for beach activities; fall, winter, and spring for migrant shorebirds.

Pets

Not allowed.

BOYD HILL NATURE PARK

The City of St. Petersburg operates the 245 acres of Boyd Hill
Nature Park as part of an 800-acre complex with Lake Maggiore.
About 15,000 people visit the park each year. It has been a lush
oasis of cool, shady serenity in the midst of the city since 1947—
an oasis for wildlife as well as humans. Park managers have an
intensive exotic plant control project and usually two prescribed
burns a year. Allow a half day to walk the trails and visit the
Nature Center.

Location, Mailing Address, and Phone

*In St. Petersburg. From I-275, exit at 54th Ave. and go east to 9th
Street. Turn left, proceed to Country Club Way, and turn left to
Nature Center.*

*1101 Country Club Way South, St. Petersburg, FL 33705; (813)
893-7326*

Facilities and Activities

*Hiking, birding, nature center, bicycling, picnic areas. Admission
fee charged. Open 9 AM to 5 PM except Thanksgiving and
Christmas (open till 8 PM Tuesdays and Thursdays in summer);
closed about two days each year for prescribed burns.*

Hiking

Six interpretive trails are based on different ecosystems: scrub,
flatwoods, oak-hammock, swamp woodlands, willow marsh,
and lake. There are 3.5 miles of handicapped-accessible trails
and two quarter-mile boardwalks.

Bald eagles nest at the park, so watch for them, particularly in
winter. Boyd Hill has the largest population of gopher tortoises

in southern Pinellas County. It also hosts Sherman's fox squirrels, indigo snakes, Florida golden asters (one of only three populations left), and orchids. There are over 46 species of herps in the park.

Fall warbler migration is excellent, especially in October. Birds heading south along the west coast reach the end of the Pinellas peninsula and pile up at this heavily treed sanctuary, resting and feeding before continuing across the water.

Wildflowers in the uplands are excellent in October, when many are flowering. Alligators nest here in the summer and may be heard bellowing in the spring. Many snakes, lizards, and other wildlife are active in the summer, making the summer a good time to visit as well.

Nature Center

The nature center packs in many exhibits of local interest. Live snakes, aquaria with baby alligators, turtles, and fish, a live beehive, and so on make it a great stop for children. Nearby, the park maintains a raptor rehabilitation center, and visitors can see permanently injured birds in flight cages.

Nature programs are also presented (call for schedule). Programs include daily tram tours, bird walks, night hikes, and wildflower walks. A limited-use group campground is available to Scouts, youth groups, churches, etc. by scheduling in advance.

Bicycling

Including the roads, there are 3.5 miles of bicycling trails. Bicyclists must stay on the paths.

Best Time of Year

October for migrating warblers and wildflowers. Summer is hot but not buggy.

Pets

Not allowed.

CHARLOTTE HARBOR ENVIRONMENTAL CENTER

The Charlotte Harbor Environmental Center is built on state land leased by four entities: the Charlotte County School Board, City of Punta Gorda, Charlotte County commissioners, and the Audubon Society. About 3,000 acres comprise the area, part of a State Buffer Preserve that protects Charlotte Harbor from the developed areas. The center was started in 1988, and visitation has been steadily increasing.

A variety of habitats can be explored on the many hiking trails. The Environmental Center is visited by many school groups and contains exhibits of local flora and fauna and native inhabitants. It houses a mini-auditorium for viewing a video and a small nature gift shop.

Location, Mailing Address, and Phone
South of Punta Gorda. From I-75 in Punta Gorda, go east on US 17 to US 41, then south to Burnt Store Road (SR 765). Proceed 1.3 miles to Center on right.

10941 Burnt Store Road, Punta Gorda, FL 33955. (941) 575-4800

Facilities and Activities
Nature trails, visitor center, educational programs, picnic shelters. No admission fee (donation suggested). Open Monday to Friday from 8 AM to 3 PM, Saturday 8 AM to 12 noon.

About 11 miles of trails are available for hikers. The trails pass through many habitats, including pine flatwoods, cabbage palm–live oak hammocks, mangroves, estuaries, salt marshes, and salt flats. Bobcats, alligators, and gopher tortoises are frequently seen. Bald eagles nest in the area, occasionally necessitating the closure of a hiking trail in the vicinity to prevent disturbance to the birds. Alligators are seen on the pond in the winter. A trail map is available from the visitor center for folks hiking on their own.

From November through April, staff and volunteers conduct

211

guided walks on the nature trails, lectures, and family programs.

Best Time of Year

Winter for better hiking weather.

Pets

Allowed on leash.

DISNEY WILDERNESS PRESERVE

The concept of environmental mitigation acquires grand meaning when applied to the Disney world. To compensate for land and wildlife that the Disney Corporation will be allowed to destroy over a 20-year period, the company must undertake an ambitious preservation and restoration project. The center of the conservation effort is the 8,500-acre former Walker Ranch, once owned by Disney but deeded to The Nature Conservancy in 1992. Disney will also pay for all the restoration costs for 20 years and will provide TNC with an endowment fund to operate the preserve after 20 years. The area is environmentally sensitive because it serves as the headwaters for the Kissimmee River.

The ranch, now known as the Disney Wilderness Preserve, will require removal of dikes and exotic species, filling of drainage ditches, and prescribed burns. Cattle grazing had previously diminished the grasses and permitted shrubs to dominate. Some wetland restoration has already begun. The preserve contains mostly scrub and some wetlands, so the variety of wildlife that can be found is exciting. Good populations of gopher tortoises, scrub jays (26 families), sandhill cranes, wood storks, and one of the largest concentrations of bald eagles in the southeastern United States (12 active nests) flourish here. Wiregrass and the rare cutthroat grass are returning amply. TNC hopes to acquire neighboring lands so it can reintroduce the red-cockaded woodpecker, which requires about 20,000 acres to support colonies.

The preserve was opened to the public in early 1995. Only a part of the preserve will be publicly accessible so that nesting eagles and other species will not be disturbed. The trail described below winds through several plant communities, including cypress swamps, scrubby flatwoods, dry prairies, and Lake Russell shoreline. TNC is gradually adding more hiking trails, so call periodically to see if there are any new ones.

Location

About 15 miles south of Kissimmee. From Kissimmee, go south on US 17/92 to Pleasant Hill Road (CR 531). Turn left and go south for 10.4 miles (bearing left at Preserve sign at 8.6 miles). From Lake Wales, take US 27-Alt. north to Haines City. At the end, go right on US 17/92 for 0.6 miles. Turn right at CR 580 (Cypress Parkway) in Haines City, then go 11.6 miles to Pleasant Hill Road. Turn right, go 2.2 miles (bearing left at Preserve sign).

Mailing Address and Phone

6075 Scrub Jay Trail, Kissimmee, FL 34759; (407) 935-0002
   The Nature Conservancy, 2699 Lee Road, Suite 500, Winter Park, FL 32789; (407) 628-5887.
   Field trip information line (407) 262-3827.

Facilities and Activities

Hiking, wildlife observation, picnicking. Open sunrise to sunset daily. No admission fee. Note: The narrow dirt road leading to the trailhead cannot accommodate vehicles larger than passenger vans. *The nearest water, restroom, and telephone are 3 miles away. Trail capacity limited to small groups.*

   The self-guided interpretive trail follows grassy roads in a loop 4.7 miles long. A guide brochure and map is available at the trailhead. The trail passes through a variety of habitats, including cypress swamps, longleaf pine flatwoods, oak hammocks, and dry prairies.

   At some of the stops along the way, the brochure explains how

Dry prairie, one of many habitat types at Disney Wilderness Preserve (Susan D. Jewell)

the restoration is being accomplished there. For example, wiregrass is returning to the pine understory because of prescribed burning. Formerly, the ranchers favored cattle forage by burning at the wrong season to favor native grasses. When TNC burned the understory at the right time of year, seeds of native plants that had lain dormant for 50 to 100 years began to sprout!

From the picnic area along the cypress shore of Lake Russell, watch for bald eagles. There is virtually no development around the lake, only part of which belongs to TNC. Lake restoration includes reversing the ranchers' practice of allowing cattle direct access to the lake, where they could urinate and defecate directly into it.

Best Time of Year

Winter for cooler weather and drier footing (trail may be wet in summer). Note: Trail may be closed in summer due to wet conditions or prescribed burns. Call (407) 262-3827 to verify trail status.

Pets

Not allowed.

EDWARD MEDARD PARK & RESERVOIR

Water-related activities are the attraction to this 1,284-acre Hillsborough County regional park. The 700-acre Pleasant Grove Reservoir was once a phosphate mine, now reclaimed. Swimming, boating, fishing, and camping are the most popular activities of the 500,000 visitors a year.

Location, Mailing Address, and Phone

About 10 miles east of Tampa city limit, on S. Turkey Creek Road. From Tampa (or I-75 north or south, Exit 51), take SR 60 east past Valrico, turn right onto S. Turkey Creek Road and go south 1 mile. 5726 Panther Loop, Plant City, FL 33566; (813) 757-3802.

Facilities and Activities

Swimming, canoeing, campground, interpretive programs, picnicking, observation tower, horse trails, fishing. No admission fee. Fee charged for camping. Handicapped-accessible. Open 6 AM to variable hours (near sunset) daily. Closed Christmas.

This recreation area is mostly popular for swimming and fishing. A boat ramp allows canoe access to the reservoir. The horse trail runs along the boundary at the north and east sides of the park. It's about 5 miles long (then return the same way). Guided walks and programs are available on request by advance arrangement. A 730-foot-long fishing pier boardwalk leads to an observation tower on a small island. The 42-site campground has two shower houses (no reservations accepted).

Best Time of Year

No preference.

Pets

Allowed on a 6-foot hand-held leash.

E.G. SIMMONS PARK

Simmons Park, established in 1964 as a Hillsborough County regional park, is a maze of mangrove-lined waterways, interrupted by narrow uplands. The core area of 469 acres, primarily developed for camping, fishing, and picnicking, happens to be an excellent location for viewing waterbirds (such as shorebirds, gulls and terns, and waders). A 1,100-acre area was recently purchased to protect the mangrove estuary habitat.

Location, Mailing Address, and Phone

In Ruskin, 18 miles south of Tampa. From Tampa, take US 41 south to 19th Ave. NW (3.3 miles south of Apollo Beach Road) and turn right. Or, from I-75 north or south, take Exit 46 and go east 3 miles on SR 674 to US 41, then north 1.5 miles to 19th Ave. NW. 2401 19th Ave. NW, Ruskin, FL 33570; (813) 671-7655.

Facilities and Activities

Birding, swimming, boat ramp, campground, picnicking, fishing. No admission fee. Fee charged for camping. Open 8 AM to sunset daily. Closed Christmas.

The open shallow waters of Tampa Bay provide excellent feeding opportunities for wading birds, ospreys, bald eagles, shorebirds, and ducks, which can be easily observed. Look for an osprey nest platform near the entrance to the park. Wood storks and roseate spoonbills may be seen wading or roosting. Manatees are also occasionally seen in the park. Some small groups of trees attract passerines, but the habitat is too open to attract many.

The campground offers 88 sites with or without electricity and has hot showers. This is the only park with camping on Tampa Bay in Hillsborough County. No reservations are taken. Expect the pesky no-see-ums at dusk.

Fishing is the primary activity, and sea trout, redfish, cobia, snook, Gulf flounder, tripletail, and grouper may be caught. Anglers can fish from boats, from along the mangrove-lined banks, or from open shores. The park offers a sizable boat ramp.

Best Time of Year

Fall, winter, and spring for birding and camping.

Pets

Allowed on a 6-foot hand-held leash.

EUREKA SPRINGS PARK

This small, specialized county park is on a site where four small springs emerge, connected by short runs. Until Albert Greenburg donated the land to Hillsborough County in 1967, he nurtured rare and unusual plants into a splendid botanical garden and dabbled in raising tropical fish in the warm waters. The county has maintained the botanical garden on the 31-acre site.

When a canal was built just west of the park, the water pressure of the aquifer feeding the springs decreased. Now the springs flow only during the rainy season.

Location, Mailing Address, and Phone

About a mile east of Tampa city limit. From Tampa, take I-4 east to Exit 6C and bear right onto Eureka Springs Rd, go north 1.5 miles. Or, from I-75, get off at the I-4 exit and go west to Exit 6C, then bear right onto Eureka Springs Road, go north 1.5 miles.

6400 Eureka Springs Road, Tampa, FL 33610; (813) 744-5536.

Facilities and Activities

Botanical garden, nature trail, boardwalk, picnicking. No admission fee. Open 8 AM to 6 PM daily. Closed Christmas.

The botanical garden, greenhouse, and trellised walks are geared for the botanically minded. Some plants are labeled. The boardwalk is 0.3 miles and is handicapped-accessible. The nature trail is about the same length but is not handicapped-accessible.

Best Time of Year

Very colorful in spring (February to late April) with blooming azaleas and other spring flowers. Something is blooming at all times of the year.

Pets

Allowed on a 6-foot hand-held leash.

FORT DESOTO PARK

Few county parks can match the attractions offered by Fort DeSoto. A waterfront campground, 7 miles of white beaches, a 400-year history, and nationally famous bird migrations are only a few of the reasons to visit. The nearly 900 acres is spread over five islands: Mullet (the largest), Bonne Fortune, St. Christopher, Madelaine, and St. Jean Keys. All are connected by man-made causeways. Open to the public since 1962, the park now attracts 2.3 million visitors a year, primarily picnickers, boaters, campers, beach-goers, and birders.

The fort was constructed in 1898 and named for the Spanish explorer Hernando DeSoto, who landed in the vicinity in 1539. The fort, which was closed in 1929, still stands and can be toured for free. In DeSoto's time, Timucuan Indians were living in the area. They left a shell mound, called the Tierra Verde Burial Mound, found on the east side of SR 697, just north of the park entrance. No artifacts have been found, just shells from the mollusks they probably subsisted on. The Timucuans disappeared shortly after the Spanish arrived.

Location, Mailing Address, and Phone

In southern Pinellas County. From north or south, take I-275 to Exit 5 (SR 682, 54th Ave. South). Go west on 682 to SR 679 (also called Pinellas Bayway). Turn left and go south about 5 miles to the park.

3500 Pinellas Bayway South, Tierra Verde, FL 33715

Park Headquarters: (813) 866-2484

Campground: (813) 866-2662

Snack bar and gift shop concession on Mullet Key: (813) 864-1376

Facilities and Activities

Self-guided nature trails, birding, shelling and swimming beach, campground, boating, fishing, snack bar and gift shop. No admission fee. (Toll fee on Pinellas Bayway does not go to the park.) Open sunrise to sunset daily. Fee charged for camping.

Hiking

The Arrowhead Trail is a self-guided nature trail at the north end of Mullet Key. It is 1.5 miles long, with another spur that can add 0.4 mile, or a short cut that can make the trail only a half-mile long. At the trailhead, pick up a copy of the "Arrowhead Nature Trail Guide," which goes into more detail about the natural history of the area than most trail guides. You will wander through slash pine, oak hammock, mangrove, and beach habitats. Look for gopher tortoises, ospreys, and eastern diamondback rattlesnakes (the latter are very secretive and shy of humans).

Birding

Birders from all over the country have discovered the exciting birding opportunities awaiting them at Fort DeSoto, which boasts 283 species on its bird list. Magnificent frigatebirds, mottled ducks, American oystercatchers, black skimmers, gray kingbirds, and black-whiskered vireos are common. Roseate spoonbills, bald eagles, marbled godwits, Caspian terns, mangrove cuckoos, scissor-tailed flycatchers, and painted buntings are occasionally seen.

The primary attraction is the spring migration. Because so many birds follow the coastline as they head north, they pass by Fort DeSoto and often stop to feed and rest. Careful observers have spotted 100 species in a single day. The migration runs from early March to mid-May, with a peak around the second week of April. During cold fronts, with their strong north winds, birds may drop from the sky and rest in the trees until the winds turn more favorable. The warblers are the stars of the spring migration—36 species have been seen. Most shorebirds and wading birds are year-round residents.

The park has an excellent publication called "Checklist of the Birds of Fort DeSoto Park and Pinellas Bayway." It includes a useful chart of where in the park you're mostly likely to see each species. Some good places to check are the causeway leading to the park (on the Bayway), the nature trail, the fishing pier in winter, and the beaches.

Camping

The 235-site campground has all the modern conveniences, including water and electrical hookups and laundry facilities. The sites are packed closely together but are well-vegetated and reasonably private. There are even some waterfront sites. A camp store sells basic camping supplies.

This is a popular campground with both locals and tourists. Reservations must be made in person, which favors Pinellas County residents. January through April is the busiest season, when the campground usually fills on weekends. The best chance of getting a campsite without a reservation is to arrive in the morning on a weekday (and not a holiday). The Campground Office is open 8 AM to 9 PM.

Boating

An 800-foot-wide boat ramp before the park entrance allows easy access to Tampa Bay and Gulf of Mexico waters. Boaters must check the local regulations, because much of the area is designated the Fort DeSoto Wetland and Aquatic Management Area. This restricts boat speed and use of combustion engines in certain areas to protect the valuable seagrass beds. Large areas around Mullet Key are good for canoeing in calm weather because of the lack of motorboats.

Beaches

One source ranked the beaches at Fort DeSoto as 19th in the world. There are 7 miles of sparkling beaches, covered with a fine sand known as "white sugar sand." Much of the sand was pumped from the ocean floor to dredge a channel for super-tankers going to Tampa. The dredgers needed somewhere to put the sand, so they built up the east and north beaches.

Shelling is a favorite activity on all the beaches, and a free park publication called "Common Shells of Fort DeSoto County Park" will aid your identification. Sharks' teeth are also found with a little closer scrutiny.

Two beaches are designated for swimming—North Beach Swim Area and East Beach Swim Area. Lifeguards are on duty only during the summer, but swimming is permitted at your own risk in other seasons.

Loggerhead sea turtles nest regularly in June and July. Usually at least 20 nests are made. Park staff protect the eggs from humans, raccoons, and ghost crabs by erecting fences around them.

Another park publication, "Beach Self Guide," was designed to be used along the beach near the fort. Since there are no particular stops, the guide can be used on any of the beaches to learn about the plants and animals inhabiting the tidal areas. Gulls, terns, sandpipers, plovers, pelicans, and many other types of birds can be found along the shore.

Fishing

The two piers, 500 and 1,000 feet long respectively, provide easy access to good fishing. In the spring and fall, Spanish mackerel can be caught from the piers. Both piers have bait-and-tackle shops. Also found are redfish, gulf flounder, seatrout, drum, sheepshead, snook, and crabs. The fishing piers are the only

EXPLORING WILD CENTRAL FLORIDA

places visitors are permitted to be after the park closes at night (other than driving to or from the piers). See "Boating" above for boat access.

Best Time of Year

Early March to mid-May for spring bird migrations. Other activities year-round.

Pets

Allowed on 6-foot hand-held leash. Not allowed at campground, beaches, picnic shelters, concession areas, fishing piers.

FRED H. HOWARD COUNTY PARK

Birders will want to explore this small park for waterbirds. The setting is ideal: a long causeway jutting into the Gulf of Mexico's Pinellas County Aquatic Preserve, with mudflats and beaches all around. The 0.75-mile long causeway leads to the swimming beach island, which can be very productive in early morning or winter, when the swimmers are absent. Sea oats, sea grapes, and cabbage palms thrive on the island. The mainland section, designed primarily for picnicking, has an overstory of oak-pine-palmetto and an open understory.

Many species of shorebirds, wading birds, and ducks can be found in the winter. Spring and fall migrations produce raptors, warblers, and other passerines which are stopping over.

Location, Mailing Address, and Phone

On the Gulf of Mexico in Tarpon Springs. From US 19 in Tarpon Springs, turn west onto Klosterman Road for 0.8 miles, then north (right) onto Carlton Road for 0.5 miles, then west (left) onto Curlew Place for 0.5 miles, then north (right) onto S. Florida

Avenue for 1 mile, and left onto Sunset Drive. Signs along the way make it easy to find the park.

1700 Sunset Dr., Tarpon Springs, FL 34689; (813) 937-4938

Facilities and Activities

Birding, swimming, picnicking. Open 7 AM to sunset daily. No admission fee.

The mainland section consists of live oaks with many picnic tables and pavilions. A causeway leads to the bathing beach on the Gulf with bathhouses. Along the beach are sea oats, sea grapes, and cabbage palms.

Birders should study the shore along the causeway for plovers (Wilson's, black-bellied, piping, semi-palmated, and snowy) as well as other shorebirds. At low tide, the extensive mud flats invite many shorebirds. Look for yellow-crowned night-herons, terns, brown pelicans, great blue herons, great egrets, and red-breasted mergansers. In spring and fall migrations, shorebirds pass through in great numbers, as well as raptors, waders, and passerines. During migration season, the tree canopy on the mainland section may be alive with warblers and other small migrants. The understory is relatively open, thus usually devoid of ground-feeding birds.

Best Time of Year

Fall, winter, and spring for birding (spring and fall for waterbird migrations; shorebirds come through in August and September); spring, summer, and fall for swimming. Try to time your birding for the falling or low tide (for exposed mudflats).

Pets

Allowed on mainland section, not allowed on causeway or beach.

JOHN CHESTNUT, SR. COUNTY PARK

Formerly called Brooker Park, this 255-acre county park on the eastern shores of Lake Tarpon offers recreation of many types. Boating and canoeing on the lake and walking on the trails are popular activities. The lake is 5 miles long and a mile wide, averaging 8 to 12 feet deep. A boardwalk meanders through a cypress swamp along Brooker Creek.

Location, Mailing Address, and Phone

In northern Pinellas County, on the east side of Lake Tarpon. Entrance is on CR 611 (E. Lake Road), 500 feet south of traffic light at Sandy Point Road. From Tarpon Springs, go east on Tarpon Road and turn right onto CR 611. From St. Petersburg, take Curlew Creek Road (SR 586) east to CR 611 and turn left.

3900 Sandy Point Road, Palm Harbor, FL 33685; (813) 784-4686

Facilities and Activities

Nature trail, canoeing, boat ramp. Open 7 AM to sunset daily. No admission fee.

Hiking

The Peggy Park Trail is 3,300 feet long and half of it is boardwalk. From the boardwalk, visitors can gaze upon some very large cypress trees heavily festooned with bromeliads. There are also wax myrtles, red maples, red bays, and many ferns. On the upland part of the trail is a pine–oak hammock. The trail passes by Brooker Creek. The trail guide (at the trailhead box) is packed with information about the flora and fauna of the trail.

Canoeing

Brooker Creek provides scenic canoeing. It can be accessed by launching at the ramp on the lake and paddling south along the shore to the mouth of the creek. You may be able to go about a mile upstream on the creek. For novice canoeists, the quarter-mile canoe trail along a 50-foot-wide canal loop may be preferable.

Best Time of Year

No preference.

Pets

Allowed on a 6-foot hand-held leash.

LAKE OKEECHOBEE SANCTUARIES

The National Audubon Society has many sanctuaries that aren't "on the map," so to speak. Two such sanctuaries are so close to each other that they're treated as one by Audubon. The Lake Okeechobee Sanctuaries consist of Northwest Shore (21,210 acres) and Observation Shoal (7,040 acres) sanctuaries. They're not listed on any road map because they can only be accessed by boat.

Audubon has maintained a lease with the state for the sanctuary area since 1938 to protect snail kites and other birds. Audubon wardens patrol the western side of Lake Okeechobee.

For people who don't have access to a private boat, the Audubon-sanctioned boat tour is a good way to experience one of the largest lakes in the country. The tour is wildlife- and conservation-oriented. The two-hour cruise travels through shallow marshes where snail kites, limpkins, bald eagles, peregrine falcons, ospreys, fulvous whistling-ducks, lesser scaup, shovelers, herons, egrets, rails, and other birds feed and nest.

Location, Mailing Address, and Phone

Sanctuary is located on the northwest shore of Lake Okeechobee. Tour operation is located on SR 78, just north of the bridge where the Kissimmee River empties into Lake Okeechobee (building is

*on the west side of the road). From Okeechobee, go south on US
441, turn right on SR 78, and go 4 miles to Swampland Tours.*

*For information on the sanctuary as well as the tour: Swamp-
land Tours, 10375 Highway 78 West, Okeechobee, FL 34974; (941)
467-4411.*

Facilities and Activities

*Boat tour, wildlife observation. Two boat tours daily, charters
available. Fee for tour.*

The 44-passenger boat takes two-hour cruises, weather permitting. It's best to call ahead for reservations and alternate
scheduling. One tour goes to the Northwest Shore and the other
to Observation Shoal. The tours are narrated by a knowledgeable
guide, usually an Audubon warden. The guide will stop any time
an unusual creature is spotted, drifting in quietly to avoid dis-
turbing it. Ducks, wading birds, raptors, rails, gulls, terns, and
bitterns are abundant. Least bitterns, limpkins, American coots,
common moorhens, purple gallinules, great blue herons, and
many other birds nest in the summer along the boat route. Bobcats occasionally are seen along the spoil banks, and alligators
are frequently seen basking on the shoreline. Infrequently, a
manatee survives the obstacle-course canals from the ocean to
arrive at the lake and be observed on the tour, usually in
November or December. Unfortunately, two exotic trees
(melaleuca and Brazilian pepper) have invaded the shoreline, so
the habitat is not pristine. However, the highlight of this tour is
the wildlife, particularly the snail kites, which nest locally. The
kites are seen regularly, making this tour one of the surest ways
to see them.

Best Time of Year

More birds are present in winter, but summer has a lot of nesting
activity.

Pets

Not allowed on tour boat.

LAKE PARK

The City of St. Petersburg and Hillsborough County joined forces to create this 589-acre park in suburban Tampa. It is a multi-use park, including such outdoor activities as motocross bicycling and archery. However, local residents may find the jogging path a good birding place.

Location, Mailing Address, and Phone

8 miles north of Tampa. The park is a half-mile south of Van Dyke Road on the west side of Dale Mabry Highway (CR 597).
17302 North Dale Mabry Hwy., Lutz, FL 33549; (813) 264-3806.

Facilities and Activities

Hiking/jogging path, boat ramp, canoeing, handicapped horseback riding, picnicking. No admission fee. Open 7 AM to 6 PM from October to March, 7 AM to 8 PM from April to September.

The hiking/jogging path is a 1.5-mile-long hard-packed dirt road. It circumnavigates a small lake and goes through several habitat types, including cypress swamp, pine flatwood, and hardwood hammock. Most of the vegetation is disturbed, with an abundance of Brazilian pepper. There is a "Vita Course" with exercise stops along the way. The path is handicapped-accessible.

Best Time of Year

No preference.

Pets

Allowed on a 6-foot hand-held leash.

LETTUCE LAKE REGIONAL PARK

Since it opened in 1982, this county park has been a local haven for nature study. Its 240 acres of hardwood swamp are part of the floodplain of the Hillsborough River, which flanks the park on two sides. Lettuce Lake is a narrow, shallow side pocket of the river, named after the exotic floating plant water lettuce. Efforts are made by Hillsborough County to preserve the area in its natural state. Over 300 species of plants have been identified in the park.

Location, Mailing Address, and Phone

In northeastern Tampa, on Fletcher Ave. (SR 582A), east of the bridge crossing the Hillsborough River. Or, from I-75, take Exit 55 and go west on Fletcher Ave.

6920 E. Fletcher Ave., Tampa, FL 33592; (813) 987-6204.

Facilities and Activities

Nature trails, biking/jogging path, boardwalks, observation tower, visitor center, picnicking. No admission fee. Handicapped-accessible. Open 8 AM to 6 PM from October to March, 8 AM to 8 PM from April to September.

A 5,000-foot-long nature trail through uplands, a 3,500-foot-long boardwalk through hardwood swamp along the river, and a 35-foot-tall observation tower give nature seekers ample opportunity to view the relatively unspoiled floodplain and its wildlife. A small visitor center near the boardwalk houses exhibits and a place for interpretive programs. The biking/jogging path is paved road over a mile long through the pines, with wheelchair-accessible exercise stations.

Best Time of Year

No preference.

Pets

Allowed on a 6-foot hand-held leash.

LITHIA SPRINGS PARK

About 200,000 people every year delight in a swim in the re-freshing clear spring waters at Lithia. Approximately 24 million gallons gush daily from the spring and flow, with other smaller springs, into the Alafia River. Against this watery setting, 200 acres of cypress swamp, hardwood hammocks, and sandhills provide a variety of habitats for naturalists to study. Originally, the springs tract was owned by a nearby company as a source of fresh water, but Hillsborough County now operates the park.

Location, Mailing Address, and Phone

About 10 miles southeast of Tampa city limit on Lithia Springs Road. Take SR 60 east to Brandon, turn right onto SR 640 (Lithia Road) and go south to Lithia Springs Road on the right. From I-75 north or south, take Exit 51 and go east on SR 60 to Brandon and follow directions above.

3932 Lithia Springs Road, Lithia, FL 33547; (813) 744-5572.

Facilities and Activities

Swimming, snorkeling, canoeing and canoe launch, camp-ground, picnicking, fishing. Admission fee charged; fee charged for camping. Handicapped-accessible. Open 8 AM to sunset daily.

Year-round swimming and snorkeling are popular in the clear, warm spring water (a constant 72°F). You can call the park to arrange interpretive guided walks and programs. There is a 40-site family campground with two shower houses. Each site has water and electricity. Two youth group campsites are available with reservations.

Canoeing

A canoe launch area is provided on the Alafia River. Canoeists can: 1) launch at Alderman's Ford Park (see **ALDERMAN'S FORD PARK** entry above) 10 miles upstream and end here, 2) go downstream for 3 miles from here to the Bell Shoals Road and return to Lithia Springs Park, or 3) go upstream and then return to Lithia. Along the river you may see alligators, water snakes, turtles, river otters, raccoons, gray and fox squirrels, herons and egrets, and wood storks. The water may be very low during dry spells (requiring short portages) or very high during heavy rains (creating dangerously fast water). Some experience is recommended. Alafia Canoe Rentals (813-689-8645), a few miles from the park entrance and not associated with the park, has rental canoes (closed Dec.-Jan. and Thursdays).

Best Time of Year

No preference. Canoeing depends on water levels (call park for conditions).

Pets

Allowed on a 6-foot hand-held leash; not allowed in water.

PINELLAS TRAIL

Quite a change from the typical park concept! Pinellas Trail is a linear park—it is *very* long and *very* narrow. In fact, the trail is 47 miles long but only 15 feet wide.

It began when the Pinellas County residents approved a one percent sales tax to build the trail along an abandoned railroad right-of-way. Construction began in 1990. The trail runs the length of the county from Tarpon Springs in the north to St. Petersburg in the south, so that anyone in the county can reach it within a few minutes. This is not a wilderness park. It passes mainly through suburban areas with occasional wooded stretches. Bicyclists, joggers, roller skaters, and dog-walkers who live in Pinellas County will find the trail a great place for some outdoor exercise. Non-residents, however, would probably have little reason to travel here just to use the trail.

Location

Northern terminus is on Jasmine Street in Tarpon Springs. Southern terminus is on 34th Street (US 19) between Fairfield Ave. and 8th Ave. South.

Mailing Address and Phone

1100 8th Ave. SW, Largo, FL 34640; (813) 581-2953

Facilities and Activities

Bicycling, jogging, walking. Handicapped-accessible. No admission fee. Open daylight hours daily.

The trail is paved and was constructed to allow bicyclists and roller skaters on one side and pedestrians and wheelchairs on the other. Believe it or not, there are speed-limit signs for cyclists, who must keep their speed down to 20 mph. There are picnic tables and occasional shelters. Many conveniences, such as restaurants and restrooms, are within a few minutes' walk from the trail. The county's planning department has produced a "Guidebook to the Pinellas Trail," which may be acquired by contacting the park. The guidebook shows the locations of drinking water, restaurants, gas stations (for bicycles needing air for tires), bicycle shops, motels and campgrounds, telephones, and restrooms.

A note for bicyclists: the trail is punctuated with cross streets at which you must stop. Thus, you won't find an uninterrupted long-distance ride.

Best Time of Year

No preference.

Pets

Allowed on a 6-foot hand-held leash.

SADDLE CREEK PARK

A maze of islands and waterways comprises this 734-acre suburban Polk County park, formerly a phosphate mine. The phosphate pits were abandoned decades ago and are now known as lakes. While the park seems to draw mostly anglers, the birding is excellent from late summer to October. Fall migrants, especially warblers, are abundant. Limpkins, herons, and egrets are commonly seen. A roost of egrets and anhingas may be visible from Saddle Creek Road at dawn or dusk.

Location, Mailing Address, and Phone

Just east of Lakeland, off US 92. Go east from Lakeland on US 92 for 0.7 mile east of the railroad crossing at Fish Hatchery Road. Turn left on Saddle Creek Park Road.

3716 Morgan Comee Road, Lakeland, FL 33801; (941) 499-2613.

Facilities and Activities

Nature trail, wildlife observation, canoeing, boating, fishing, campground, swimming area. No admission fee. Open 5 AM to 9 PM daily.

A 3-mile (one way) wooded nature trail is located just north of the campground. The landscape is heavily wooded. The trail was cut through a swamp but is on high ground, with a few low spots. Former phosphate pits may be seen on both sides. Canoeists and boaters have a choice of three ramps. The lakes are small interconnected waterways that can engross a canoeist for hours. The campground has separate tent and camper/trailer areas with showers at the bathrooms. A swimming area at the back of the park is open during the summer (usually May through September).

Best Time of Year
No preference.

Pets
Allowed on a leash.

SAVANNAS OUTDOOR RECREATION AREA

This distinctive St. Lucie county park is located next to "The Savannas," a long, narrow freshwater marsh nestled between a sand ridge to the east and pine flatwoods to the west. Most of the 550-acre park includes part of the marsh, but about 100 acres is upland. Canoeing is the best way to see the Savannas. (See also **SAVANNAS STATE RESERVE**)

The area was originally developed as a drinking-water reservoir for Fort Pierce. Impoundments were created by building dikes. In 1963, the county started the recreation area around the impoundments, primarily for fishing, with a ramp for small boats. They cleared the canals of weeds, created islands, and graded the roads. The state fisheries managers still stock bass.

St. Lucie County has done well at keeping costs to the public down. Most people visit the recreation area to canoe and camp. Birding can be productive, with snail kites, roseate spoonbills, and black-crowned night-herons occasionally seen.

Location, Mailing Address, and Phone

7 miles south of Fort Pierce, on Midway Road between US 1 and Indian River Drive (CR 707). Take Exit 64 from I-95 to CR 712 (Midway Road), go east on 712 for 1.25 miles past US 1.

Savannas Recreation Area, 1400 Midway Road, Fort Pierce, FL 33482; (407) 464-7855

Camping adjacent to the Savannas marsh is a lure for naturalists to this county park (Susan D. Jewell)

Facilities and Activities

Canoeing and canoe rentals, campground, nature trail, picnicking. Admission fee charged. Fee extra for camping (discount for St. Lucie Co. residents) and canoe rentals. Open 8 AM to sunset daily.

Canoeing

The Savannas is at the tip of your paddle. From the boat ramp near the entrance station, you can paddle around the northern part of this vast marsh. The grassy waters attract many wading birds, shore birds, and ducks. In spring, a small colony of wading birds forms at the east side of the marsh. It can be seen from land by going out of the park's entrance, going east on Midway Road to the railroad tracks, then walking north on the west side of the tracks (outside of the railroad right-of-way) for a few hundred yards until you see the birds to the left. In summer, several pairs of snail kites nest in the marsh around here. Water depths are generally 2 to 4 feet. Canoe rentals are available at a refreshingly low fee.

Small motorboats may also be launched here. The maximum motor size is 7.5 horsepower.

Camping

The campground has 68 campsites, some with water only, some with water and electricity, some with water, electricity, and sewage disposal. They are fairly exposed (no privacy, but good breeze). Some of the sites are directly beside the water on the savannas. A chorus of frogs and other nocturnal creatures will lull you to sleep (in between the roaring trains on the far side of the marsh). Reservations are accepted. The bathrooms have hot showers. There are even a few relic clothes washers and driers. Chips, charcoal, laundry soap, and mosquito repellent are for sale at the entrance station. A separate group site for up to 20 people is available for tax-exempt groups.

Nature Trail

This trail deserves mention only for those people who have already come to the park for the camping or canoeing. It is a half-mile zigzag walk across the mowed dikes of the impoundments. Follow the numbered posts that accompany the interpretive brochure available at the entrance station. One of the stops is at a 15-foot-tall observation tower that overlooks the Savannas. Some of the native plants you'll see are dahoon holly, Virginia chain fern, marsh mallow, sawgrass, redbay, cabbage palm, laurel oak, and slash pine. Of course, melaleuca, Australian-pine, and Brazilian pepper are ever-present exotics.

Best Time of Year

Winter for overwintering birds (but campground more crowded; may be full on weekends); snail kites in summer (but some mosquitoes also); fall and spring for migrants.

Pets

Allowed on a leash.

SAWGRASS LAKE PARK

The 400 acres of red maple swamp, live oak hammock, channel, and lake create this haven surrounded by urban sprawl. Sawgrass Park is a cool, lush place for a naturalist's stroll. Boardwalks provide a nonintruding view of the wetlands. The area was named in the 1800s, when the maple swamp had not encroached so much on the marsh. Thus, there is only a little sawgrass left now.

The area was developed for flood protection for the nearby Pinellas City Park. It was acquired by the Pinellas-Anclote River Basin Board of the Southwest Florida Water Management District in 1979. It is maintained and operated by the Pinellas County Park Department and the Pinellas County School Board. The marsh acts as a natural filter for the water before it flows into Tampa Bay.

As many as 31 species of warblers seek the swamp during their spring migrations, and most of them return in the fall. A pair of bald eagles arrives in November and may nest nearby. Waterfowl favor the pond in winter. Alligators nest in the summer but are present all year. The park has an active environmental education program for schools and visitors.

Location, Mailing Address, and Phone

In St. Petersburg. From I-275, take the exit for 54th Ave. North, turn right on 28th Street North, turn right on 62nd Ave. North, then left on 25th Street North.

7400 25th Street North, St. Petersburg, FL 33702; (813) 527-3814

Facilities and Activities

Environmental education center, nature trails, birding, picnic shelter. No admission fee. Open 7 AM to sunset daily. Handicapped-accessible.

The John Anderson Environmental Education Center has excellent exhibits and dioramas on birds of prey, historic/prehistoric Native American life, life on the beach, soil types, bird eggs, butterflies, and so on. A large central aquarium displays local freshwater animals, such as turtles, sirens, and fish, and smaller tanks house some live snakes. Classroom and laboratory facilities for Pinellas schools are also present.

Trails

The Sawgrass Trail, about a half mile long, is a boardwalk through a red maple swamp that leads to the Overlook Tower. The tower (not handicapped-accessible) provides a view across a pond with common moorhens, alligators, and other marsh animals. Along the trail you may see giant leather ferns, Spanish moss, and mistletoe. The Maple Trail, over a half mile long, is also a boardwalk through red maple swamp. The Hammock Trail is the longest of the three. It is partly boardwalk but mostly a rough trail over higher elevations. Look for armadillos and gopher tortoise burrows. On the drier land are sand live oak, hickory, tallowwood, goldenrod, sedge, and bracken fern. Slightly downhill are pignut hickory, saw palmetto, staggerbush, beauty berry, and red bay. Still lower on the hill are rouge plant, red mulberry, wild coffee, dahoon holly, Boston fern, marsh fern, and royal fern.

Over 200 bird species have been seen in this small park. The park is an oasis of green in an otherwise heavily developed county, attracting not only the birds but the birders as well. Many species, such as most warblers, are absent in the summer. By December, up to 17 species of ducks (such as shoveler, pintail, canvas-backed, and redhead) have arrived on the pond. Mottled, wood, and ring-necked ducks are residents. Amphibian and reptile activity peaks in the summer, when many species perform their courtship displays. Alligators occasionally build their nests in view of visitors.

Best Time of Year

Year-round for hiking and observing plants and wildlife. Birding best in fall (September, October) and spring (March, April) for small birds; winter for waterfowl.

Pets

Allowed on a 6-foot hand-held leash in picnic area but not on trails or boardwalks.

STARKEY WILDERNESS PARK

This minimally developed Pasco County park protects the environment around a city water supply. The 8,069-acre park protects the watersheds of the Anclote and Pithlachascotee Rivers, which flow through it. Fourteen wells provide drinking water (after treatment) for 163,000 residents daily.

The land was formerly owned by J.B. Starkey, who ranched and lumbered it. Starkey donated the original 250 acres to the state to preserve it. The Southwest Florida Water Management District purchased the rest from Starkey's family. In 1989, the SWFWMD signed an agreement with Pasco County for the county to develop and manage the property for passive recreation. Most of the intensive-use recreational facilities are concentrated in the 65-acre tract owned by Pasco County. A variety of habitats, including pine flatwoods and sandhills, provide homes for turkeys, bobcats, deer, and other wildlife.

Location, Mailing Address, and Phone

In southwestern Pasco County, just east of New Port Richey. From SR 54 at Seven Springs, go north on Little Road for 1 mile, turn east onto River Crossing Road.

10500 Wilderness Park Road, New Port Richey, FL 34653; (813) 834-3247

Facilities and Activities

Hiking, horseback riding, wildlife observation, campground, bicycling, primitive backpack and horseback camping, rental cabins, picnicking. No admission fee. Open daylight hours daily. Fee for campground and cabins.

Thirteen miles of marked hiking trails are in short, medium, and long loops. Along the way are three primitive campsites. There is no fee for the backcountry campsites, but campers must register at the information kiosk. Reservations are not necessary but are accepted. There are 9 miles of equestrian trails and two backcountry equestrian campsites. The bicycle trail is a 3.2-mile paved road that passes the wellfields. Bicyclists may ride on any paved or shell roadway.

The 16-site campground is for tents only (no generators, pop-up tents, or RVs). Water spigots and shower facilities are nearby. Eight primitive cabins (one handicapped-accessible) are available for rent. They have no electricity, plumbing, or indoor cooking. Restroom/shower facilities are located nearby. Reservations may be made for cabins or tent camping in person up to 30 days in advance at the park's information kiosk. This low-impact camping keeps the overnight fees modest.

Best Time of Year

November and December are nice months for hiking and camping (fewer insects and people, cooler and drier weather), but January to April are also good.

Pets

Allowed on a leash. Not allowed in camping area.

THE HAMMOCK

The state's first designated natural feature is in a small, unassuming suburban park. It was chosen in 1976 to preserve the hammock as a representative of Florida's original forests. The 80 acres of hammock provide a shady retreat in hot weather and a source of shelter and food for migrating songbirds. Three self-guided nature trails and several unmarked trails provide access into the hammock.

Location, Mailing Address, and Phone

In the city of Dunedin, about 10 miles north of St. Petersburg. From SR 586 (Curlew Road), go south on US 19-Alt. to Mira Vista Drive. Turn left and go 0.2 mile to end (crossing the Pinellas Trail), then left onto San Mateo.

Department of Leisure Services, 903 Michigan Boulevard, Dunedin, FL 34698

Facilities and Activities

Nature trails, birding, picnicking, restrooms. No admission fee. Open 7:30 AM to sunset daily.

The dense canopy in the hammock supports many migrating and wintering warblers, vireos, and other passerines. The three self-guided trails (Cedar, Palm, and Sugarberry) are a mile or less round-trip. Signs at the trailheads explain the numbered stops, or you can obtain a trail guide by writing to the above address. The Cedar Trail is the only handicapped-accessible one, composed of firmly-packed shell and boardwalk. It is named for the southern redcedar, a type of juniper, found here. It grows in moist soils in central and northern Florida and has droopier twigs than the eastern redcedar. Other trees and plants on this trail include slash pine, pignut hickory, live oak, resurrection fern, and beauty berry. Besides the cabbage palms for which the trail is named, the Palm Trail also bypasses tallowwoods, which are thorny shrubs with edible, yellow, plum-like fruits. Tallowwood, also known as hog plum, is a tropical species that is usually found in coastal hammocks or in scrub. The Sugarberry Trail is named for the tree of that name, also known as southern hackberry, which prefers bottomlands and floodplains. Around the bottomlands in the park, you may see herons and egrets, ospreys, skimmers, and gulls.

Best Time of Year

Fall through spring for migrating and wintering songbirds.

Pets

Allowed on a leash.

TIGER CREEK PRESERVE

Located on the Lake Wales Ridge, the Tiger Creek watershed has been the target of land acquisition by The Nature Conservancy since 1968. The pristine creek flows from the ridge into Lake Weohyakapka. The swamps, hammocks, pine and oak scrubs, pine flatwoods, and sandhill communities surrounding the creek complete the 4,700-acre preserve. Three hiking trails allow the visitor an opportunity to explore the variety of habitats.

The Lake Wales Ridge contains more listed species of plants and animals than anywhere else in Florida. Some of the species you may see are Florida scrub lizard, sand skink, scrub jay, pygmy fringe tree, and large-flowered bonamia (or scrub morning-glory). To enhance populations of rare species, TNC's staff manages the property with prescribed burns and other activities.

Location, Mailing Address, and Phone

Southeast of Lake Wales, near Babson Park. From Babson Park, go south on US 27A for about 2 miles to Murray Road and turn left. Go 2.2 miles to Pfundstein Road and turn left again. George Cooley Trail is at the second power pole on the left. For Tiger Creek Preserve Hiking Trail, go to first left off Pfundstein Road and proceed 0.1 mile to parking area. For Jenkins Trail, take SR 60 east from Lake Wales for about 9 miles to Walk-in-Water Road. Turn right and go 3.5 miles south to Wakeford Road. Then right again and proceed to parking area at end. Or Jenkins Trail can be reached from Frostproof: go east on CR 630 to Walk-in-Water Road, turn left and go 5.2 miles to Wakeford Road, then left to end.

For more information, contact The Nature Conservancy, 225 East Stuart Avenue, Lake Wales, FL 33853; (941) 678-1551

Facilities and Activities

Nature trails; guided nature walks available through The Nature Conservancy. No admission fee. Open daylight hours daily.

The George Cooley Trail is a loop footpath that traverses scrubs, hardwood swamps, pine flatwoods, and cutthroat seeps. The slight change in elevation from scrub to wetland is anything but subtle. In fact, the demarcation can even be seen by noting where the trail changes from sand to dark, rich soil. A short side spur goes to a bayhead with lush ferns, such as cinnamon fern. Hiking time: 30 to 60 minutes.

The Jenkins Trail is a slightly longer loop of the Florida Trail that traces along Tiger Creek. The black water of Tiger Creek is pristine because almost the entire watershed is within the preserve boundaries. The trail passes through pine flatwoods to swampy bottomlands, where the trail gets rough (from feral hogs and tree roots) and may be wet. Hiking time: one to two hours.

The Tiger Creek Preserve Trail (Pfundstein Trail) is a sandy footpath, also maintained by the Florida Trail Association, that goes to the ridge area. Patrick Creek, a wide blackwater stream, is just a mile from the trailhead. The Highland Loop is 5.5 miles. Hiking time: one to six hours.

Best Time of Year

October to April for best weather.

Pets

Not allowed.

UPPER TAMPA BAY PARK

This 2,144-acre Hillsborough County park is operated as a nature preserve with limited recreational facilities. The varied habitat includes freshwater ponds, salt marshes, oyster bars, mangroves, oak hammocks, and pine flatwoods. Indigenous peoples thrived on the rich lands and waters—their bountiful shellfish harvests reflected in the numerous shell mounds found within the park today. After the native people disappeared from the area, European settlers discovered the prime locations around Tampa Bay, which they and their descendants rapidly developed. The development interfered with the function of the estuaries around the bay, leading to a decline of the bay's health. The park was designed for minimal impact on the ecosystem while providing a way for visitors to see the area and to learn about the importance of estuaries.

An environmental study center, operated with Hillsborough Community College, is open to the public.

Location, Mailing Address, and Phone

Just west of Tampa International Airport. From SR 589 in Tampa, go west on SR 580 (Hillsborough Ave.) for 6.2 miles (about a mile east of the Pinellas County line). At Double Branch Road, turn left and go south 0.4 mile to entrance.

8001 Double Branch Road, Tampa, FL 33615; (813) 855-1765.

Facilities and Activities

Canoeing, nature trails, nature center, boardwalk, group campsite, picnic and playground area, saltwater fishing. No admission fee (donation requested). Trails are handicapped-accessible. Open 8 AM to 6 PM daily. Closed Christmas.

The park is on a peninsula in Upper Tampa Bay that provides scenic canoeing. Canoeists can explore the protected mangrove coves and salt marshes but should have a compass and consider the wind and tides. Some canoeing experience is recommended. Look for bald eagles, ospreys, northern harriers, wood storks, roseate spoonbills (in summer), and herons and egrets.

Three short self-guided nature trails and boardwalks, each about a 20-minute leisurely walk, guide visitors through a variety of upland and wetland habitats. The Eagle Trail (0.4 mile one-way) goes through pine flatwoods, xeric hammocks (oak-palmetto), freshwater marshes, salt marshes, and mangroves. The Otter Trail (0.6-mile loop) connects two picnic areas through pine flatwoods and xeric hammocks. The Bobcat Trail (0.4-mile loop) is a boardwalk along mangroves, salt barrens, and around a large salt marsh. In the Tampa area, the mangroves' height is determined by climate. The frosts that occur in several-year intervals are enough to keep the trees from growing any taller. Only about five percent of the original pine flatwoods in Hillsborough County are left, which is why they're protected by this park. Around the freshwater marshes, look for coots, mottled ducks, American widgeons, blue-winged teals, pintails, and ringnecked ducks.

The nature center houses interpretive exhibits, including saltwater aquaria, live snakes, computer games, and wall displays. An unusual semi-spherical tank displays remoras and stingrays in a most effective way. One display on native peoples includes a reconstructed kitchen midden. Outside are a butterfly garden and a classroom building used by Hillsborough County schoolchildren and by Hillsborough Community College students.

A primitive campsite for organized groups is available by prior arrangement on a seasonal basis.

Best Time of Year

Winter for hiking and birding; August to September for migrating shorebirds, October to November for other migrating birds.

Pets

Allowed on a 6-foot hand-held leash.

WEEDON ISLAND PRESERVE

Formerly known as Weedon Island State Preserve, the park was transferred to the Pinellas County park system on October 1, 1993. Full of human history, the area was the home of Timucuan people for 10,000 years until the Spaniards arrived in the 1500s. Hernando DeSoto's expedition landed nearby in 1539. The exact location is unknown. Shell mounds and burial mounds have been excavated by the Smithsonian, which removed 250 human skeletons. Since the European settlers arrived, Weedon Island's soils have supported development schemes, an airport, and a movie studio. Dr. Leslie Weedon, who owned the island from 1898 to 1923, wanted it to be a park. His wish came true posthumously in the 1970s.

In July 1972, Weedon Island was added to the National Register of Historic Sites. The state purchased the island and adjacent smaller ones, and after several years of cleaning up the garbage that had been dumped, filling in mosquito ditches, and removing the exotic plants, the preserve opened to the public in 1980. The shallow estuary waters around the islands are now an aquatic preserve, protecting the seagrass beds by prohibiting motorboats in the shallow waters. The 1,300-acre Weedon Island Preserve is currently known for its fine birding, canoeing, and fishing, and is enjoyed by 136,000 visitors a year.

Location, Mailing Address, and Phone

On Tampa Bay. From Gandy Boulevard (US 92) in St. Petersburg, turn south onto San Martin Blvd., which is south of the Gandy Bridge. Go 0.9 mile to Weedon Drive, turn left and go 1 mile to the preserve entrance.

Weedon Island Preserve, 1500 Weedon Island Drive, St. Petersburg, FL 33702; (813) 579-8360

Facilities and Activities

Canoeing, hiking, birding, wildlife observation, fishing. No admission fee. Open 7 AM to sunset daily.

Hiking

Four miles of firebreaks afford the hiker the opportunity to see the upland habitats. Gopher tortoises, indigo snakes, Florida cotton mice, rattlesnakes, and kingsnakes are among the animals you may see. Two hundred acres are uplands, which the preserve staff is restoring to pine flatwoods. A 2-mile boardwalk is planned for 1996.

Canoeing

Canoeists may bring their own canoes and launch at the ramp at the end of Weedon Drive (no motorboats allowed). This is the start of the 4-mile self-guided canoe trail. Ask for the written guide at the preserve entrance. The trail takes about 2 1/2 hours and affords the opportunity to observe roseate spoonbills, wood storks, American oystercatchers, brown pelicans, bald eagles, terns, herons, egrets, and many other birds. The trail passes mangroves, seagrass beds, shell mounds, hammocks, and pine flatwoods. The eastern end of the island is a no-motor zone.

Fishing

Anglers can fish from the pier at the end of Weedon Drive or by canoe or rowboat. Catches include snook, sea trout, and sheepshead. Despite the plentiful oyster bars, shellfish harvesting is prohibited due to possible contamination.

Best Time of Year

Canoeists, hikers, and anglers seem to have little seasonal preference. The no-see-ums are pesky in the summer (dawn and dusk). Birders can find more of interest from fall to spring.

Pets

Allowed on a 6-foot hand-held leash.

WILDERNESS PARK

Hillsborough County has a novel concept with its Wilderness Park. At 16,000 acres, it is the largest park in the county system. Although it is managed as one park, it is separated into six disjunct sites, each with a different name. About 20 miles of the Hillsborough River flow through four of the sites, inviting many local canoeists. The land is leased from the Southwest Florida Water Management District for recreation. Some of the visitor facilities are still under development. Habitats include uplands with pine flatwoods and bottomlands with cypress swamps. You may see alligators, otters, turkeys, deer, feral hogs, barred owls, and wading birds.

Location, Mailing Address, and Phone

See separate entries below for each site. For information on the park in general, contact the Hillsborough County Parks and Recreation Administrative Office at 1101 E. River Cove Street, Tampa, FL 33604; (813) 975-2160.

Facilities and Activities

Hiking, canoeing, fishing, camping, picnicking. No admission fee. Hours of operation vary for each site (call ahead to Administrative Office in Tampa or individual site office). Restrooms at all sites. All sites are handicapped-accessible. See separate entries below for each site.

Best Time of Year

Varies for activity.

Pets

Allowed on a 6-foot hand-held leash. Not permitted in buildings or on boardwalks.

Dead River Park

Hiking trails, fishing, youth group camping site, picnicking, primitive canoeing (expect portages, pullovers, and low branches). Open Friday to Sunday from 9 AM to 5:30 PM. This 378-acre park is primarily a youth camp, but it is open to the public on weekends. It was set aside as "Environmentally Sensitive" land which supports gopher tortoises, indigo snakes, and other rare species. A 2-mile hiking trail leads to Hillsborough River State Park.

Located about 15 miles northeast of Tampa. Take I-75 to Fowler Ave. (SR 582) exit, go east to US 301, then north on 301 for 8 miles to Dead River Road (1 mile south of Hillsborough River State Park). Turn left and go 2 miles to end of road.

Office and mailing address—15098 Dead River Road, Thonotosassa, FL 33592; (813) 987-6210.

Flatwoods Park

Interpretive Center, hiking trails, three camping areas, picnicking, 9-mile paved bike loop.

Located on Morris Bridge Road. From Tampa, take SR 579 (Morris Bridge Road) north to 1 mile north of Hillsborough River.

Office and mailing address—16400 Morris Bridge Road, Thonotosassa, FL 33592; (813) 987-6211.

John B. Sargeant, Sr. Park   *very nice*

Canoeing (with launch), boardwalk through cypress forest, picnicking, fishing. Easy access to Hillsborough River for canoeing or boating. This is the farthest upstream site for reasonable canoeing (rapids are upstream).

Located on US 301 and Stacy Road, about 5 miles south of Hillsborough River State Park and about 4 miles north of SR 582.

Office and mailing address—12702 Hwy. 301, Thonotosassa, FL 33592; (813) 987-6208.

Morris Bridge Park

Canoeing (with launch), boardwalks, hiking trails, picnicking. The canoeing is on the Hillsborough River.

Located on Morris Bridge Road at the Hillsborough River. From Tampa, take SR 579 (Morris Bridge Road) north to the Hillsborough River.

Office and mailing address—13330 Morris Bridge Road, Thonotosassa, FL 33592; (813) 987-6209.

Trout Creek Park

Canoeing (with launch), boardwalk, fishing, picnicking. The canoeing is on the Hillsborough River.

Located on Morris Bridge Road and the Tampa Bypass Canal (Palm River/Sixmile Creek). From Tampa, take SR 579/582A (Fletcher Ave.) east to Morris Bridge Road and the Tampa Bypass Canal.

Office and mailing address—12550 Morris Bridge Road, Thonotosassa, FL 33592; (813) 987-6200.

Veteran's Memorial Park

0.7-mile bicycle and bank fishing trail along canal, military museum, picnicking. This is more of an urban park.

Located on US 301 at the Tampa Bypass Canal (Palm River/Sixmile Creek), south of SR 574.

Office and mailing address—3602 Hwy. 301, Tampa, FL 33619; (813) 744-5502.

WITHLACOOCHEE RIVER PARK

Like Starkey Wilderness Park, the 606-acre Withlacoochee River Park is jointly owned and managed by Pasco County and the Southwest Florida Water Management District to protect water resources. A variety of habitats, from low riverine swamps to pine flatwoods to sandhills, and access to the Withlacoochee River and its cypress swamps make this an interesting day or weekend visit. Bald eagles have been seen, as well as alligators, indigo snakes, turkeys, owls, and deer.

Location, Mailing Address, and Phone

In the Green Swamp area of eastern Pasco County. From Dade City, take River Road almost 4 miles east to Auton Road, turn right, then left on Withlacoochee Blvd. to park entrance.

12449 Withlacoochee Blvd., Dade City, FL 33525; (904) 567-0264 or 521-4182

Facilities and Activities

Nature trails, boardwalks, canoeing, primitive campground, observation tower, picnicking, Native American villages. Open daylight hours daily. No admission fee.

The campground has ten primitive sites and it is accessible only by foot trail—about a half mile from the closest parking lot. You must walk back to the day-use area for bathrooms and potable water (a pump in the campground has non-potable water). There is no charge for camping. A 1.7-mile hiking trail that goes to the river is maintained by the Florida Trail Association. About 3 more miles of trails throughout the park are maintained by the county. Three boardwalks lead from the observation tower to a swamp. The wooden canoe launch on the Withlacoochee requires a 100-foot portage from the parking lot. The river is narrow here and offers opportunities to practice steering. A Native American village is being constructed by Native American volunteers for educational purposes.

Best Time of Year

November and December are nice months for hiking and camping (fewer insects and people, cooler and drier weather), but January to April are also good.

Pets

Allowed on a leash.

VIII
ADDITIONAL
INFORMATION

WILDLIFE CHECKLISTS

The following checklists are intended to include the known native and some of the more common naturalized exotic vertebrates (except fish) found in central Florida. Species of unknown status, accidentals, those numbering only a few individuals, or obscure subspecies may be excluded. The ranges given are for each species' range within the whole state. The population status, however, is only for central Florida.

Population status is given in relative terms as follows:

abundant—likely to be seen in the right habitat; population dense

common—often seen in the right habitat; population numerous

uncommon—infrequently seen; population low

rare—not likely to be seen; population very small or endangered

resident (bird checklist only)—present year-round

migrant (bird checklist only)—passes through on way to wintering/ summering grounds

visitor (bird checklist only)—central Florida is the final migration destination

+ = known breeder in central Florida (bird checklist only)

* = exotic species (breeds in central Florida)

E = endangered species

BIRD CHECKLIST

The following list of 352 bird species includes some which have occurred rarely in the central Florida region but which may be expected to occur in the future. Some naturally occurring species reported in the region are less likely to be found in the future and have been omitted. Some exotic species having uncertain reproductive success in central Florida have been omitted. Readers who desire detailed information should refer to *Florida Bird Species: An Annotated List* by William B. Robertson, Jr. and Glen E. Woolfenden (order from: Glen Woolfenden, Editor of Special Publications, Archbold Biological Station, Venus, FL 33960). Another resource is *Florida's Birds: A Handbook and Reference*, by Herbert W. Kale and David S. Maehr, available through Pineapple Press, Inc., P.O. Drawer 16008, Sarasota, Florida 34239. Wayne Hoffman contributed expertise to the following list.

Loons and Grebes

- ☐ **Red-throated loon** (*Gavia stellata*)—rare winter visitor; Atlantic and Gulf coasts of northern half of Florida
- ☐ **Common loon** (*Gavia immer*)—variably common migrant and winter visitor; ocean and bays, occasionally large lakes
- ☐ **+Pied-billed grebe** (*Podilymbus podiceps*)—common migrant and winter visitor, some resident all year; mainly fresh water
- ☐ **Horned grebe** (*Podiceps auritus*)—uncommon to locally common winter visitor; chiefly coastal, occasionally lakes in central Florida
- ☐ **Eared grebe** (*Podiceps nigricollis*)—rare winter visitor; deeper lakes

Shearwaters and Storm-petrels

- ☐ **Cory's shearwater** (*Calonectris diomedea*)—uncommon summer and fall migrant; pelagic, Atlantic
- ☐ **Greater shearwater** (*Puffinus gravis*)—rare to uncommon late spring and summer migrant; pelagic, chiefly Atlantic
- ☐ **Sooty shearwater** (*Puffinus griseus*)—rare summer migrant; pelagic, chiefly Atlantic
- ☐ **Audubon's shearwater** (*Puffinus lherminieri*)—uncommon spring-fall visitor; pelagic, chiefly Atlantic

☐ **Wilson's storm-petrel** (*Oceanites oceanicus*)—uncommon late spring and summer migrant; pelagic

☐ **Leach's storm-petrel** (*Oceanodroma leucorhoa*)—rare summer visitor; pelagic

☐ **Band-rumped storm-petrel** (*Oceanodroma castro*)—rare summer and fall visitor; pelagic

Pelicans and Allies

☐ **White-tailed tropicbird** (*Phaethon lepturus*)—rare summer visitor; pelagic

☐ **Masked booby** (*Sula dactylatra*)—rare (less in spring); pelagic, more on Atlantic south of Canaveral and on Gulf

☐ **Brown booby** (*Sula leucogaster*)—uncommon visitor; pelagic off southern half of Florida

☐ **Red-footed booby** (*Sula sula*)—very rare summer and fall visitor; pelagic

☐ **Northern gannet** (*Morus bassanus*)—common migrant and winter visitor; chiefly pelagic, sometimes close to shore

☐ **American white pelican** (*Pelecanus erythrorhynchos*)—common winter visitor, some in summer; bays and inland lakes, except northeastern Florida

☐ **+Brown pelican** (*Pelecanus occidentalis*)—abundant resident; coasts and bays

Cormorants and Anhingas

☐ **Great cormorant** (*Phalacrocorax carbo*)—rare winter visitor, more on Atlantic than Gulf

☐ **+Double-crested cormorant** (*Phalacrocorax auritus*)—abundant resident; coasts, bays, and inland waters

☐ **+Anhinga** (*Anhinga anhinga*)—common resident; fresh water marshes, canals, and ponds

Frigatebirds

☐ **Magnificent frigatebird** (*Fregata magnificens*)—variably common resident; coasts and bays

Herons, Egrets, and Other Waders

☐ **American bittern** (*Botaurus lentiginosus*)—rare to common migrant and winter visitor; interior and coastal marshes

☐ **+Least bittern** (*Ixobrychus exilis*)—locally common resident; interior and coastal marshes, especially central Florida lakes and Lake Okeechobee

☐ **+Great blue heron** (*Ardea herodias*)—common resident; shallow fresh and salt water

☐ **+"Great white heron"** (*Ardea "occidentalis"*)—locally common resident in southern Florida; usually shallow salt water; some post-breeding dispersal northward to central Florida, often in freshwater marshes [considered by some the same species as *Ardea herodias*]

☐ **+Great egret** (*Casmerodius albus*)—common resident; shallow fresh and salt water

☐ **+Snowy egret** (*Egretta thula*)—common resident; shallow fresh and salt water

☐ **+Little blue heron** (*Egretta caerulea*)—common resident; shallow fresh and salt water

☐ **+Tricolored heron** (*Egretta tricolor*)—common resident; shallow fresh and salt water

☐ **+Reddish egret** (*Egretta rufescens*)—uncommon resident; shallow salt water

☐ **+Cattle egret** (*Bubulcus ibis*)—abundant resident, less common in winter; margins and fields

☐ **+Green heron** (*Butorides virescens*)—common resident; shaded shallow freshwater and saltwater shorelines

☐ **+Black-crowned night-heron** (*Nycticorax nycticorax*)—fairly common resident; shallow fresh and salt water

☐ **+Yellow-crowned night-heron** (*Nyctanassa violacea*)—common resident; shallow salt and fresh water

☐ **+White ibis** (*Eudocimus albus*)—common resident; shallow fresh and salt water, agricultural fields and lawns

☐ ***Scarlet ibis** (*Eudocimus ruber*)—occasional escapees or hybrids from past introductions; shallow fresh and salt water

☐ **+Glossy ibis** (*Plegadis falcinellus*)—uncommon resident; shallow fresh water

☐ **+Roseate spoonbill** (*Ajaia ajaja*)—locally common resident (breeds Tampa Bay and Merritt Island); shallow salt water, occasionally inland (especially Lake Okeechobee)

☐ **+Wood stork** (*Mycteria americana*)—uncommon resident; freshwater margins and swamps **E**

Waterfowl

☐ **+Fulvous whistling-duck** (*Dendrocygna bicolor*)—common visitor and local resident; freshwater marshes, especially Lake Okeechobee, Kissimmee River, and St. Johns River marshes

☐ **+Black-bellied whistling-duck** (*Dendrocygna autumnalis*)—possibly becoming established; flooded farmlands, especially east of Sarasota

☐ **Snow goose** (*Chen caerulescens*)—rare winter visitor; freshwater and saltwater marshes, more common in northern Florida than southern

☐ **Brant** (*Branta bernicla*)—rare winter visitor; shallow bays and estuaries, more common in northern Florida than southern

☐ **+Canada goose** (*Branta canadensis*)—rare winter visitor (feral breeders); marshes in northern Florida

☐ ***Muscovy duck** (*Cairina moschata*)—locally common resident; urban ponds statewide; nuisance

☐ **+Wood duck** (*Aix sponsa*)—variably common resident; wooded swamps

☐ **Green-winged teal** (*Anas crecca*)—variably uncommon winter visitor; ponds and flooded pastures

☐ **American black duck** (*Anas rubripes*)—rare winter visitor; freshwater and saltwater marshes, mostly northern Florida

☐ **+Mottled duck** (*Anas fulvigula*)—common resident; ponds and marshes, central and southern Florida

☐ **+Mallard** (*Anas platyrhynchos*)—fairly common winter migrant and domesticated resident; urban ponds [historically, wild mallards never nested in Florida and still don't]

☐ **White-cheeked pintail** (*Anas bahamensis*)—rare winter and spring visitor, also some escapees; mangrove ponds

☐ **Northern pintail** (*Anas acuta*)—variably uncommon migrant and winter visitor; ponds, bays, and marshes

☐ **Blue-winged teal** (*Anas discors*)—common to abundant migrant and winter visitor, some summer; ponds, bays, and marshes

☐ **Cinnamon teal** (*Anas cyanoptera*)—very rare visitor from West Indies; marshes

☐ **Northern shoveler** (*Anas clypeata*)—variably uncommon migrant and winter visitor; freshwater wetlands

☐ **Gadwall** (*Anas strepera*)—uncommon migrant and winter visitor; freshwater wetlands

☐ **Eurasian wigeon** (*Anas penelope*)—rare winter visitor; coastal marshes, especially around Merritt Island

☐ **American wigeon** (*Anas americana*)—fairly common migrant and winter visitor; ponds and bays

☐ **Canvasback** (*Aythya valisineria*)—uncommon winter migrant and winter visitor; lakes and estuaries

☐ **Redhead** (*Aythya americana*)—uncommon winter migrant and winter visitor; bays and estuaries, especially around Merritt Island

☐ **+Ring-necked duck** (*Aythya collaris*)—fairly common migrant and winter visitor (rare breeder); lakes and ponds

☐ **Greater scaup** (*Aythya marila*)—rare to uncommon winter migrant; mostly coasts in northern Florida

☐ **Lesser scaup** (*Aythya affinis*)—common migrant and winter visitor; estuaries, bays, and lakes (common on lakes of central ridge)

☐ **Oldsquaw** (*Clangula hyemalis*)—rare winter visitor; mostly coastal

☐ **Black scoter** (*Melanitta nigra*)—rare migrant and winter visitor; mostly coastal

☐ **Surf scoter** (*Melanitta perspicillata*)—rare winter visitor; coastal and occasionally inland waters of northern Florida

☐ **Common goldeneye** (*Bucephala clangula*)—uncommon winter visitor; mostly coastal waters of northern Florida

☐ **Bufflehead** (*Bucephala albeola*)—uncommon winter visitor; mostly coastal waters of northern Florida

☐ **+Hooded merganser** (*Lophodytes cucullatus*)—uncommon migrant and winter visitor; varied coastal and inland wetlands

☐ **Red-breasted merganser** (*Mergus serrator*)—common migrant and winter visitor, some summer; ocean and bays, occasionally lakes

☐ **+Ruddy duck** (*Oxyura jamaicensis*)—variably common migrant and winter visitor; ponds, bays, inland impoundments

☐ **Masked duck** (*Oxyura dominica*)—very rare winter visitor; freshwater marshes in southern Florida

Hawks, Falcons, Kites, and Other Raptors

☐ **+Black vulture** (*Coragyps atratus*)—locally common resident; many habitats

☐ **+Turkey vulture** (*Cathartes aura*)—abundant winter visitor, fewer resident; many habitats

☐ **+Osprey** (*Pandion haliaetus*)—fairly common resident and migrant; bays, canals, and ponds

☐ **+American swallow-tailed kite** (*Elanoides forficatus*)—common spring and summer breeder; wet and dry woodlands

☐ **+White-tailed kite** (*Elanus leucurus*)—very rare resident; dried-out sawgrass prairies, pasturelands

☐ **+Snail kite** (*Rostrhamus sociabilis*)—variably uncommon resident; freshwater marshes, primarily Kissimmee–Okeechobee-Everglades region E

☐ **Mississippi kite** (*Ictinia mississippiensis*)—rare spring and fall migrant

☐ **+Bald eagle** (*Haliaeetus leucocephalus*)—fairly common resident; mainly bays and large lakes (formerly E)

☐ **Northern harrier** (*Circus cyaneus*)—common migrant and winter visitor; agricultural fields and marshes

☐ **Sharp-shinned hawk** (*Accipiter striatus*)—common migrant, uncommon winter visitor; woodlands

☐ **+Cooper's hawk** (*Accipiter cooperii*)—uncommon resident and winter visitor; woodlands

☐ **+Red-shouldered hawk** (*Buteo lineatus*)—common resident; woodlands and edges

☐ **Broad-winged hawk** (*Buteo platypterus*)—common migrant and rare winter visitor; fields and edges

☐ **+Short-tailed hawk** (*Buteo brachyurus*)—uncommon fall and winter visitor south of L. Okeechobee, resident most of peninsula; woodlands, usually near grasslands or marshes

☐ **Swainson's hawk** (*Buteo swainsoni*)—rare winter visitor; open habitats

☐ **+Red-tailed hawk** (*Buteo jamaicensis*)—common migrant and winter visitor, common summer resident; open habitats

☐ **Golden eagle** (*Aquila chrysaetos*)—very rare winter visitor; chiefly northern Florida

☐ **+Crested caracara** (*Caracara plancus*)—uncommon resident; prairies and cattle ranches north and west of L. Okeechobee

☐ **+American kestrel** (*Falco sparverius*)—common migrant and winter visitor throughout, also former or rare breeder (southern peninsula); fields and edges

☐ **Merlin** (*Falco columbarius*)—fairly common migrant and uncommon winter visitor; chiefly near coasts

☐ **Peregrine falcon** (*Falco peregrinus*)—fairly common migrant and uncommon winter visitor; chiefly near coasts E

Turkeys and Quails

☐ **+Wild turkey** (*Meleagris gallopavo*)—locally common resident; undisturbed woodlands

☐ **+Northern bobwhite** (*Colinus virginianus*)—common resident; chiefly old fields, groves, and pinelands

Rails, Limpkins, and Cranes

☐ **Yellow rail** (*Coturnicops noveboracensis*)—rare winter visitor; shallow freshwater and saltwater marshes

☐ **+Black rail** (*Laterallus jamaicensis*)—resident and winter migrant; extensive damp freshwater and saltwater marshes

☐ **+Clapper rail** (*Rallus longirostris*)—common resident and winter visitor; mangroves and salt marshes

☐ **+King rail** (*Rallus elegans*)—uncommon resident and winter visitor; freshwater marshes

☐ **Virginia rail** (*Rallus limicola*)—rare winter visitor; freshwater marshes

☐ **Sora** (*Porzana carolina*)—common migrant and uncommon winter visitor; freshwater marshes and concealed margins

☐ **+Purple gallinule** (*Porphyrula martinica*)—variably common migrant and local resident; freshwater marshes

☐ **+Common moorhen** (*Gallinula chloropus*)—common resident; fresh and brackish water ponds and marshes

☐ **+American coot** (*Fulica americana*)—variably common migrant and abundant winter visitor, uncommon in summer; bays, ponds, and marshes

☐ **+Limpkin** (*Aramus guarauna*)—locally common resident; freshwater swamps and margins

☐ **+Sandhill crane** (*Grus canadensis*)—locally common resident (Florida Sandhill Crane) and winter visitor (Greater Sandhill Crane); prairies, marshes, and ranch lands

☐ **Whooping crane** (*Grus americana*)—extirpated in Florida; reintroduced by wildlife authorities in 1993 at Three Lakes Wildlife Management Area

Plovers, Sandpipers, and Other Shorebirds

☐ **Black-bellied plover** (*Pluvialis squatarola*)—common migrant and winter visitor, some summer; coastal and interior shallow water, fields, and lake shores

☐ **Lesser golden-plover** (*Pluvialis dominica*)—rare migrant; usually interior fields or coastal

☐ **+Snowy plover** (*Charadrius alexandrinus*)—rare winter visitor, former or rare breeder; undisturbed sandy beaches, chiefly Gulf coast

☐ **+Wilson's plover** (*Charadrius wilsonia*)—locally common resident; coastal beaches, spoil banks, and mud flats

☐ **Semipalmated plover** (*Charadrius semipalmatus*)—com-mon migrant and winter visitor; coastal flats, sometimes inland

☐ **Piping plover** (*Charadrius melodus*)—uncommon migrant and winter visitor; saltwater banks, occasionally pond edges, chiefly Gulf coast

☐ **+Killdeer** (*Charadrius vociferus*)—common resident and winter visitor; agricultural fields and freshwater margins

☐ **+American oystercatcher** (*Haematopus palliatus*)—locally common resident and winter visitor; saltwater flats, chiefly Gulf coast of central and southern Florida

☐ **+Black-necked stilt** (*Himantopus mexicanus*)—uncommon to locally abundant summer breeder, uncommon and local in winter; chiefly shallow fresh water and flooded agricultural fields

☐ **American avocet** (*Recurvirostra americana*)—uncommon migrant and winter visitor; usually coastal flats, occasionally flooded fields

☐ **Greater yellowlegs** (*Tringa melanoleuca*)—common migrant, less common winter visitor; coastal and inland flats and margins

☐ **Lesser yellowlegs** (*Tringa flavipes*)—common migrant, less common winter visitor; coastal and inland flats and margins

☐ **Solitary sandpiper** (*Tringa solitaria*)—uncommon migrant, rare winter visitor; freshwater margins

☐ **+Willet** (*Catoptrophorus semipalmatus*)—common migrant and winter visitor, less common in summer; chiefly salt marshes and flats

☐ **Spotted sandpiper** (*Actitis macularia*)—fairly common migrant and winter visitor; saltwater or freshwater margins

☐ **Upland sandpiper** (*Bartramia longicauda*)—uncommon migrant; fields, sod farms, and airports

☐ **Whimbrel** (*Numenius phaeopus*)—uncommon migrant and winter visitor, occasionally summer; beaches and saltwater flats

☐ **Long-billed curlew** (*Numenius americanus*)—rare winter visitor; saltwater flats, chiefly Gulf coast

☐ **Marbled godwit** (*Limosa fedoa*)—common migrant and winter visitor; saltwater beaches and mud flats, chiefly Gulf coast

☐ **Ruddy turnstone** (*Arenaria interpres*)—common migrant and winter visitor, some summer; beaches and rocky areas

☐ **Red knot** (*Calidris canutus*)—common to abundant migrant, common winter and summer visitor; beaches, salt ponds, and flats, chiefly Gulf coast

☐ **Sanderling** (*Calidris alba*)—common migrant and winter visitor, some summer; beaches

☐ **Semipalmated sandpiper** (*Calidris pusilla*)—common migrant, rare winter visitor; flats and margins

☐ **Western sandpiper** (*Calidris mauri*)—abundant migrant and winter visitor, uncommon summer visitor; flats and margins, chiefly salt water

☐ **Least sandpiper** (*Calidris minutilla*)—common migrant and winter visitor; flats and margins, fresh and salt water

☐ **White-rumped sandpiper** (*Calidris fuscicollis*)—uncommon migrant (more common in spring); beaches, flats, lawns, and grassy areas

☐ **Baird's sandpiper** (*Calidris bairdii*)—very rare migrant; usually fields and freshwater margins

☐ **Pectoral sandpiper** (*Calidris melanotos*)—common migrant, rare winter visitor; fields, flats, and margins (usually fresh water)

☐ **Purple sandpiper** (*Calidris maritima*)—rare winter visitor; rock jetties, Atlantic

☐ **Dunlin** (*Calidris alpina*)—abundant migrant and winter visitor, uncommon in summer; flats and margins (usually salt water)

☐ **Stilt sandpiper** (*Calidris himantopus*)—uncommon migrant, usually rare in winter; flats and shallow ponds (often fresh water)

☐ **Buff-breasted sandpiper** (*Tryngites subruficollis*)—rare to uncommon migrant, chiefly fall; coastal and inland

☐ **Short-billed dowitcher** (*Limnodromus griseus*)—abundant migrant and winter visitor, uncommon summer visitor; chiefly flats and shallow salt ponds

☐ **Long-billed dowitcher** (*Limnodromus scolopaceus*)—variably common migrant and winter visitor; usually shallow freshwater ponds

☐ **Common snipe** (*Gallinago gallinago*)—fairly common migrant, less common in winter; freshwater margins

☐ **+American woodcock** (*Scolopax minor*)—uncommon migrant and winter visitor, some breed; wet forests, old fields

☐ **Wilson's phalarope** (*Phalaropus tricolor*)—uncommon migrant; freshwater margins

☐ **Red-necked phalarope** (*Phalaropus lobatus*)—rare migrant or winter visitor; usually pelagic, sometimes ashore

☐ **Red phalarope** (*Phalaropus fulicaria*)—rare to locally common migrant and winter visitor; usually pelagic, rarely ashore

Gulls and Terns

☐ **Pomarine jaeger** (*Stercorarius pomarinus*)—fairly common migrant; usually pelagic, chiefly Atlantic

☐ **Parasitic jaeger** (*Stercorarius parasiticus*)—fairly common migrant, some may winter or summer; usually pelagic, sometimes coastal

☐ **Long-tailed jaeger** (*Stercorarius longicaudus*)—rare migrant, usually pelagic

☐ **+Laughing gull** (*Larus atricilla*)—abundant resident; chiefly coasts and bays, sometimes inland

☐ **Franklin's gull** (*Larus pipixcan*)—rare migrant and winter visitor; mainly coasts

☐ **Bonaparte's gull** (*Larus philadelphia*)—variably uncommon migrant and winter visitor; usually coasts, bays, and interior lakes

☐ **Ring-billed gull** (*Larus delawarensis*)—abundant migrant and winter visitor, some immatures summer; coasts, bays, and inland ponds and fields

☐ **Herring gull** (*Larus argentatus*)—common migrant and winter visitor, some immatures summer; coasts, bays, and lakes

☐ **Lesser black-backed gull** (*Larus fuscus*)—uncommon winter visitor; coasts, bays, and landfills

☐ **Glaucous gull** (*Larus hyperboreus*)—rare winter visitor; coasts

☐ **Great black-backed gull** (*Larus marinus*)—uncommon winter visitor; coasts and landfills, especially Atlantic coast

☐ **Black-legged kittiwake** (*Rissa tridactyla*)—uncommon (Atlantic) to rare (Gulf) winter visitor; coasts and offshore

☐ **+Gull-billed tern** (*Sterna nilotica*)—locally common summer breeder; salt marshes and flats, freshwater lakes

☐ **+Caspian tern** (*Sterna caspia*)—common migrant and winter visitor, some resident; lakes, marshes, and estuaries

☐ **+Royal tern** (*Sterna maxima*)—abundant migrant and winter visitor, many summer (nest Tampa Bay area, Merritt Island); coasts and occasionally inland lakes

☐ **+Sandwich tern** (*Sterna sandvicensis*)—abundant migrant and uncommon winter visitor, locally common in summer (nest Tampa Bay area; coasts (chiefly Gulf) and inland lakes

☐ **Roseate tern** (*Sterna dougallii*)—rare migrant; coastal

☐ **Common tern** (*Sterna hirundo*)—fairly common migrant, rare winter visitor; coasts and rarely inland

☐ **Forster's tern** (*Sterna forsteri*)—common migrant and abundant winter visitor, some summer; coastal marshes and bays, occasionally inland lakes

☐ **+Least tern** (*Sterna antillarum*)—fairly common spring and summer breeder, leaves in winter; coastal and inland, nests on urban rooftops

☐ **Bridled tern** (*Sterna anaethetus*)—uncommon spring to early fall visitor; pelagic

☐ **Sooty tern** (*Sterna fuscata*)—variably uncommon spring to fall visitor, absent late fall and winter; pelagic

☐ **Black tern** (*Chlidonias niger*)—locally common migrant and summer visitor (very rare in winter); inland and coastal wetlands

☐ **Brown noddy** (*Anous stolidus*)—rare to uncommon summer visitor; pelagic

☐ **+Black skimmer** (*Rynchops nigra*)—locally common resident; coastal flats and spoil islands, inland lakes

Doves and Pigeons

☐ ***Rock dove** (*Columba livia*)—abundant resident; urban areas

☐ **White-crowned pigeon** (*Columba leucocephala*)—rare (a few straggle north to Lee and St. Lucie counties; around fruiting trees

☐ ***Eurasian collared-dove** (*Streptopelia decaocto*)—locally abundant (and increasing) resident statwide; suburbs

☐ ***White-winged dove** (*Zenaida asiatica*)—locally uncommon resident; groves and suburban areas, common in Lake Placid; probably introduced

☐ **+Mourning dove** (*Zenaida macroura*)—abundant resident; open areas, suburbs

☐ **+Common ground-dove** (*Columbina passerina*)—locally common resident; fields and suburbs

Parakeets

☐ ***Budgerigar** (*Melopsittacus undulatus*)—locally common from Tampa to Fort Myers and southward from St. Lucie Co.; suburban and urban areas

☐ ***Monk parakeet** (*Myiopsitta monachus*)—locally common resident; suburban areas with fruiting trees

☐ ***Canary-winged parakeet** (*Brotogeris versicolurus*)—locally uncommon resident; suburbs, mainly Tampa area

Cuckoos and Anis

☐ **Black-billed cuckoo** (*Coccyzus erythropthalmus*)—rare migrant; woodlands

☐ **+Yellow-billed cuckoo** (*Coccyzus americanus*)—common migrant and uncommon summer breeder; woodlands

☐ **+Mangrove cuckoo** (*Coccyzus minor*)—uncommon resident, seldom seen in fall and winter; hammocks and mangroves, chiefly Gulf coast from Anclote Key southward

☐ **+Smooth-billed ani** (*Crotophaga ani*)—local and declining uncommon resident; brushy areas, chiefly southern half of Florida

☐ **Groove-billed ani** (*Crotophaga sulcirostris*)—rare winter visitor; brushy areas

Owls

☐ **+Barn owl** (*Tyto alba*)—common resident and winter visitor; often nest and roost in unused buildings

☐ **+Eastern screech-owl** (*Otus asio*)—common resident; many habitats, including suburbs

☐ **+Great horned owl** (*Bubo virginianus*)—common resident; chiefly pine woodlands, but many habitats

☐ **+Burrowing owl** (*Speotyto cunicularia*)—locally common resident; airports, campuses, and other open grassy areas

☐ **+Barred owl** (*Strix varia*)—common resident; mesic woodlands

☐ **Long-eared owl** (*Asio otus*)—rare winter visitor

☐ **Short-eared owl** (*Asio flammeus*)—rare winter and spring visitor; grassy marshes and fields

Nightjars

☐ **+Common nighthawk** (*Chordeiles minor*)—common migrant and summer breeder; open areas and urban rooftops

☐ **+Chuck-will's-widow** (*Caprimulgus carolinensis*)—common migrant and uncommon winter visitor, fairly common summer breeder; woodlands

☐ **Whip-poor-will** (*Caprimulgus vociferus*)—common migrant and winter visitor; woodlands

Swifts

☐ **+Chimney swift** (*Chaetura pelagica*)—fairly common migrant and uncommon summer breeder; suburbs

Hummingbirds

☐ **+Ruby-throated hummingbird** (*Archilochus colubris*)—common migrant and winter visitor, uncommon breeding resident; around flowering plants near coasts

☐ **Black-chinned hummingbird** (*Archilochus alexandri*)—rare winter visitor

Kingfishers

☐ **+Belted kingfisher** (*Ceryle alcyon*)—common late summer to spring visitor (rare resident in northern central Florida); many types of freshwater and saltwater areas

Woodpeckers

☐ **+Red-headed woodpecker** (*Melanerpes erythrocephalus*)—uncommon resident; pine-oak woodlands

☐ **+Red-bellied woodpecker** (*Melanerpes carolinus*)—common resident; suburbs and wooded areas

☐ **Yellow-bellied sapsucker** (*Sphyrapicus varius*)—uncommon to fairly common migrant and winter visitor; suburbs and wooded areas

☐ **+Downy woodpecker** (*Picoides pubescens*)—fairly common resident; suburbs and wooded areas

☐ **+Hairy woodpecker** (*Picoides villosus*)—rare resident; pinelands

☐ **+Red-cockaded woodpecker** (*Picoides borealis*)—rare resident; old-growth pinelands E

☐ **+Northern flicker** (*Colaptes auratus*)—common resident and winter visitor; suburbs and wooded areas

☐ **+Pileated woodpecker** (*Dryocopus pileatus*)—uncommon resident; suburbs and wooded areas

Flycatchers

☐ **+Eastern wood-pewee** (*Contopus virens*)—uncommon migrant and summer breeder; pine and pine-oak woodlands

☐ **Yellow-bellied flycatcher** (*Empidonax flaviventris*)—rare migrant, chiefly fall; hardwood swamps and thickets, chiefly Gulf coast

☐ **+Acadian flycatcher** (*Empidonax virescens*)—variably common summer breeder; swamps, northern and central Florida

☐ **Willow flycatcher** (*Empidonax traillii*)—status uncertain (hard to distinguish from Alder (*E. alnorum*), rare migrant?, chiefly fall; swamps

☐ **Least flycatcher** (*Empidonax minimus*)—uncommon migrant and winter visitor; second growth, edges, *Ludwigia* thickets

☐ **Eastern phoebe** (*Sayornis phoebe*)—common fall and winter visitor; suburban and wooded areas, utility wires

☐ **Vermilion flycatcher** (*Pyrocephalus rubinus*)—rare winter visitor; hardwoods near lake shores

☐ **+Great crested flycatcher** (*Myiarchus crinitus*)—common migrant and summer resident, rare winter visitor in central Florida, common winter visitor in south Florida; suburbs and wooded areas

☐ **La Sagra's flycatcher** (*Myiarchus sagrae*)—very rare winter visitor and spring migrant; Atlantic coastal hammocks

☐ **Western kingbird** (*Tyrannus verticalis*)—variably uncommon migrant and winter visitor; open areas, usually near coasts

☐ **+Eastern kingbird** (*Tyrannus tyrannus*)—uncommon spring migrant and summer breeder; woodland edges, utility wires

☐ **+Gray kingbird** (*Tyrannus dominicensis*)—uncommon migrant and common summer breeder; suburbs and wooded areas, chiefly near mangroves

☐ **Scissor-tailed flycatcher** (*Tyrannus forficatus*)—locally uncommon migrant and winter visitor; open areas around fruiting trees, utility wires

Swallows

☐ **+Purple martin** (*Progne subis*)—common summer breeder, spring and fall migrant; open areas, mostly nests in man-made nesting structures (usually near water)

☐ **Tree swallow** (*Tachycineta bicolor*)—variably abundant late fall through early spring visitor; marshes and open areas

☐ **+Northern rough-winged swallow** (*Stelgidopteryx serripennis*)—common migrant and uncommon summer breeder (in holes near water); open areas

☐ **Bank swallow** (*Riparia riparia*)—uncommon spring, common late summer and fall migrant; open areas

☐ **+Cliff swallow** (*Hirundo pyrrhonota*)—rare to uncommon migrant; open areas

☐ **+Barn swallow** (*Hirundo rustica*)—abundant migrant and rare summer breeder; open areas, under highway bridges over water

Jays and Crows

☐ **+Blue jay** (*Cyanocitta cristata*)—common resident; suburbs and wooded areas

☐ **+Scrub jay** (*Aphelocoma coerulescens*)—uncommon resident; scrub areas

☐ **+American crow** (*Corvus brachyrhynchos*)—common resident; wilder wooded areas, prairies

☐ **+Fish crow** (*Corvus ossifragus*)—common to abundant resident; suburbs, chiefly near coasts

Chickadees and Titmice

☐ **+Carolina chickadee** (*Parus carolinensis*)—uncommon resident; woodlands

☐ **+Tufted titmouse** (*Parus bicolor*)—common resident; many habitats

Nuthatches

☐ **+White-breasted nuthatch** (*Sitta carolinensis*)—rare resident; woodlands

☐ **+Brown-headed nuthatch** (*Sitta pusilla*)—rare resident; pinelands

Creepers

☐ **Brown creeper** (*Certhia americana*)—rare winter visitor; open pinelands

Wrens

☐ **+Carolina wren** (*Thryothorus ludovicianus*)—abundant resident; woodlands

☐ **House wren** (*Troglodytes aedon*)—common migrant and winter visitor; suburban and brushy areas

☐ **Winter wren** (*Troglodytes troglodytes*)—rare winter visitor; woodlands

☐ **Sedge wren** (*Cistothorus platensis*)—variably uncommon winter visitor; coastal and inland marshes

☐ **+Marsh wren** (*Cistothorus palustris*)—variably uncommon winter visitor and summer breeder; coastal reedy marshes

Kinglets and Gnatcatchers

☐ **Ruby-crowned kinglet** (*Regulus calendula*)—uncommon winter visitor; woodlands

☐ **+Blue-gray gnatcatcher** (*Polioptila caerulea*)—common migrant, winter visitor, and summer breeder; suburbs and woodlands

Thrushes and Allies

☐ **+Eastern bluebird** (*Sialia sialis*)—uncommon resident and common winter visitor; pine-oak woodland edges

☐ **Veery** (*Catharus fuscescens*)—variably uncommon migrant; mixed hardwoods

☐ **Gray-cheeked thrush** (*Catharus minimus*)—variably uncommon migrant; woodlands and swamps, chiefly Gulf coast

☐ **Swainson's thrush** (*Catharus ustulatus*)—variably uncommon migrant; woodlands and swamps

☐ **Hermit thrush** (*Catharus guttatus*)—variably common winter visitor; woodlands and thickets

☐ **Wood thrush** (*Hylocichla mustelina*)—variably uncommon migrant, rare in winter; woodlands

☐ **+American robin** (*Turdus migratorius*)—variably abundant winter visitor; suburbs and wooded areas

Mockingbirds, Thrashers, and Allies

☐ **Gray catbird** (*Dumetella carolinensis*)—abundant migrant and common winter visitor; brushy areas and thickets
☐ **+Northern mockingbird** (*Mimus polyglottos*)—abundant resident; suburbs and open wooded areas
☐ **+Brown thrasher** (*Toxostoma rufum*)—uncommon resident and common winter visitor; brushy wooded edges

Pipits

☐ **American pipit** (*Anthus rubescens*)—variably uncommon winter visitor; fields

Waxwings

☐ **Cedar waxwing** (*Bombycilla cedrorum*)—variably common winter and spring visitor; in fruiting trees

Shrikes

☐ **+Loggerhead shrike** (*Lanius ludovicianus*)—uncommon resident and common winter visitor; open areas with brushy edges, agricultural fields

Starlings and Mynas

☐ ***European starling** (*Sturnus vulgaris*)—abundant resident; suburbs
☐ ***Common myna** (*Acridotheres tristis*)—locally uncommon resident; chiefly large parking lots

Vireos

☐ **+White-eyed vireo** (*Vireo griseus*)—common migrant, winter visitor, and resident; brushy woodlands

- [ ] **Bell's vireo** (*Vireo bellii*)—rare migrant and winter visitor; brushy woodlands
- [ ] **Solitary vireo** (*Vireo solitarius*)—variably common migrant and winter visitor; woodlands
- [ ] **+Yellow-throated vireo** (*Vireo flavifrons*)—uncommon migrant and rare winter visitor, common summer resident; woodlands
- [ ] **Warbling vireo** (*Vireo gilvus*)—rare migrant, chiefly spring; chiefly Gulf coast
- [ ] **Philadelphia vireo** (*Vireo philadelphicus*)—rare migrant; chiefly on Gulf coast
- [ ] **+Red-eyed vireo** (*Vireo olivaceus*)—common migrant and summer breeding visitor; mesic woodlands
- [ ] **+Black-whiskered vireo** (*Vireo altiloquus*)—common summer breeding visitor (absent in winter); coastal woodlands, mangroves

Warblers

- [ ] **Blue-winged warbler** (*Vermivora pinus*)—variably uncommon migrant and rare winter visitor; woodlands
- [ ] **Golden-winged warbler** (*Vermivora chrysoptera*)—rare migrant; woodlands
- [ ] **Tennessee warbler** (*Vermivora peregrina*)—abundant fall and common spring migrant; brushy woodlands
- [ ] **Orange-crowned warbler** (*Vermivora celata*)—fairly common winter visitor; brushy woodlands
- [ ] **Nashville warbler** (*Vermivora ruficapilla*)—variably uncommon migrant and rare winter visitor; brushy woodlands
- [ ] **+Northern parula** (*Parula americana*)—common migrant and winter visitor, summer breeder; mesic woodlands
- [ ] **Yellow warbler** (*Dendroica petechia*)—common fall and uncommon spring migrant; willows, old fields
- [ ] **Chestnut-sided warbler** (*Dendroica pensylvanica*)—uncommon migrant (chiefly fall and along Gulf coast); old fields, woodlands
- [ ] **Magnolia warbler** (*Dendroica magnolia*)—variably common migrant and rare winter visitor; woodlands
- [ ] **Cape May warbler** (*Dendroica tigrina*)—abundant migrant, rare winter visitor; in flowering and fruiting trees

☐ **Black-throated blue warbler** (*Dendroica caerulescens*)—common migrant and rare winter visitor; woodlands

☐ **Yellow-rumped warbler** (*Dendroica coronata*)—variably abundant winter visitor; brushy and wooded areas

☐ **Black-throated gray warbler** (*Dendroica nigrescens*)—rare migrant and winter visitor; woodlands

☐ **Black-throated green warbler** (*Dendroica virens*)—variably uncommon migrant and rare winter visitor; woodlands

☐ **Blackburnian warbler** (*Dendroica fusca*)—uncommon migrant; woodlands

☐ **+Yellow-throated warbler** (*Dendroica dominica*)—common migrant and winter visitor, some resident; woodlands and palms

☐ **+Pine warbler** (*Dendroica pinus*)—common resident and common winter visitor; pine woodlands

☐ **+Prairie warbler** (*Dendroica discolor*)—common resident (in mangroves), common migrant and uncommon winter visitor; brushy woodlands

☐ **Palm warbler** (*Dendroica palmarum*)—abundant migrant and winter visitor; brushy areas and lawns

☐ **Bay-breasted warbler** (*Dendroica castanea*)—variably uncommon migrant; deciduous woodlands

☐ **Blackpoll warbler** (*Dendroica striata*)—uncommon spring and abundant fall migrant; woodlands

☐ **Cerulean warbler** (*Dendroica cerulea*)—rare migrant; mesic woodlands, swamps

☐ **Black-and-white warbler** (*Mniotilta varia*)—common migrant and fairly common winter visitor; woodlands

☐ **American redstart** (*Setophaga ruticilla*)—common migrant and fairly rare winter visitor; woodlands

☐ **+Prothonotary warbler** (*Protonotaria citrea*)—fairly common migrant and rare winter visitor, summer breeding visitor; cypress and hardwood swamps

☐ **Worm-eating warbler** (*Helmitheros vermivorus*)—common migrant and very rare winter visitor; brushy woodlands

☐ **Swainson's warbler** (*Limnothlypis swainsonii*)—uncommon migrant; on damp leaf litter, usually near coasts

☐ **Ovenbird** (*Seiurus aurocapillus*)—common migrant and uncommon winter visitor; woodlands

☐ **Northern waterthrush** (*Seiurus noveboracensis*)—common migrant and uncommon winter visitor; damp margins, woodlands near water, and mangroves

☐ **Louisiana waterthrush** (*Seiurus motacilla*)—uncommon migrant and rare winter visitor; slightly damp margins, usually fresh water

☐ **Kentucky warbler** (*Oporornis formosus*)—rare migrant; woodlands, chiefly Gulf coast

☐ **Connecticut warbler** (*Oporornis agilis*)—uncommon spring and rare fall migrant, mostly Atlantic coast; brushy leaf litter

☐ **Mourning warbler** (*Oporornis philadelphia*)—rare migrant, chiefly fall; brushy areas

☐ **+Common yellowthroat** (*Geothlypis trichas*)—common migrant and common winter visitor, fairly common summer breeder; marshes, wet prairies, and moist brushy areas

☐ **Hooded warbler** (*Wilsonia citrina*)—uncommon migrant and rare winter visitor; woodlands

☐ **Wilson's warbler** (*Wilsonia pusilla*)—variably uncommon migrant and very rare winter visitor; brushy areas

☐ **Canada warbler** (*Wilsonia canadensis*)—variably uncommon migrant; dense woodlands, chiefly Gulf coast

☐ **+Yellow-breasted chat** (*Icteria virens*)—variably uncommon migrant and rare winter visitor; brushy areas

Tanagers

☐ **+Summer tanager** (*Piranga rubra*)—uncommon migrant and rare winter visitor, summer breeding visitor; pine-oak woodlands

☐ **Scarlet tanager** (*Piranga olivacea*)—variably uncommon migrant; deciduous woodlands

☐ **Western tanager** (*Piranga ludoviciana*)—rare winter visitor

Cardinals, Grosbeaks, and Buntings

☐ **+Northern cardinal** (*Cardinalis cardinalis*)—common resident; suburbs and wooded areas

☐ **Rose-breasted grosbeak** (*Pheucticus ludovicianus*)—variably uncommon migrant; woodlands

☐ **+Blue grosbeak** (*Guiraca caerulea*)—variably uncommon migrant and rare winter visitor; brushy areas

☐ **+Indigo bunting** (*Passerina cyanea*)—common migrant and uncommon winter visitor; brushy areas

☐ **+Painted bunting** (*Passerina ciris*)—common migrant and winter visitor, breeds in northern Florida; brushy areas

☐ **Dickcissel** (*Spiza americana*)—uncommon migrant and rare winter visitor; brushy areas

Towhees and Sparrows

☐ **+Rufous-sided towhee** (*Pipilo erythrophthalmus*)—common resident and winter visitor; chiefly pine woodlands and scrub

☐ **+Bachman's sparrow** (*Aimophila aestivalis*)—uncommon resident; pinelands, palmettos, and scrub

☐ **Chipping sparrow** (*Spizella passerina*)—variably common migrant and winter visitor; brushy areas and lawns

☐ **Clay-colored sparrow** (*Spizella pallida*)—uncommon to rare migrant and winter visitor; brushy areas

☐ **Field sparrow** (*Spizella pusilla*)—uncommon migrant and winter visitor; brushy areas

☐ **Vesper sparrow** (*Pooecetes gramineus*)—uncommon migrant and winter visitor; brushy fallow fields

☐ **Lark sparrow** (*Chondestes grammacus*)—variably rare migrant and winter visitor; brushy areas

☐ **Savannah sparrow** (*Passerculus sandwichensis*)—common migrant and winter visitor; grasslands

☐ **+Grasshopper sparrow** (*Ammodramus savannarum*)—rare resident, uncommon migrant and winter visitor; brushy fallow fields [Florida grasshopper sparrow *A. s. floridanus* E]

☐ **Le Conte's sparrow** (*Ammodramus leconteii*)—rare winter visitor; grassy fields

☐ **Sharp-tailed sparrow** (*Ammodramus caudacutus*)—locally common winter visitor; salt marshes

☐ **+Seaside sparrow** (*Ammodramus maritimus*)—uncommon resident, common winter visitor; salt marshes [Cape Sable seaside sparrow *A. m. maritimus* E]

☐ **Fox sparrow** (*Passerella iliaca*)—uncommon winter visitor (absent southern half Florida); dense undergrowth in forests and brushy areas

☐ **Song sparrow** (*Melospiza melodia*)—rare to uncommon winter visitor; fields and edges

☐ **Lincoln's sparrow** (*Melospiza lincolnii*)—uncommon migrant and winter visitor; brushy areas

☐ **Swamp sparrow** (*Melospiza georgiana*)—common winter visitor; swampy areas

☐ **White-throated sparrow** (*Zonotrichia albicollis*)—common winter visitor; brushy areas, many habitats

☐ **White-crowned sparrow** (*Zonotrichia leucophrys*)—locally uncommon migrant and winter visitor; brushy areas

☐ **Dark-eyed junco** (*Junco hyemalis*)—rare migrant and uncommon winter visitor (latter northern Florida); open woodlands, fields

Blackbirds and Orioles

☐ **Bobolink** (*Dolichonyx oryzivorus*)—common migrant; fields and agricultural areas

☐ **+Red-winged blackbird** (*Agelaius phoeniceus*)—abundant resident and winter visitor; brushy fields and marshes

☐ **+Eastern meadowlark** (*Sturnella magna*)—common resident and winter visitor; fields

☐ **Yellow-headed blackbird** (*Xanthocephalus xanthocephalus*)—rare migrant and winter visitor; fields and marshes

☐ **Rusty blackbird** (*Euphagus carolinus*)—rare winter visitor; many habitats

☐ **Brewer's blackbird** (*Euphagus cyanocephalus*)—rare winter visitor; fields

☐ **+Boat-tailed grackle** (*Quiscalus major*)—abundant resident; marshes and fields

☐ **+Common grackle** (*Quiscalus quiscula*)—common resident and abundant winter visitor; suburbs and fields

☐ **+Shiny cowbird** (*Molothrus bonariensis*)—Uncommon resident; suburbs and fields

☐ **Bronzed cowbird** (*Molothrus aeneus*)—rare winter visitor; open areas

☐ **+Brown-headed cowbird** (*Molothrus ater*)—common migrant and winter visitor, some breed; fields and edges

☐ **Orchard oriole** (*Icterus spurius*)—variably common migrant; woodlands

☐ ***Spot-breasted oriole** (*Icterus pectoralis*)—uncommon resident; suburbs with fruiting trees, chiefly Atlantic coastal counties from Brevard to Dade

☐ **Northern oriole** (*Icterus galbula*)—common (chiefly spring) migrant, rare winter visitor; wooded areas

Finches

☐ **House finch** (*Carpodacus mexicanus*)—rare winter visitor

☐ **Purple finch** (*Carpodacus purpureus*)—rare winter visitor; feeders, woodlands, chiefly northern Florida

☐ **Pine siskin** (*Carduelis pinus*)—variably rare winter visitor; wooded edges

☐ **American goldfinch** (*Carduelis tristis*)—variably uncommon winter visitor; wooded edges, old fields

Old World Sparrows

☐ ***House sparrow** (*Passer domesticus*)—common resident; urban areas

MAMMAL CHECKLIST

Marsupials

☐ **Opossum** (*Didelphis virginiana pigra*)—abundant; most habitats, including urban

Insectivores

☐ **Southeastern shrew** (*Sorex longirostris longirostris, S.l. eionis*)—rare?; many habitats, preferably moist, in peninsula south to Highlands Co. area

- [ ] Short-tailed shrew (*Blarina carolinensis (brevicauda) carolinensis, B.c. peninsulae*)—common; many habitats, statewide except Everglades
- [ ] **Sherman's short-tailed shrew** (*Blarina carolinensis shermani*)—status unknown; southwest Florida
- [ ] **Least shrew** (*Cryptotis parva floridana*)—common; grassy and brushy areas and marshes statewide
- [ ] **Eastern mole** (*Scalopus aquaticus anastasae, S. a. bassi, S. a. parvus, S. a. porteri*)—common to abundant; moist lawns and pine flatwoods statewide except southwest

Bats

- [ ] **Southeastern brown bat** (*Myotis austroriparius*)—abundant; primarily in caves (also trees) in northern Florida south to Volusia and Sarasota counties
- [ ] **Eastern pipistrelle** (*Pipistrellus subflavus floridanus*)—uncommon to common; in caves, trees, and crevices (rocks, structures) in peninsula
- [ ] **Big brown bat** (*Eptesicus fuscus fuscus*)—rare; in buildings and trees in northern and central Florida to Lake Okeechobee
- [ ] **Seminole bat** (*Nycteris seminola*)—rare to common; in trees and Spanish moss south to Miami, except extreme southwestern Florida
- [ ] **Northern yellow bat** (*Nycteris intermedia floridana*)—uncommon to abundant; in trees and Spanish moss statewide except extreme southwest
- [ ] **Red bat** (*Nycteris borealis borealis*)—common; in trees and Spanish moss or caves in northern and north central Florida
- [ ] **Evening bat** (*Nycticeius humeralis subtropicalis*)—common; in trees and buildings in south central and southern peninsula
- [ ] **Hoary bat** (*Nycteris cinerea cinerea*)—common; in trees in northern and north central Florida
- [ ] **Rafinesque's big-eared bat** (*Plecotus rafinesquii macrotis*)—status unknown; in caves and buildings in forested wetlands statewide
- [ ] **Brazilian free-tailed bat** (*Tadarida brasiliensis cynocephala*)—status unknown (probably common); in buildings, trees, and crevices (rocks, structures) statewide

☐ **Florida mastiff bat** (*Eumops glaucinus floridanus*)—rare; in buildings and trees in Broward, Charlotte, and Dade counties (the most restricted range of any Florida mammal) E

Edentates

☐ ***Nine-banded armadillo** (*Dasypus novemcinctus mexicanus*)—abundant; drier areas statewide, except extreme southwest

Lagomorphs

☐ **Marsh rabbit** (*Sylvilagus palustris paludicola*)—abundant; many habitats (prefers marshes) in peninsula

☐ **Eastern cottontail** (*Sylvilagus floridanus ammophilus, S. f. floridanus, S. f. mallurus,* and *S. f. paulsoni*)—abundant; brushy fields and edges statewide

Rodents

☐ **Gray squirrel** (*Sciurus carolinensis carolinensis, S. c. extimus*)—abundant; woodlands and hammocks statewide except part of central Florida

☐ **Mangrove fox squirrel** (*Sciurus niger avicennia*)—uncommon; mangroves, cypress, and pinelands southwest of Lake Okeechobee

☐ **Sherman's fox squirrel** (*Sciurus niger shermani*)—uncommon; mature longleaf pine–turkey oak sandhills and flatwoods over much of peninsula except southwest of Lake Okeechobee

☐ **Southern flying squirrel** (*Glaucomys volans querceti*)—common to abundant; woodlands of mostly deciduous trees in peninsula

☐ **Southeastern pocket gopher** (*Geomys pinetis austrinus, G. p. floridanus, G. p. goffi*)—common to abundant; dry soils, e.g., longleaf pine-turkey oak-wiregrass communities in drier regions of central and northern Florida

☐ **Marsh rice rat** (*Oryzomys palustris coloratus, O. p. natator, O. p. planirostris, O. p. sanibel*)—abundant; freshwater and saltwater marshes statewide

☐ **Eastern harvest mouse** (*Reithrodontomys humilis humilis*)—common?; fields, marshes, and wet meadows statewide except south and southwest

☐ **Oldfield** (or southeastern beach) **mouse** (*Peromyscus polionotus decoloratus, P. p. niveiventris, P. p. rhoadsi, P. p. subgriseus*)—rare, some subspecies common; coastal dunes and interior sandy ridges

☐ **Cotton mouse** (*Peromyscus gossypinus, P. g.palmarius, P. g. restrictus, P. g. telmaphilus*)—abundant; many habitats statewide

☐ **Florida mouse** (*Peromyscus floridanus*)—uncommon; along coastal uplands and interior xeric uplands in most of peninsula except southwest

☐ **Golden mouse** (*Ochrotomys nuttali floridanus*)—common; many habitats, including forests, thickets, and canebrakes, south to Lake Okeechobee

☐ **Hispid cotton rat** (*Sigmodon hispidus floridanus, S. h. insulicola*)—abundant; fields statewide

☐ **Eastern woodrat** (*Neotoma floridana floridana*)—common; forests and other habitats, south to Vero Beach and Fort Myers

☐ **Round-tailed muskrat** (*Neofiber alleni alleni, N. a. nigrescens, N. a. struix*)—uncommon; marshes and sloughs in most of peninsula

☐ ***Black (Roof) rat** (*Rattus rattus*)—abundant; near development statewide

☐ ***Norway rat** (*Rattus norvegicus*)—common; near development statewide

☐ ***House mouse** (*Mus musculus*)—common; near development statewide

Cetaceans

☐ **Atlantic bottle-nosed dolphin** (*Tursiops truncatus*)—common; shallow marine waters and estuaries of Atlantic and Gulf [Note: other cetaceans are present in our marine waters, but this dolphin is the only species to appear in shallow waters regularly]

Carnivores

☐ **Gray fox** (*Urocyon cinereoargenteus floridanus*)—common; many habitats, including near development statewide

☐ ***Red fox** (*Vulpes vulpes*)—transplanted, uncommon; fields, local in interior, not in southern Florida

☐ **Black bear** (*Ursus americanus floridanus*)—uncommon; uplands in scattered regions across the state (common around Wekiwa Springs and some other areas)

☐ **Raccoon** (*Procyon lotor elucus, P. l. marinus*)—abundant; virtually all habitats statewide

☐ **Long-tailed weasel** (*Mustela frenata peninsulae*)—rare; variety of habitats in central Florida south to Indian River and Collier counties

☐ **Mink** (*Mustela vison evergladensis* and *M. v. lutensis*)—rare; freshwater wetlands (mostly marshes) statewide

☐ **Spotted skunk** (*Spilogale putorius ambarvalis*)—uncommon; palmetto scrub and hammocks statewide

☐ **Striped skunk** (*Mephitis mephitis elongata*)—uncommon; uplands statewide

☐ **River otter** (*Lutra canadensis lataxina*)—common; freshwater wetlands statewide

☐ **Florida panther** (*Felis concolor coryi*)—very rare; pinelands, cypresses, and hammocks in primarily Glades, Hendry, Collier, and Lee counties **E**

☐ **Bobcat** (*Lynx rufus floridanus*)—common; many habitats statewide

Artiodactyls

☐ **White-tailed deer** (*Odocoileus virginianus osceola, O. v. seminolus*)—common to abundant; many habitats statewide

☐ ***Feral hog** (*Sus scrofa*)—abundant; many habitats statewide; nuisance

Sirenians

☐ **West Indian manatee** (*Trichecus manatus latirostris*)—rare; in shallow marine and estuary waters of Gulf and Atlantic coasts, Caloosahatchee and St. Johns Rivers, and St. Lucie Canal **E**

REPTILE CHECKLIST

Crocodilians

☐ **American crocodile** (*Crocodylus acutus*)—rare; coastal mangroves in Lee Co. and southern Broward Co. and south E

☐ **American alligator** (*Alligator mississippiensis*)—abundant; freshwater wetlands and brackish estuaries statewide

Turtles

☐ **Florida snapping turtle** (*Chelydra serpentina osceola*)—common; freshwater marshes and ponds in peninsula

☐ **Alligator snapping turtle** (*Macroclemys temminckii*)—common?; lakes and rivers in panhandle to Chassahowitzka

☐ **Striped mud turtle** (*Kinosternon baurii*)—common; fresh to slightly brackish wetlands in peninsula

☐ **Florida mud turtle** (*Kinosternon subrubrum steindachneri*)— common; freshwater wetlands and salt marshes in peninsula

☐ **Common musk turtle or stinkpot** (*Sternotherus odoratus*)— common; fresh water statewide

☐ **Loggerhead musk turtle** (*Sternotherus minor minor*)—common; clear springs in north central Florida

☐ **Florida box turtle** (*Terrapene carolina bauri*)—common; pinelands and hammocks in peninsula, except large wetland systems

☐ **Gulf Coast box turtle** (*Terrapene carolina major*)—uncommon?; marshes and palmetto–pine woods of Gulf coast around Chassahowitzka and north

☐ **Florida east coast diamondback terrapin** (*Malaclemys terrapin tequesta*)—uncommon; mangroves and salt marshes of Atlantic coast

☐ **Ornate diamondback terrapin** (*Malaclemys terrapin macrospilota*)— uncommon; mangroves and salt marshes of Gulf coast

☐ **Spotted turtle** (*Clemmys guttata*)—rare; shallow freshwater ponds and sloughs south to Polk Co.

☐ **Peninsula cooter** (*Pseudemys floridana peninsularis*)—abundant; variety of aquatic habitats in peninsula

☐ **River cooter** (*Pseudemys concinna suwanniensis*)—rare; limited to few Gulf-side rivers (Withlacoochee, Crystal, Chassahowitzka, and Alafia rivers)

- [ ] **Florida redbelly turtle** (*Pseudemys nelsoni*)—abundant; mostly freshwater wetlands, also mangrove borders in peninsula
- [ ] **Florida chicken turtle** (*Deirochelys reticularia chrysea*)—common; freshwater marshes and ponds in peninsula
- [ ] **Gopher tortoise** (*Gopherus polyphemus*)—locally common but rapidly declining; pinelands and scrub south to Lake Okeechobee, Atlantic coastal ridge to Broward Co.
- [ ] **Atlantic leatherback turtle** (*Dermochelys coriacea*)—rare; in marine waters, nests on Atlantic coast E
- [ ] **Green turtle** (*Chelonia mydas*)—uncommon to rare; in marine waters, nests on Atlantic coast E
- [ ] **Atlantic hawksbill turtle** (*Eretmochelys imbricata*)—rare; in marine waters, nests on Atlantic coast E
- [ ] **Loggerhead turtle** (*Caretta caretta*)—common; marine waters near sandy beaches, nests on both coasts
- [ ] **Atlantic Ridley turtle** (*Lepidochelys kempi*)—rare; in marine waters, nests in Mexico E
- [ ] **Florida softshell turtle** (*Apalone ferox*)—common; freshwater marshes statewide

Lizards

- [ ] ***Mediterranean gecko** (*Hemidactylus turcicus turcicus*)—locally common; developed areas in parts of Atlantic coast, Tampa area, and isolated areas in central Florida
- [ ] ***Indopacific gecko** (*Hemidactylus garnotii*)—locally common; developed areas (in buildings) from Seminole Co. south in east and Charlotte Co. south in west
- [ ] **Green anole** (*Anolis carolinensis*)—common; many habitats statewide
- [ ] ***Brown anole** (*Anolis sagrei*)—abundant; many habitats over most of peninsula
- [ ] **Southern fence lizard** (*Sceloporus undulatus undulatus*)—common; often in pine woods in north central Florida
- [ ] **Florida scrub lizard** (*Sceloporus woodi*)—rare; open sand pine scrub and sandhills along Atlantic coastal ridge, so. Lee Co. coast, and Lake Wales Ridge
- [ ] **Six-lined racerunner** (*Cnemidophorus sexlineatus*)—locally common; uplands statewide

☐ **Ground skink** (*Scincella lateralis*)—common; hammocks and pinelands

☐ **Broadhead skink** (*Eumeces laticeps*)—common; mesic or xeric woodlands in northern Florida to Brevard County

☐ **Southeastern five-lined skink** (*Eumeces inexpectatus*)—common; often seen on trails statewide

☐ **Peninsula mole skink** (*Eumeces egregius onocrepis*)—uncommon; sandy scrub in most of peninsula, except Kissimmee-Everglades system and Lake Wales Ridge

☐ **Bluetail mole skink** (*Eumeces egregius lividus*)—rare; sandy scrub on Lake Wales Ridge E

☐ **Sand skink** (*Neoseps reynoldsi*)—rare; open scrub with loose sand in Lake Wales Ridge and other central Florida ridges

☐ **Eastern glass lizard** (*Ophisaurus ventralis*)—locally common; pinelands and hammocks statewide

☐ **Slender glass lizard** (*Ophisaurus attenuatus*)—locally common; dry grasslands or woods statewide

☐ **Island glass lizard** (*Ophisaurus compressus*)—common; marshes and pinelands in peninsula

Amphisbaenians

☐ **Florida worm lizard** (*Rhineura floridana*)—common, fossorial; dry, sandy habitats in northern peninsula and central ridges

Snakes

☐ ***Brahminy blind snake** (*Ramphotyphlops braminus*)—wormlike burrower, locally common; southeast coast and Charlotte Harbor area

☐ **Florida green water snake** (*Nerodia floridana*)—common; fresh or brackish marshes statewide

☐ **Brown water snake** (*Nerodia taxispilota*)—common; clear, quiet waters in entire state except southeastern Atlantic coastal ridge

☐ **Florida water snake** (*Nerodia fasciata pictiventris*)—common; marshes and canals in peninsula

☐ **Mangrove salt marsh snake** (*Nerodia clarkii compressicauda*)—common; mangrove swamps and salt marshes on both coasts

☐ **Atlantic salt marsh snake** (*Nerodia clarkii taeniata*—rare; mangrove swamps and salt marshes in Indian River Lagoon, Volusia County E

☐ **North Florida swamp snake** (*Seminatrix pygaea pygaea*)—common; under debris in freshwater wetlands in northern peninsula south to Brevard Co. and Tampa

☐ **South Florida swamp snake** (*Seminatrix pygaea cyclas*)—common; under debris in freshwater wetlands in southern peninsula from Indian Co. and Tampa south

☐ **Florida brown snake** (*Storeria dekayi victa*)—common; pinelands, hammocks, and freshwater marshes in peninsula

☐ **Bluestripe garter snake** (*Thamnophis sirtalis similis*)—common; many habitats, Gulf coast north from Tampa

☐ **Eastern garter snake** (*Thamnophis sirtalis sirtalis*)—common; many habitats statewide except Gulf coast from Apalachee Bay to Tampa

☐ **Bluestripe ribbon snake** (*Thamnophis sauritus nitae*)—common; marshes, pine flatwoods, and hammocks in Gulf coast from Withlacoochee River north

☐ **Peninsula ribbon snake** (*Thamnophis sauritus sackenii*)—common; many habitats in peninsula (except bluestripe ribbon's range)

☐ **Eastern earth snake** (*Virginia valeriae valeriae*)—uncommon; isolated populations around central Florida, damp woods or marshes

☐ **Glossy crayfish snake** (*Regina rigida*)—uncommon; freshwater habitats in north central Florida

☐ **Striped crayfish snake** (*Regina alleni*)—locally common; very aquatic, dense vegetation in fresh water in peninsula

☐ **Eastern hognose snake** (*Heterodon platyrhinos*)—uncommon to common; sandy areas statewide

☐ **Southern hognose snake** (*Heterodon simus*)—rare to uncommon; variety of dry habitats south to Tampa and Lake Okeechobee

☐ **Pine woods snake** (*Rhadinaea flavilata*)—rare; damp woodlands under debris in peninsula south to Lake Okeechobee

☐ **Southern ringneck snake** (*Diadophis punctatus punctatus*)—common; under debris in woodlands near water statewide

- [ ] **Eastern mud snake** (*Farancia abacura abacura*)—locally common; near freshwater marshes, ponds, and canals statewide (usually seen on rainy nights)
- [ ] **Rainbow snake** (*Farancia erytrogramma erytrogramma*)— uncommon; in or near water such as cypress swamps in north Florida and Pinellas Co. area
- [ ] **South Florida rainbow snake** (*Farancia erytrogramma seminola*)— status unknown; fresh water, only at Fisheating Creek in Glades Co.
- [ ] **Southern black racer** (*Coluber constrictor priapus*)—abundant; many habitats, all peninsula except Everglades and Cape Canaveral area
- [ ] **Everglades racer** (*Coluber constrictor paludicola*)—abundant; many habitats in Everglades and Cape Canaveral area
- [ ] **Eastern coachwhip** (*Masticophis flagellum flagellum*)—locally common; many habitats statewide
- [ ] **Rough green snake** (*Opheodrys aestivus*)—abundant; many habitats statewide
- [ ] **Eastern indigo snake** (*Drymarchon corais couperi*)—uncommon; primarily dry areas statewide
- [ ] **Corn snake or red rat snake** (*Elaphe guttata guttata*)—common; mostly around development statewide
- [ ] **Everglades rat snake** (*Elaphe obsoleta rossalleni*)—locally common; freshwater marshes, hammocks, and pinelands from Martin County south
- [ ] **Yellow rat snake** (*Elaphe obsoleta quadrivitatta*)—common; many habitats in peninsula (except Everglades)
- [ ] **Florida pine snake** (*Pituophis melanoleucus mugitis*)—uncommon; very dry oak–pine woodlands and scrub south to Lake Okeechobee and along Atlantic coastal ridge to Broward Co.
- [ ] **Eastern kingsnake** (*Lampropeltis getula getula*)—common; pine flatwoods and other habitats in northern and eastern Florida
- [ ] **Florida kingsnake** (*Lampropeltis getula florida*)—uncommon; freshwater marshes, hammocks, and pinelands in most of peninsula
- [ ] **Scarlet kingsnake** (*Lampropeltis triangulum*)—uncommon; pinelands and hammocks statewide
- [ ] **South Florida mole kingsnake** (*Lampropeltis calligaster occipitolineata*)—rare, fossorial; several isolated populations in a variety of habitats in northeast central Florida

☐ **Florida scarlet snake** (*Cemophora coccinea coccinea*)—uncommon; pinelands and hammocks in peninsula

☐ **Short-tailed snake** (*Stilosoma extenuatum*)—rare and declining; primarily longleaf pine–turkey oak woodlands of Lake Wales ridge and northwest central Florida

☐ **Peninsula crowned snake** (*Tantilla relicta relicta*)—common; scrub of Lake Wales ridge and isolated coastal scrubs

☐ **Central Florida crowned snake** (*Tantilla relicta neilli*)—common; sandhills and moist hammocks of northwest peninsula

☐ **Coastal dunes crowned snake** (*Tantilla relicta pamlica*)—uncommon; coastal dunes and scrub of central Atlantic coast

☐ **Eastern coral snake** (*Micrurus fulvius*)—uncommon; pinelands and hammocks statewide; venomous

☐ **Florida cottonmouth or water moccasin** (*Agkistrodon piscivorus conanti*)—common; freshwater marshes and mangroves statewide; venomous

☐ **Dusky pygmy rattlesnake** (*Sistrurus miliarius*)—common; pinelands and freshwater marshes statewide; venomous

☐ **Eastern diamondback rattlesnake** (*Crotalus adamanteus*)—locally common; many habitats statewide; venomous

AMPHIBIAN CHECKLIST

Salamanders

☐ **Two-toed amphiuma** (*Amphiuma means*)—uncommon; freshwater marshes and sloughs statewide

☐ **One-toed amphiuma** (*Amphiuma pholeter*)—rare; deep muck of stream drainages in western Citrus and Hernando Co.

☐ **Greater siren** (*Siren lacertina*)—common; freshwater marshes, sloughs, and ponds statewide

☐ **Eastern lesser siren** (*Siren intermedia*)—common; in debris at the bottom of shallow stagnant water, north central Florida south through Kissimmee River drainage and possibly eastern Everglades

☐ **Narrow-striped dwarf siren** (*Pseudobranchus striatus axanthus*)—common; in floating vegetation in shallow stagnant water, peninsula south to Lake Okeechobee

☐ **Everglades dwarf siren** (*Pseudobranchus striatus belli*)—uncommon; in floating vegetation in shallow stagnant water, Lake Okeechobee south

☐ **Gulf Hammock dwarf siren** (*Pseudobranchus striatus lustricolus*)—status unknown (probably rare); stagnant freshwater ponds of extreme northwest corner of Citrus Co., possibly extending to Hernando and Sumter counties

☐ **Mole salamander** (*Ambystoma talpoideum*)—common; under ground, logs, and debris in damp places in northern Florida possibly to Orange Co.

☐ **Eastern tiger salamander** (*Ambystoma tigrinum tigrinum*)—status unknown (probably rare); mixed woodlands near temporary ponds in northwest range

☐ **Peninsula newt** (*Notophthalmus viridescens piaropicola*)—abundant; freshwater marshes and ponds in peninsula

☐ **Striped newt** (*Notophthalmus perstriatus*)—rare; sinkholes and cypress ponds in north central Florida

☐ **Southern dusky salamander** (*Desmognathus auriculatus*)—common; ponds, bogs, streams of northern central Florida

☐ **Southeastern slimy salamander** (*Plethodon glutinosus grobmani*)—abundant; moist woodlands and hillsides in northern central Florida

☐ **Rusty mud salamander** (*Pseudotriton montanus floridanus*)—status unknown (probably uncommon); under wet leaves and logs in northern central Florida

☐ **Dwarf salamander** (*Eurycea quadridigitata*)—common; variety of wet habitats, northern and central Florida and Kissimmee and Everglades drainages

Toads and Frogs

☐ **Eastern spadefoot toad** (*Scaphiophus holbrookii holbrookii*)—common, secretive; sandy, dry areas statewide except Kissimmee and Everglades drainages

☐ **Southern toad** (*Bufo terrestris*)—abundant; yards, hammocks, pinelands, and freshwater marshes statewide

☐ **Oak toad** (*Bufo quercicus*)—common; dry hammocks, pine flatwoods, and scrub statewide

☐ ***Giant** (Marine) toad (*Bufo marinus*)—common; breeds in fresh or brackish water in Tampa area and coastal southeastern Florida

☐ ***Greenhouse frog** (*Eleutherodactylus planirostris*)—common, may be immigrant; found under leaf litter in peninsula

☐ **Florida cricket frog** (*Acris gryllus dorsalis*)—abundant; freshwater wetlands statewide

☐ **Green treefrog** (*Hyla cinerea*)—abundant; hammocks, pinelands, and freshwater marshes statewide

☐ **Barking treefrog** (*Hyla gratiosa*)—common, secretive; habitat not well-known, statewide except Everglades

☐ **Pine woods treefrog** (*Hyla femoralis*)—common; often around artificial lights, variety of habitats statewide except Everglades

☐ **Squirrel treefrog** (*Hyla squirella*)—abundant; yards and all freshwater habitats in all Florida

☐ ***Cuban treefrog** (*Osteopilus septentrionalis*)—may be immigrant, locally abundant; often around buildings on Atlantic and southern Gulf coasts, Glades and Orange counties

☐ **Southern spring peeper** (*Pseudacris crucifer bartramiana*)—common; woodlands near small ponds or swamps in northern Florida and Orange Co.

☐ **Florida chorus frog** (*Pseudacris nigrita verrucosa*)—common; freshwater swamps, marshes, and ditches in peninsula

☐ **Ornate chorus frog** (*Pseudacris ornata*)—common; many freshwater habitats and pinelands in north Florida south to Lake County

☐ **Little grass frog** (*Pseudacris ocularis*)—abundant; freshwater swamps, marshes, and temporary ponds in peninsula

☐ **Eastern narrowmouth toad** (*Gastrophryne carolinensis*)—common, secretive burrower; under leaf litter in hammocks statewide

☐ **Bullfrog** (*Rana catesbiana*)—uncommon; permanent freshwater bodies in northern and north central Florida

☐ **River frog** (*Rana heckscheri*)—common; riverine swamps and other permanent freshwater habitats south to Volusia and Hillsborough counties

☐ **Pig frog** (*Rana grylio*)—abundant, commercially exploited; all permanent freshwater habitats statewide

☐ **Bronze frog** (*Rana clamitans clamitans*)—common; variety of freshwater habitats in north Florida south to Lake Co.

☐ **Southern leopard frog** (*Rana utricularia*)—abundant; terrestrial, fresh and brackish water habitats statewide

☐ **Florida gopher frog** (*Rana capito aesopus*)—uncommon and rapidly declining; found in gopher tortoise burrows, south to Lake Okeechobee and Atlantic coastal ridge to Broward Co. (same range as tortoise)

SCIENTIFIC NAMES OF FISH

The following is a list of the scientific names of the saltwater and freshwater fish mentioned in the text. All the fish are found in central Florida. However, this is not intended to be a complete list of the fish found in the region covered by this book.

Bluegill (*Lepomis macrochirus*)
Catfish (*Ictalurus* spp.)
Cobia (*Rachycentron canadum*)
Crevalle jack (*Caranx hippos*)
Foureye butterflyfish (*Chaetodon capistratus*)
Grouper (Family Serranidae)
Gulf flounder (*Paralichthys albigutta*)
Largemouth bass (*Micropterus salmoides*)
Mangrove (gray) snapper (*Lutjanus griseus*)
Margate (*Haemulon album*)
Ocean surgeon (*Acanthurus bahianus*)
Redfish or red drum (*Sciaenops ocellatus*)
Sea trout (*Cynoscion nebulosus*)
Sergeant major (*Abudefduf saxatilis*)
Sheepshead (*Archosargus probatocephalus*)
Snook (*Centropomus undecimalis*)
Spanish mackerel (*Scomberomorus maculatus*)
Stingray (Family Dasyatidae)
Striped mullet (*Mugil cephalus*)
Tarpon (*Megalops atlantica*)
Tripletail (*Lobotes surinamensis*)

SCIENTIFIC NAMES OF PLANTS

The following is a list of the scientific names of the plants mentioned in the text. All the plants are found in central Florida. However, this is not intended to be a complete list of the plants found in the region covered by this book. There would be too many to list comfortably.

* = exotic species
E = endangered species

TREES, SHRUBS, AND WOODY PLANTS

Gymnosperms:
CUPRESSACEAE—Cypress family
southern redcedar (*Juniperus silicicola*)

CYCADACEAE—Cycad family
coontie (*Zamia* spp.)

PINACEAE—Pine family
slash pine (*Pinus elliottii var. elliottii, P.e. var. densa*)
sand pine (*Pinus clausa*)
loblolly pine (*Pinus taeda*)
longleaf pine (*Pinus palustris*)
pond pine (*Pinus serotina*)

TAXODIACEAE—Redwood family
bald-cypress (*Taxodium distichum*)
pond-cypress (*Taxodium ascendens* or *T. distichum var. nutans*)

Angiosperms:

ACERACEAE—Maple family
red maple (*Acer rubrum*)

ANACARDIACEAE—Cashew family
Brazilian pepper (*Schinus terebinthifolius*)*

poison-ivy (*Toxicodendron radicans*)

ANNONACEAE—Custard-apple family
pond-apple (*Annona glabra*)

AQUIFOLIACEAE—Holly family
dahoon holly (*Ilex cassine*)
gallberry or inkberry (*Ilex glabra*)
sand holly (*Ilex ambigua*)

ARECACEAE—Palm family
cabbage palm (*Sabal palmetto*)
scrub palmetto (*Sabal etonia*)
saw palmetto (*Serenoa repens*)

AVICENNIACEAE—Black mangrove family
black mangrove (*Avicennia germinans*)

BURSERACEAE—Torchwood family
gumbo-limbo (*Bursera simaruba*)

CASUARINACEAE—Beefwood family
Australian-pine (*Casuarina litorea and C. glauca*)*

CHRYSOBALANACEAE—Coco-plum family
coco-plum (*Chrysobalanus icaco*)
gopher apple (*Licania michauxii*)

COMBRETACEAE—Combretum family
buttonwood (*Conocarpus erectus*)
white mangrove (*Laguncularia racemosa*)

ERICACEAE—Heath family
gallberry (*Ilex glabra*)
rusty lyonia (*Lyonia fruticosa*)
sparkleberry (*Vaccinium arboreum*)
staggerbush (*Lyonia ferruginea*)
FABACEAE—Pea family
coral bean (*Erythrina herbacea*)

FAGACEAE—Beech family
Chapman's oak (*Quercus chapmanni*)

live oak (*Quercus virginiana*)
laurel oak (*Quercus laurifolia*)
myrtle oak (*Quercus myrtifolia*)
sand live oak (*Quercus geminata*)
scrub (or inopina) oak (*Quercus inopina*)
turkey oak (*Quercus laevis*)
water oak (*Quercus nigra*)

HAMAMELIDACEAE—Witch-hazel family
sweetgum (*Liquidambar styraciflua*)

HYPERICACEAE—St. John's-wort family
St. John's-wort (*Hypericum fasciculatum*)

JUGLANDACEAE—Walnut family
pignut hickory (*Carya glabra*)
scrub hickory (*Carya floridana*)

LAURACEAE—Laurel family
redbay (*Persea borbonia*)
silk bay (*Persea humilis*)
swamp bay (*Persea palustris*)

LORANTHACEAE—Mistletoe family
mistletoe (*Phoradendron serotinum*)

MAGNOLIACEAE—Magnolia family
sweet bay (*Magnolia virginiana*)

MORACEAE—Mulberry family
red mulberry (*Morus rubra*)
strangler fig (*Ficus aurea*)

MYRICACEAE—Bayberry family
wax myrtle (*Myrica cerifera*)

MYRTACEAE—Myrtle family
melaleuca, cajeput (*Melaleuca quinquenervia*)*

white stopper (*Eugenia axillaris*)
Simpson's stopper (*Eugenia simpsonii*)

NYSSACEAE—Tupelo family
black gum or tupelo (*Nyssa sylvatica*)

OLACACEAE—Tallowwood family
tallowwood or hog plum (*Ximenia americana*)

OLEACEAE—Olive family
Carolina ash (*Fraxinus caroliniana*)
pygmy fringe tree (*Chionanthus pygmaeus*) **E**

POLYGONACEAE—Buckwheat family
sea grape (*Coccoloba uvifera*)

RHAMNACEAE—Buckthorn family
black ironwood (*Krugiodendron ferreum*)
Florida ziziphus (*Ziziphus celata*) **E**

RHIZOPHORACEAE—Mangrove family
red mangrove (*Rhizophora mangle*)

ROSACEAE—Rose family
scrub plum (*Prunus geniculata*) **E**

RUBIACEAE—Madder family
wild coffee (*Psychotria nervosa*)

RUTACEAE—Citrus family
wild-lime (*Zanthoxylum fagara*)

SALICACEAE—Willow family

coastal plain willow (*Salix caroliniana*)
SIMAROUBACEAE—Quassia family
paradise-tree (*Simarouba glauca*)

SURIANACEAE—Bay-cedar family
bay-cedar (*Suriana maritima*)

THEACEAE—Tea family

loblolly bay (*Gordonia lasianthus*)

ULMACEAE—Elm family
sugarberry (*Celtis laevigata*)

NON-WOODY PLANTS

AGAVACEAE—Yucca family
Florida beargrass (*Nolina atopocarpa*) E
scrub beargrass (*Nolina brittoniana*) E
yucca or Spanish bayonet (*Yucca aloifolia*)

AIZOACEAE—Carpetweed family
sea purslane (*Sesuvium portulacastrum*)

ALISMATACEAE—Water-plaintain family
arrowhead (*Sagittaria graminea*)

ASTERACEAE—Aster family
goldenrod (*Solidago* spp.)
sea ox-eye daisy (*Borrichia frutescens*)
scrub blazing star (*Liatris ohlingerae*) E

BATACEAE—Saltwort family
saltwort (*Batis maritima*)

BROMELIACEAE—Air plant family
bromeliad (*Tillandsia* spp.)
giant wild pine (*Tillandsia utriculata*)
needle-leaved wild pine (*Tillandsia setacea*)
Spanish moss (*Tillandsia usneoides*)
ball moss (*Tillandsia recurvata*)

CACTACEAE—Cactus family
prickly-pear (*Opuntia* sp.)
fragrant wool-bearing cereus (*Cereus eriophorus* var. *fragrans*) E

CAMPANULAEAE—Bluebell family

glades lobelia (*Lobelia glandulosa*)

CHENOPODIACEAE—glasswort (*Salicornia virginica*)

CONVOLVULACEAE—Morning-glory family
large-flowered bonamia (*Bonamia grandiflora*) E

CRUCIFERAE—Mustard family
Carter's mustard (*Warea carteri*) E
clasping warea (*Warea amplexifolia*) E

CYPERACEAE—Sedge family
sawgrass (*Cladium jamaicense*)
spike rush (*Eleocharis* sp.)
Tracy's beakrush (*Rhynchospora tracyi*)
white-topped sedge (*Dichromena colorata*)

DIOSCORACEAE—Yam family
air-potato (*Dioscorea bulbifera*)*

DROSERACEAE—Sundew family
round-leaved sundew (*Drosera rotundifolia*)

EMPETRACEAE—Crowberry family
rosemary (*Ceratiola ericoides*)

FABACEAE—Pea family
kudzu (*Pueraria lobata*)*
GENTIANACEAE—Gentian family
white sabatia (*Sabatia brevifolia*)

HALORAGACEAE—Watermilfoil family
water milfoil (*Myriophyllum spicatum*)

HYDROCHARITACEAE—Frog's-bit family
hydrilla (*Hydrilla verticillata*)*
turtle grass (*Thalassia testudinum*)

IRIDACEAE—Iris family

celestial lily (*Nemastylis floridana*) **E**

LAMIACEAE—Mint family
scrub mint or large-flowered rosemary (*Conradina grandi-flora*) **E**

LENTIBULARIACEAE—Bladderwort family
bladderwort (*Utricularia* spp.)
butterwort (*Pinguicula* spp.)

LILIACEAE—Lily family
pine lily (*Lilium catesbaei*)

LYCOPODIACEAE—Clubmoss family
whisk fern (*Psilotum nudum*)

NAJADACEAE—Water nymph family
southern naiad (*Najas guadalupensis*)

NYMPHEAECEAE—Waterlily family
spadderdock (*Nuphar lutea*)
white waterlily (*Nymphaea odorata*)

OPHIOGLOSSACEAE—Adders-tongue family
hand fern (*Ophioglossum palmatum*) **E**

ORCHIDACEAE—Orchid family
butterfly orchid (*Encyclia tampensis*)
spider orchid (*Brassia caudata*)

OSMUNDACEAE—Royal fern family
royal fern (*Osmunda regalis*)

PHYTOLACCACEAE—Pokeweed family
rouge plant (*Rivina humilis*)

POACEAE—Grass family
cordgrass (*Spartina bakeri*)
cutthroat grass (*Panicum abscissum*)
muhly grass (*Muhlenberghia filipes*)
sea oats (*Uniola paniculata*)

wiregrass (*Aristida stricta*)

POLYGALACEAE—Milkwort family
bog bachelor-button (*Polygala lutea*)

POLYPODIACEAE—Polypodium family
Boston fern (*Nephrolepis exaltata*)
bracken fern (*Pteridium caudatum*)
giant leather fern (*Acrostichum danaeifolium*)
marsh fern (*Thelypteris palustris*)
resurrection fern (*Polypodium polypodioides*)
shoestring fern (*Vittaria lineata*)

PONTEDERIACEAE—Pickerelweed family
pickerel-weed (*Pontederia cordata*)
water hyacinth (*Eichhornia crassipes*)*

RUBIACEAE—Madder family
beach creeper (*Ernodia littoralis*)

RUPPIACEAE—Ruppia family
widgeon grass (*Ruppia maritima*)

SARRACENIACEAE—pitcherplant
pitcherplant (*Sarracenia* sp.)

SCHIZAEACEAE—Climbing fern family
Old World climbing fern (*Lygodium microphyllum*)*
TYPHACEAE—Cattail family
cattail (*Typha latifolia* and *T. dominguensis*)

VERBENACEAE—Verbena family
beauty berry (*Callicarpa americana*)
coastal vervain (*Verbena maritima*) **E**

ZANNICHELLIACEAE—Horned pondweed family
horned pondweed (*Zannichellia palustris*)

NON-VASCULAR PLANTS

LICHEN
Florida perforate lichen (*Cladonia perforata*)

A strangler fig embraces a cypress at Barley Barber Swamp. (Susan D. Jewell)

SUGGESTED READING

Asterisk denotes sources used in preparation of this book.

Andrews, Evangeline Walker, and Charles McLean Andrews (eds.). 1985. *Jonathan Dickinson's Journal or, God's Protecting Providence.* Port Salerno, FL: Florida Classics Library. 109 pp.

Ashton, Ray E., Jr., and Patricia Sawyer Ashton. 1981. *Handbook of Reptiles and Amphibians of Florida. Part One: The Snakes.* Miami: Windward Publishing. 176pp. *

Ashton, Ray E., Jr., and Patricia Sawyer Ashton. 1985. *Handbook of Reptiles and Amphibians of Florida. Part Two: Lizards, Turtles, and Crocodilians.* Miami: Windward Publishing. 191pp.*

Ashton, Ray E., Jr., and Patricia Sawyer Ashton. 1988. *Handbook of Reptiles and Amphibians of Florida. Part Three: The Amphibians.* Miami: Windward Publishing. 191pp. *

Austin, Daniel. 1993. *Scrub Plant Guide.* South Palm Beach County, FL: The Gumbo Limbo Nature Center. 70pp. *

Bell, C. Ritchie, and Bryan J. Taylor. 1982. *Florida Wild Flowers and Roadside Plants.* Chapel Hill, NC: Laurel Hill Press. 308pp. *

Carter, Elizabeth F. 1987. *A Hiking Guide to the Trails of Florida.* Birmingham, AL: Menasha Ridge Press. 129pp.

Cerulean, Susan, and Ann Morrow. 1993. *Florida Wildlife Viewing Guide.* Helena, MT: Falcon Press Publishing, Inc. 136pp.

Gerberg, Eugene J., and Ross H. Arnett. 1989. *Florida Butterflies.* Baltimore, MD: Natural Science Publications. 90pp.

Gildersleeve, Nancy B., and Susan K. (eds.). 1991. *Florida Hiking Trails.* Gainesville, FL: Maupin House. 171pp.

Gingerich, Jerry Lee. 1994. *Florida's Fabulous Mammals.* Tampa, FL: World Publications. 128pp.

Glaros, Lou, and Doug Sphar. 1987. *A Canoeing and Kayaking Guide to the Streams of Florida, Volume II, Central and South Peninsula*. Birmingham, AL: Menasha Ridge Press. 136pp.

Gluckman, David. 1995. *Sea Kayaking in Florida*. Sarasota, FL: Pineapple Press. 186pp.

Grow, Gerald. 1993. *Florida Parks: a Guide to Camping in Nature*. Tallahassee, FL: Longleaf Publications. 257pp.

Henry, James A., Kenneth M. Portier, and Jan Coyne. 1994. *The Climate and Weather of Florida*. Sarasota, FL: Pineapple Press. 280 pp.

Holt, Harold R. 1990. *Lane's A Birder's Guide to Florida*. Distr. by ABA Sales, P.O. Box 6599, Colorado Springs, Colo. 80934. 164pp. (Revised late 1995.)

Humphrey, Stephen R. (ed.) 1992. *Rare and Endangered Biota of Florida*. Volume I: Mammals. Gainesville, FL: University Press of Florida. 392pp. *

Kale, Herbert W., II, and David S. Maehr. 1990. *Florida's Birds*. Sarasota, FL: Pineapple Press. 288pp. *

Lakela, Olga, and Richard Wunderlin. 1980. *Trees of Central Florida*. Miami, FL: Banyan Books. 208pp.

Meyers, Ronald L., and John J. Ewel (eds.). 1990. *Ecosystems of Florida*. Orlando, FL: University of Central Florida Press. 763pp. *

Moler, Paul E. (ed.) 1992. *Rare and Endangered Biota of Florida. Volume III: Amphibians and Reptiles*. Gainesville, FL: University Press of Florida. 291pp. *

Morton, Julia F. 1982. *Wild Plants for Survival in South Florida*. Miami: Fairchild Tropical Garden. 80pp.

Neill, Wildfred T. 1956. *Florida's Seminole Indians*. St. Petersburg, FL: Great Outdoors Publishing Company. 128pp.

Nelson, Gil. 1994. *The Trees of Florida*. Sarasota, FL: Pineapple Press. 338pp.

Rodgers, James A., Jr., H. W. Kale II, and Henry T. Smith (eds.). *Rare and Endangered Biota of Florida. Volume V: Birds*. Gainesville, FL: University Press of Florida. (Due late 1995.)

Stiling, Peter D. 1989. *Florida's Butterflies and Other Insects*. Sarasota, FL: Pineapple Press. 95pp.

Tomlinson, P. B. 1980. *The Biology of Trees Native to Tropical Florida.* Allston, MA: Harvard University Printing Office. 480pp. *

Toops, Connie M. 1988. *The Alligator: Monarch of the Marsh.* Homestead, FL: Florida National Parks and Monuments Assn. 58pp.

Winsberg, Morton D. 1990. *Florida Weather.* Orlando, FL: University of Central Florida Press. 171pp. *

ADDITIONAL SOURCES USED IN THE PREPARATION OF THIS BOOK
(TECHNICAL OR NOT READILY AVAILABLE)

MMWR. 1989. Seizures temporally associated with DEET insect repellent—New York and Connecticut. Morbidity and Mortality Weekly R. 38(39):678–680.

NOAA. 1992. Monthly normals of temperature, precipitation, and heating and cooling degree days for Florida. Ashville, NC: National Climatic Center.

OTHER SOURCES OF INFORMATION

Florida—General

DeLorme Mapping Company
P.O. Box 298
Freeport, ME 04032
(207) 865-4171
publishes "Florida Atlas & Gazetteer" (detailed road maps with guide to outdoor recreation)

Florida Association of Canoe Liveries & Outfitters
Box 1764
Arcadia, FL 33821
(941) 494-1215
free list of canoe outfitters

Florida Audubon Society
  460 Hwy. 436, Suite 200
  Casselberry, FL 32707
  (407) 260-8300
Florida Board of Tourism
  Department of Commerce
  126 West Van Buren St.
  Tallahassee, FL 32399-2000
  (904) 487-1462
  free road map of Florida
Florida Department of Environmental Protection
  Division of Recreation and Parks
  3900 Commonwealth Blvd.
  Tallahassee, FL 32399-3000
  (904) 487-4784 or (904) 488-6131
  information on state parks, free canoe trail guides and map with access points of 36 Florida canoe trails
Florida Game and Fresh Water Fish Commission
  620 S. Meridian Street
  Tallahassee, FL 32399-1600
  (904) 488-4674 for general information
  (904) 488-1960 for Florida freshwater fishing handbook
Florida Sierra Club
  462 Fernwood Road
  Key Biscayne, FL 33149
  (305) 361-1292
Florida Trail Association, Inc.
  P.O. Box 13708
  Gainesville, FL 32604
  (904) 378-8823
  (800) 343-1882 (Florida only)
Florida Wildlife Federation
  2545 Blairstone Pines Drive
  P.O. Box 6870
  Tallahassee, FL 32314-6870
  (904) 656-7113
Save the Manatee Club
  500 N. Maitland Avenue

Maitland, FL 32751
(800) 432-JOIN
The Nature Conservancy
Florida Field Office
2699 Lee Rd., Suite 500
Winter Park, FL 32789
(407) 628-5887
U.S. Fish & Wildlife Service
6620 South Point Drive, South
Suite 310
Jacksonville, FL 32216-0912
(904) 232-2580

Florida—Central

Florida Game and Fresh Water Fish Commission
South Region
3900 Drane Field Road
Lakeland, FL 33811
(941) 648-3203
Hillsborough County Parks and Recreation Administrative Office
1101 E. River Cove Street
Tampa, FL 33604
(813) 975-2160
Pasco County Parks Administrative Office
Central Pasco Professional Center
4111 Land O'Lakes Boulevard
Land O'Lakes, FL 34639
(813) 929-1260
Pinellas County Park Department
631 Chestnut Street
Clearwater, FL 34616
(813) 462-3347
Polk County Parks and Recreation Division
P.O. Box 60
Bartow, FL 33830
(941) 534-4341

Rails to Trails of the Withlacoochee, Inc.
P.O. Box 807
Inverness, FL 34451-0807
South Florida Water Management District
P.O. Box 24680
3301 Gun Club Road
West Palm Beach, FL 33416-4680
(407) 686-8800
(800) 432-2045
Southwest Florida Water Management District
2379 Broad Street
Brooksville, FL 34609-6899
(904) 796-7211
(800) 423-1476
St. Johns River Water Management District
P.O. Box 1429
Palatka, FL 32178-1429
(904) 329-4500

GLOSSARY

aquifer an underground porous rock formation containing water; the source of water for wells and springs.

barrier island a low-lying island, usually long and narrow, paralleling the coastal shore, that protects the mainland from heavy surf and winds.

bayhead a tree island in a freshwater marsh that may be inundated during the wet season; so named because it usually contains redbay, sweet bay, or other bay trees.

brackish describes water that contains some salts and may vary considerably in salinity; usually found where rivers meet an ocean.

bromeliad (pronounced "bro-me'-li-ad") a type of epiphyte (airplant); a plant from the pineapple family that is an epiphyte. Examples: Spanish moss, ball-moss, needle-leaved airplant, banded wildpine.

carapace the upper shell of a turtle.

deciduous plants that drop their leaves seasonally.

endangered species a species of plant or animal that has been declared (by a state or federal agency) in danger of becoming extinct if not protected.

endemic originating in a particular locality, indigenous; growing nowhere else in the world.

epiphyte a plant growing upon or attached to another plant or nonliving structure but is not parasitic; airplant. Florida has numerous epiphytic bromeliads, orchids, and ferns.

estuary a shallow brackish wetland formed where a river meets an inlet of the sea; among the most productive habitats in the world.

exotic species any species of plant or animal that was introduced (intentionally or unintentionally) by humans to an area it did not previously inhabit. Undesirable because they may outcompete or deplete native species. Examples are melaleuca, Brazilian pepper, domestic cat, common pigeon.

extinct vanished from existence.

feral refers to an animal of a domesticated species that has reverted to the wild.

hammock a tree island; a well-drained tract of land slightly higher than the surrounding wetlands, vegetated with hardwood trees.

herp short for 'herpetofauna,' which means reptiles and amphibians (may refer to either class).

hurricane a cyclone forming in the Atlantic Ocean and having wind speeds of 74 mph or greater.

key a small, low-lying island; occasionally used to mean a hammock. From the Spanish *cayo* ("small island").

midden a mound or small hill made by Indians, usually from discarding shells of oysters, clams, snails, or other staple food.

mitigation as relates to environmental practices: the restoration or improvement of one land area to a healthier natural state to compensate for destroying another area through human activities.

GLOSSARY

native species of plants or animals indigenous to an area.

prescribed burn an intentionally set fire on an undeveloped area, planned and controlled by fire ecologists to maintain a healthy habitat.

run (noun) the section of water between a spring and where it flows into a river.

sinkhole a depression in the ground caused by the collapse of underlying material, often when the limestone bedrock dissolves beneath a layer of soil.

slough (pronounced "slew") a channel of slow-moving water, slightly deeper than the surrounding freshwater marsh.

solution hole a depression in surface limestone rock formed by the dissolving action of acidic water, which is created by rainwater mixing with decomposing vegetation.

xeric dry environment, well-drained soil; can refer to plants that require little water to thrive.

INDEX